S0-AVK-999

MIRRORS
OF THE
SELF

This *New Consciousness Reader*
is part of a new series of original
and classic writing by renowned experts on
leading-edge concepts in personal development,
psychology, spiritual growth, and healing.

MIRRORS

OF THE

SELF

Archetypal Images That Shape Your Life

EDITED BY

CHRISTINE DOWNING

JEREMY P. TARCHER, INC.
Los Angeles

Library of Congress Cataloging-in-Publication Data

Mirrors of the self : archetypal images that shape your life / edited
by Christine Downing. — 1st ed.
    p.   cm. — (New consciousness reader)
  Includes bibliographical references.
  ISBN 0-87477-664-3 : $12.95
  1. Archetype (Psychology)   2. Self-actualization (Psychology)
I. Downing, Christine, 1931-   . II. Series.
BF175.5.A72M57   1991
155.2'64—dc20   91-24850
                                                                    CIP

Copyright © 1991 by Christine Downing

All rights reserved. No part of this work may be reproduced or transmitted
in any form by any means, electronic or mechanical, including photocopying
and recording, or by any information storage or retrieval system, except
as may be expressly permitted by the 1976 Copyright Act or in writing
by the publisher. Requests for such permissions should be addressed to:

Jeremy P. Tarcher, Inc.
5858 Wilshire Blvd., Suite 200
Los Angeles, CA 90036

Distributed by St. Martin's Press, New York

Copyrights and Permissions appear on pages 280–283,
which constitute a continuation of the copyright page.

Manufactured in the United States of America
10 9 8 7 6 5 4 3 2 1

First Edition

For

Richard Arnold Underwood

*"For we have been a conversation and have been able
to hear from one another"*

Contents

Christine Downing

Prologue

Archetypal images reveal a rich mirroring of our inner experience and our interactions with the world outside ourselves. As Jung discovered when he went in search of "the myth that was living him," the encounter with a dimension of the unconscious, which is a living, creative, transpersonal source of inexhaustible energy and direction, is life-changing.

Many people, when we first read Jung, feel we recognize immediately the dimension of experience for which he used the word *archetypal*. I remember my own first reading of him when I was in my early twenties and imagined myself as fully and fulfillingly defined by the roles of wife and mother. Suddenly my self-understanding was opened up as I began to pay attention to my dreams, which introduced me to an unsuspected multitude of unlived potentialities waiting to be acknowledged and nurtured. I discovered also how these roles had archetypal and numinous dimensions (both threatening and life-giving) to which I had been blinded by my involvement with their more trivial aspects. I felt myself in touch with elements of my own experience that were not mine alone. The recognition that I shared my deepest feelings, my most profound hopes and fears, my most valued accomplishments and most regretted failures with others gave me an entirely new sense of being connected to all humanity not just through outward relationships but at the very core of my being.

This experience felt very real. Jung had introduced me to a new word and, more important, to a new vision of myself that I recognized as both liberating and challenging. Although I have many theoretical reservations about the details of his presentation, reflection on Jung's theory of archetypes still renews my gratitude for the way it helps us—both personally and theoretically—to move beyond the limits of a psychology focused only on personal history and pathological issues.

Jung named the images through which the collective unconscious manifests itself "archetypal images." He used the word *archetypal* to communicate the power some images have to bring us in touch with what feels like the very source of our being. The Greek root, *arche*, refers to beginnings, to origins; *type* derives from a Greek verb meaning "to strike" and from the related noun that refers to an impression or model. *Archetype* thus signifies the model from which copies are cast, the underlying pattern, the beginning point from which something develops. Though Jung sometimes writes of archetypes as imprinted on our psyches, he also applies this etymology in a more dynamic way when he defines archetypal images as having the power to impress us: "These typical images and associations . . . impress, influence, and fascinate us."[1]

Jung distinguished between archetypes and archetypal images. He recognized that what comes into individual consciousness are always *archetypal images*—particular, concrete manifestations that are influenced by sociocultural and individual factors. However, the archetypes themselves are formless and unrepresentable, psychoid rather than, properly speaking, psychic: "The archetype as such is a psychoid factor that belongs, as it were, to the invisible, ultraviolet end of the psychic spectrum . . . One must consistently bear in mind that what we mean by 'archetype' is in itself irrepresentable, but that it has effects which enable us to visualize it, namely, the archetypal images."[2] Archetypes themselves, Jung says, are empty and without form; we can never really see them except as they become conscious, except when filled with individual content.

What it means to posit the reality of archetypes apart from their manifestations is a much-debated issue whose metaphysical dimensions I will mostly sidestep. Because I tend to see archetypes as abstractions from the concrete, diversified images, like many other recent appreciators and critics of Jung I find myself not very interested in them—precisely because I *am* interested in psyche, soul, and the imagining activity which I take to be the psyche's most characteristic activity.

Jung's interest in archetypal images reflects his emphasis on the *form* of unconscious thought rather than on the content. Our capacity to respond to experience as image-making creatures is inherited, given to us with our humanness. Archetypal images are not remnants of archaic thought, not a dead deposit, but part of a living system of interactions between the human psyche and the outer world. The archetypal images that appear in my dreams spring from the same human capacity that gave rise to ancient mythologies among our remote ancestors. The myths are not causes of the contemporary and individual manifestations, but rather exist on the same plane as analogies.

The focus on the archetypal emphasizes the importance of our images in making us who we are. Our lives are shaped by our thoughts and deeds and, even more powerfully, our fantasies and dreams, and the complex feeling-toned associations with which we respond to the persons and events we encounter everyday. I am not merely what I have thought, as Descartes proposed, nor simply what I have done, as the existentialists claim, but also, as Gaston Bachelard has so powerfully shown, what I have imagined and remembered.[3]

When we speak of archetypal images we are not referring simply to dream images or to mythological or literary images. We are, instead, speaking of a way to respond to our ordinary lives with our imaginations, rather than only pragmatically or logically. We are speaking of a way of being in the world that is open to many dimensions of meaning, open to resonances, echoes, to associative and synchronous connections, not only causal ones. We are speaking of a world discovered to be full of sign-ificance—of signs, symbols, metaphors, images.

Thus, the point of attending to the archetypal is to bring us to appreciate and nurture the natural, spontaneous human capacity to respond to the world not only conceptually but also symbol-ically. Image-making is as fundamental a human way of responding to the world as are the categories of space, time, and causality as described by Kant. Symbolic thinking is associational, analogical, concrete, feeling-toned, animistic, anthropomorphic. It may seem more passive, more simply receptive than organizing conceptual thought, because images, unlike ideas, feel given to us rather than made by us and may, therefore, as Jolande Jacobi suggests, feel like revelations, "convincing by virtue of their immediacy."[4] Or, our involvement with archetypal images may lead us to feel ourselves engaged with an *inner* world, a world of interior objects. But actually, as Jung clearly saw, symbolic or archetypal thinking is a mode of response *to* the world, which may help free us from entrapment by the illusion of the separation between inner and outer and the disjunction of subject from object.

For Jung this capacity for symbol-making, not reason, is the truly human-making function. Attending to these images (which are not translated ideas but the natural speech of the soul, its authentic *logos*) helps get us beyond the tyranny of the verbal and rational modes, which have issued in the suppression of those human faculties we encounter as "unconscious."

When we focus on archetypal as adjective rather than on archetype as noun, the question, according to James Hillman, becomes "What is it about an image that draws the modifier archetypal?"[5] His answer is that so much wealth can be gotten from it, that it is experienced as rich, deep, fecund, generative. *Archetypal* is a word that connotes the value and importance we attach to particular images. It means we endow them with the deepest possible significance. Calling something archetypal is a *valuing* process, not the positing of an ontological fact. Archetypal refers then to a way of seeing. We don't so much look *at* archetypes as *through* them. To call an image archetypal is not to say it is some special, different kind of image but a different way of viewing or valuing the image.

Whether an image is archetypal or not depends chiefly on the attitude of the observing consciousness, on our *response* to the image, rather than any inherent quality. I also believe that there are some common features of human life, such as the birth of a first child or the appearance of a rainbow after a storm, that seem to compel or often evoke this kind of response. There are situations in which it is difficult to respond rationally or pragmatically; these situations stir us as whole human beings. Though it is often said that archetypal images are formed in response to recurrent typical experiences and to widespread, relatively constant, and consequential aspects of human experience,

Hillman reverses this theory: images that merit our repeated attention are archetypal. The repetition pertains not to what instigates the image but to what it engenders.

When we focus on the archetypal *image*, it becomes clear that there is no absolute distinction between the personal and the collective, for the archetypal image marks the juncture where inner and outer, personal and collective meet. It represents the continual dynamic interaction between the conscious and the unconscious, the personal and the collective. Jacobi suggests that archetypal images exist on a continuum from the more particularized to the more general: "The more personal and current a problem is, the more intricate, detailed, and clearly defined is the archetypal figure by which it is expressed; the more impersonal and universal the situation it concretizes, the simpler or more blurred it will be."[6]

Which aspect we emphasize will depend on our purposes, situations, and needs. Yet it is important to recognize that archetypal images will always carry a personal valence and appear in a specific context. Apprehending their meaning for us will always require paying attention to their particularity and not simply their generality.

Then what makes us respond to an image as archetypal? As I recall my discovery of the power of the engagement with the imaginal to transform my very being, I conclude that what is important is not that archetypal images *are* a priori, universal or numinous, but that we *feel* that they are. Archetypal images feel basic, necessary, and generative. They are connected to something original, not in the sense of what they are caused by, but rather in what they help to cause or make possible. They seem to give energy and direction. Archetypal images give rise to associations and lead us to other images; and we therefore experience them as having resonance, complexity, and depth.

They feel universal. June claimed, "From the unconscious there emanate determining influences . . . which, independently of tradition, guarantee in every single individual a similarity and even a sameness of experience, and also of the way it is represented imaginatively."[7] Though I question the accuracy (or even the relevance) of the claim to literal universality, I nonetheless believe that the sense of being in touch with something that feels collective, shared, is indeed part of what *archetypal* connotes.

Perhaps "transpersonal" is a better designation for this than "universal" because it does not imply that the experience or the imaginative representation of it is necessarily apropos of all cultures or all individuals.

But quite apart from the possibility of establishing literal universality, I am troubled by the manner in which claims to universality so often proceed from a view that the socially (or individually) specific aspects of an archetypal image are somehow nonessential. This implies a prioritizing of the abstract over the concrete, the spiritual over the embodied. It also ignores the social oppressions that may seem to be sanctioned by the supposedly sacrosanct universal image, for we are all likely to be unconscious of our involvement in our own culture's assumptions. The relegation of women to subservient roles, for example, may appear sanctioned by traditional notions of archetypal femininity.

Archetypal images feel objective, in some way given, not dependent on prior personal experience, not explicable on the basis of our conscious knowledge. We feel in touch with something hitherto unknown and are often amazed to discover parallels between the images and motifs that appear in our own dreams and those that figure prominently in myths or folktales we know nothing about. The impact of these correspondences is powerful. To experience the unconscious as an objective rather than simply a subjective realm may help free us from the ego's view of the unconscious as "my" unconscious.

These images feel numinous, magic, fascinating, daemonic, or divine. They seem to have a transcendent, autonomous source beyond individual consciousness, beyond ourselves. There is a dangerous aspect to this feeling, the danger of being inflated or possessed, the danger of taking this to mean that these images are sacred and thus inviolable, unchangeable, that they come endowed with a cosmic endorsement.[8]

All archetypal images seem to evoke ambivalence in us. We are both drawn to and repelled by them; they have dark, fearsome, destructive aspects as well as a benign, creative side. We often try to deny this, to emphasize only the creative aspect, or to moralize and divide the archetype into good and bad parts—the positive mother and the negative mother, for example—and thereby lose some of the dynamic energy intrinsic to the images.

They feel transformative. Jung always emphasized that

archetypal images are connected to future as well as past: "The self... not only contains the deposit and totality of all past life, but is also a point of departure, the fertile soil from which all future life will spring. This premonition of futurity is as clearly impressed upon our innermost feelings as is the historical aspect."[9] He warns against taking this teleological aspect literally. We are not to think of archetypal images as having a ready-made meaning; rather we should think of them as indicators; otherwise we degrade them to being the mental equivalents of fortune tellers. The images present us with lifelines to be followed provisionally, for "life does not follow lines that are straight, nor lines whose course can be seen far in advance."[10]

It remains important, however, to recall that *we* give archetypal images this value, this significance. We are so easily led to separate the archetype from the psyche, to act as though we could freeze the ever-changing context in which the images appear.

Archetypal images are not absolute or unchanging. Indeed, when we treat them as if they are, we make them into *stereotypes*. Literally, a stereotype is a metal duplicate of a relief printing, the imprint taken from a mold. Stereotypes are rigid; they have lost the flexibility of the living archetype, the dynamism inherent in the image. Archetypes can become stereotypes when the images are no longer functioning as living images. Paradoxically, it is precisely when the socially or subjectively constructed aspect of the archetypal image is ignored, when the image is ontologized and given normative, universal sanction, that it may function as a stereotype. When this happens, we experience archetypal images as constrictive and confining, shaping us in ways that are not compatible with our ego-ideals or with our soul's deepest longings. For example, the hero archetype can be crippling when it becomes rigidified in this way, and the mother archetype can be oppressive to a modern woman in search of her soul.

Jung's way of working with archetypal images was not interpretation, translation into conceptual language, or reduction to some more abstract, general image, but what he called *amplification*—connecting the image to as many associated images as possible—and so, keeping us imagining. The point is to bring us in touch with their multiplicity, their fecundity, the sense of lively interconnectedness among them, not with their dependence on some common origin. Amplifying helps us get beyond our narrow personal selves and helps us "remember ourselves with a wider imagination."[11]

Archetypal images provide us with a "self-portrait" of the psyche and to reveal its protean, many-faceted character. They provide energy and direction for the continual renewal of life. To attend to them is to honor the many parts of ourselves that enrich and deepen our lives but may also add complexity and bring confusion. There are aspects of ourselves that we don't see; if we do see them, we don't like them, or we don't know how to harmonize them with our more familiar aspects. Some of these aspects may appear during particular periods in our lives and then seem to disappear. Some feel familiar and friendly, others alien and frightening.

There is no and can be no definitive list of archetypes or archetypal images. After his break with Freud, Jung spoke of going in search of the myth that was living him. Actually, our lives are shaped by a *plurality* of archetypal images. To be informed by only one is to be in its thrall and to abdicate from the living tension of their interplay, for the different images do not always arrange themselves in a neatly ordered, hierarchical pantheon. Often we will find them to be in conflict with one another. Many women artists, for example, have spoken of themselves as torn between the archetypal images of woman and artist.

Jung said that there are as many archetypes as there are typical situations in life.[12] This book focuses on a particular group of archetypal images that serve as mirrors of the self, images that help us see ourselves from many angles. The psyche is composed of various interacting subpersonalities that live within us. We will see how archetypal family figures—mother and father, orphaned child and benevolent grandfather—play active roles in our inner lives. We will discover the archetypal aspects of the various life stages through which we move as we experience childhood, youth, maturity, and old age. We will also explore the archetypal dimension of the roles that define our social identities and shape our interactions with others.

Throughout, we will examine personified images, how the self appears as a dramatic interaction among various personlike forms—the strutting self-important ego; the socially compliant persona; the elusive, fascinating anima. We will look not at youth but at puers and maidens, not at old age but at senexes and crones. None of these figures exists in isolation; each is in dramatic interaction with one another. As Jung put it, "In the unconscious the individual archetypes are not insulated from one another, but are in a state of contamination, of complete mutual interpenetration and fusion."[13] He sees that it is often "a well-nigh impossible undertaking to tear a single archetype out of the living tissue of the psyche."[14]

We need to learn to look at the images ecologically to see how they interpret and change one another. We probably all have had the experience of seeing how a situation in our lives or a figure in a dream changes its meaning as soon as we look at it through another myth or archetypal image. Often archetypal figures appear as part of a tandem: anima and animus, puer and senex, mother and son.[15] The anima appears differently when we link her with the animus rather than the shadow. Mothers appear differently to sons than to daughters, and being a daughter means something different to daughters than it does to mothers.

Thus there occurs an endless mirroring among the many different archetypal images. As in a funhouse or in Hesse's Magical Theater, these images reflect and shape one another, sometimes in distorted ways.

Sometimes we act as though Jung's description of the psyche provides us with a sacred map that cannot be redrawn. I have deliberately sought to break out of the notion that an archetypal description issues in canonically fixed entities by including James Hillman's essay on the anima and Demaris Wehr's essay on the animus, which radically challenge the received understanding of these figures, and by adding figures such as that of the double and the friend, which Jung does not include. I hope thereby to help us recover a sense of psyche as an activity, the activity of image-making, and of archetypal images as not static things, but as patterns in motion.

Jung always recognized the importance of conscious, active involvement with the archetypal images, of opening up a dialogue between consciousness and the unconscious. This entails neither repudiating nor identifying with the image or the ego. The point of conscious engagement with archetypal images is not to strengthen the ego, but rather to relativize it, to come to see that ego, too, is an archetype. For this reason, in looking at archetypal images that shape the self, we must begin with the ego. The archetypal perspective liberates us from viewing the ego's perspective as the only one. An archetypal view is inherently pluralistic, polytheistic, and thus inevitably critical of the dominance of the psyche by ego, hero, king, father. The very notion of archetype challenges the supremacy of the conscious, literal, fixed mind.

The point of archetypal images, like the point of myths, is not problem solving but "imagining, questioning, going deeper." [16] Archetypal images free us from identifying ourselves with our literal failures and successes or from seeing our lives as banal or trivial. The aim in attending to these images is to awaken us to a sense of our yet unrealized latent possibilities, to save us from our sense of isolation and meaninglessness. It is to open up our lives to renewal and reshaping.

Attending to the images creates a new bond between our personal lives and the collective experience of humankind. This accounts for the liberating effect so many people can testify to. As Jung said: "Life is crazy and meaningful at once. And when we do not laugh over the one aspect and speculate about the other, life is exceedingly drab, and everything is reduced to the littlest scale. There is then little sense and little nonsense either." [17]

There are many modes of access to the archetypal images that shape and have the power to help us reshape our lives. Among the situations that serve to constellate or activate such imagining are our own dreams and fantasies, our relationships with others, our moments of failure, and our moments of ecstasy. Sometimes a piece of literature come upon accidentally or a myth assiduously sought will arouse our own imagining, awaken us to analogies between our experience and that recorded in the discovered work. Sometimes reading an account of another's experience—such as those in this book—may open us to hitherto unexplored possibilities in our own lives. Sometimes it is just a matter of luck, of grace. . . .

I

Archetypal Figures in the Inner World

For most of us the introduction to an archetypal perspective comes with the discovery that, in a profound sense, *I* am *we*. The aspect of self, which I had naively thought of as *me*, the ego, is one late-appearing, self-important figure among many others. Jung compares the ego to "the ignorant demiurge who imagined he was the highest divinity."[1] He suggests that the discovery of the psyche's other aspects is like the discovery, once the sun has set, of the "star-strewn nightsky."[2]

We discover the archetypal realm first as we move toward a more complex understanding of our inner selves. We learn that our total personality includes not only the easily acknowledged ego but also the mask we put on to win social acceptance—the persona. We make reluctant acquaintance with a same-sex inner figure that embodies those of our attributes which the ego disowns—the shadow—and may also meet a same-sex alter ego that offers us companionship and support—the double. We meet an inner figure of the opposite sex that teaches us that strengths and vulnerabilities we may have thought belonged to women (if we are men) or to men (if we are women) are actually part of our own psychological potentiality—the anima and animus. We discover that we carry within us an intimation of a whole Self that can never become fully conscious or actualized but that draws us toward a richer, fuller life. And we find that these many inner figures are not peculiar to ourselves but are archetypal images, typically or perhaps universally appearing figures.

Having been introduced to the archetypal realm by these figures of our inner world, we are then prepared to see that our responses to intimate others, to the various lifestages through which we move, and to the various roles we play also have an archetypal dimension. All may be colored by hitherto unconscious associations, memories, and expectations, by imaginal connections that are not simply personal but have a collective dimension.

Jung's archetype-based psychology offers us a phenomenology of the self, a description based on what appears and on how the unconscious psyche *shows itself* to consciousness. Jung seeks to do psychology from the psyche's rather than the ego's perspective, from the inside rather than the outside. He invites us to see with the help of the unconscious, rather than just look at it.

As Jung tries to describe how the psyche appears to us once we adopt an archetypal perspective, he offers an account of the psyche as a list of *dramatis personae*. The psyche's own version of itself is animated, anthropomorphic, and dramatic, as though it consists of a group of persons actively interacting to support, challenge, undermine, betray, or complement one another.

Jung admits that this is a rather comical yet nonetheless accurate view because the unconscious always shows itself to consciousness in the form of personified images.[3] The psyche's own privileged symbol for itself is that of a dramatic play rather than of a space divided up into areas, with consciousness representing one subfield and the personal unconscious and the collective unconscious other subfields. Jung's way of representing the psyche helps us see it as an energy field, as a dynamic process rather than as a static structure.

The particular persons, or subpersonalities, whom Jung includes in the cast of characters are drawn from his own experience. In the chapter "Encounter with the Unconscious" in his autobiography *Memories, Dreams, Reflections*, Jung recalls the dream figures that provided him with the experiential basis for his theoretical writings about the shadow, the anima, the wise old man, and the Self. In the course of his clinical work he found that his patients' dreams were filled with similar figures, and so he came to believe that they were, indeed, archetypal or universal, rather than peculiar to himself, that these persons represent natural, typically occurring psychological processes.

Recognition of these figures makes it possible to picture the archetypes of the unconscious in this personified mode. This transforms the "rushing phantasmagoria of fugitive images"[4] into figures with whom the conscious ego can engage in dialogue so that the complementary, compensatory function of the unconscious may be effective. To discover these figures at work in our own inner lives is to be freed from an identification of ourselves with the most familiar side of our personality. We are brought in touch with other modes of perception and feeling, with forgotten memories, neglected or devalued capacities, and repressed energies, which have the power to enrich and deepen our lives.

When we meet these other parts of ourselves as inner persons, we can engage them as we do persons in the outer world. In fact, we may find that our initial encounter with these inner figures is through our engagements with actual others on whom we've projected parts of ourselves. The intense irritation I feel at my bossy, hypercritical colleague, which I know to be exaggerated, may introduce me to my own supercilious shadow side. The erotic pull I feel toward gentle, poetic men may teach me that what I seek from them I can discover within myself. Paying attention to our most charged responses to others may provide us with clues about ourselves, as happens when we attend to figures appearing in our dreams. The sinister drug-runner or the sexy nightclub singer whom I remember with startling clarity upon wakening may guide me to unsuspected aspects of myself.

We can encourage these inner figures to speak more directly and clearly to us by communicating that we are, indeed, ready to listen. To start, we can simply observe our emotional reactions and our dreams more closely, more lovingly. We might then go on to imagine these figures as actively present, as available for us to converse with, to argue against and learn from. We can try to learn *their* needs, to understand *their* perspectives, to value *their* strengths. As we establish a more conscious relation to these archetypal images that live within our own souls, we can free ourselves from being driven by *their* fears and desires, by impulses whose power in our lives we may never before have directly confronted. We may also learn how to make use of their wisdom and their energy.

Jung's most clearly worked-out archetypal description of the psyche appears in *Aion*, the 1950 work subtitled *Researches into the Phenomenology of the Self*. He includes short chapters on the ego, the shadow, the syzygy (anima and animus), and the Self. I have borrowed that ordering and added to it. It seems important, however, to insist that we rarely encounter these figures in a neat and simple order; we don't first engage the shadow, move on to anima, and then find ourselves ready to move toward integration with the Self. Instead, we find ourselves simultaneously engaged on many fronts, and often not able to discern clearly what or who is shadow or animus or double.

We begin with Jung's own description of the ego, the conscious part of the self. Jung wants us to understand that, although we experience the ego as the most unique and individual aspect of our personality, the very insistence on our individuality is archetypal! The voice in me that shouts "I, I, I" is actually a collective voice. The need to insist on my specialness is something I share with almost everyone else. The wish that all I need to acknowledge as "me" is the familiar and acceptable part, the rational and in-control part, is well-nigh universal. The ego is that part of us which claims to be the whole and yet is actually just a part of the total personality (which Jung calls the Self.) Depth psychology *relativizes* the ego by making us aware of how much of the psyche lies outside consciousness.

We then move to a description of the *persona* by Jungian analyst Edward C. Whitmont, taken from his book *The Symbolic Quest*, which remains one of the clearest summaries and interpretations of the classic Jungian perspective. As Whitmont notes, we are often introduced to the archetypal realm with the discovery that we have identified ourselves with the mask we have put on in order to conform to social expectations.

This insight opens us to a recognition of how much more there is to us than this mask and to a discovery of the *shadow*, all those aspects of ourselves we have disowned and rejected—our rage, sexuality, or fragility. Jung suggests that the shadow is a close equivalent to Freud's repressed unconscious and to what he himself calls "the personal unconscious." But to meet these aspects of ourselves as shadow is to meet them in a vividly present, condensed personified form. It is also to meet this aspect of ourselves as a typical dimension of the human psyche, rather than as a shamefully isolating unique burden.

The shadow is my dark other self and, as Jung suggests, usually appears as a same-sex figure. We may first meet the shadow in our dreams but are even more likely initially to encounter it as projected on someone in the outer world toward whom we have exaggeratedly negative feelings. Infidelity, anger, or vulnerability are all more easily seen in persons other than ourselves. Once seen as internal, however, we are forced to recognize the presence in us of a hitherto unsuspected personlike entity, one who has memories, desires, and fears as complexly organized as those of our familiar ego-self and yet radically different. This shadow-self has grown up with little nurture or care and so is a strangely misshapen creature. When first met, the shadow is ugly, disruptive, and fearsome, like the toad in the Grimms' fairy tale whom the princess must take to bed. Yet if we can learn to acknowledge "this, too, is me," the shadow may provide us with continually new energies and perspectives.

The excerpt from poet and storyteller Robert Bly's *A Little Book on the Human Shadow* gives us a vivid sense of what he calls "the long bag we drag behind us." Bly helps us see how the shadow is formed, why it is so frightening when we catch glimpses of it in adult life, and the cost to us of continuing to reject it. The next selection, excerpts from Jungian analyst Patricia Berry's book *Echo's Body*, suggests that the truly threatening shadow aspect—and therefore the one with the power to create psychic tension and stimulate transformation—is not the obvious, neatly balanced, expected polar opposite of our ego-ideal, not the announced-ahead-of-time total stranger, but a more unexpected and most unwelcome close cousin.

Jung introduced the terms *anima* and *animus* to refer to what he calls the unconscious contrasexual elements within the psyche: *anima* designates the feminine aspects (or inner woman) in the male psyche, *animus* the masculine aspects (or inner man) in the female psyche. Jung seems to have taken for granted that men are socialized to identify consciously with those psychological capacities our culture views as masculine and to have left undeveloped or unconscious the psychological capacities usually thought of as feminine. He believed that a parallel process occurs for women. The discovery that these consciously disavowed capacities nevertheless live within as nascent potentialities may initially be even more frightening than engagement with our shadow-selves. For a man to acknowledge his own hitherto hidden femininity—his tender, receptive, nurturing qualities—may seem to threaten gender identity. Yet it also may yield access to an enormous store of untapped energy. The inner woman may thus appear dangerous but alluring; she threatens ego-dissolution and yet promises to serve as a guide to the depths of the soul.

Gender roles are no longer as clearly defined as they were in Jung's time. Today our very understanding of masculine and feminine is in question. Therefore, this part of his theory has occasioned much discussion and re-visioning in recent years. Some of what he wrote about anima and animus still seems very right and liberating; other parts feel wrong and even oppressive. Again we turn to Edward C. Whitmont and *The Symbolic Quest* for a lucid and vivid restatement of Jung's perspective, though even Whitmont suggests it might be helpful to name this aspect of the psyche the "Yin element" rather then the "feminine."

A more radical recasting of anima theory is offered by James Hillman, who has written challenging essays on many aspects of archetypal theory. In his book *Anima: An Anatomy of a Personified Notion*, from which I have extracted a few pages, he proposes that we would do better to move beyond the culturebound contrasexual assumptions of Jung's theory to a recognition of anima as "an archetypal structure of consciousness" present in the psyches of women as well as men. He emphasizes not the "inner woman" aspect of the anima but rather anima as "soul guide," representing that part of ourselves which might teach us to be present in the world not on the basis of rational ego-consciousness but *imaginally*. Anima, he says, "provides a specifically structured mode of being in the world, a way of behaving, perceiving, feeling that gives events the significance not of love but of soul." It is anima-consciousness that lends soul-stirring significance to the events of ordinary life. Like any man, I as a woman, have much to learn from this figure that lives within me, and being female does not mean I can do without her guidance.

Hillman notes that every archetype always seems to imply another, although not always the same other. Our understanding is enhanced and deepened as we may look at anima as paired first with ego and then with shadow, as contrasted with persona and with Self. Most often, however, anima is paired with animus, "as though to do her full justice one has to give him equal time."[5] But anima and animus are not as parallel as they might appear, for the pairing implies that female psychology can be *deduced* from male psychology, and that women's psyches are but the logical obverse of men's. Many recent writers have observed that contrasexuality may play a less central role in the psychology of women than it does in men's psychology, in part because the first primary attachment figure for women is a same-sex other, the mother.

Jung discovered the anima through reflection on his own experience but inferred that a comparable contrasexual figure, the animus, must play a parallel role in the psychology of women. Traditional animus theory seems to tell us more about men's views of women than about women's own self-understanding. In an essay that originally appeared in *Anima*, Demaris Wehr, a professor of religion and psychology and author of *Jung and Feminism*, examines what Jung has to say about the animus and tries to articulate why so many women, beginning with Jung's own female patients, have rejected most of his definition of this archetype. Wehr nevertheless acknowledges that an "inner man" does figure in our inner lives, albeit not as the guide to the deepest depths of our soul, not as centrally as anima in the inner lives of men.

In fact, it may be, as Hillman has suggested, that just as anima appears in the psyches of both women and men, so does animus. He suggests that what we mean by animus is really the ego freed of its self-pretensions, its claim to be the whole of the self. Animus then becomes a name for an ego in touch with anima, an ego paired with anima. The ego is radically transformed when the qualities traditionally associated with it—consciousness, focused attention, intellect, will, self-assurance—are brought into paired relationship with a more diffuse and image-based awareness, with feeling and receptivity.[6] Such re-visionings help us reflect on how well the traditional descriptions of the archetypes accord with our own experience; they may help us see how trying to fit our experience into ready-made definitions may sometimes prove distorting. Nevertheless, the more traditional understanding of anima and animus may by now be so well established that *anima* will continue mostly to mean "the inner woman" and *animus* "the inner man."

In the traditional Jungian understanding, anima is a function of male psychology and animus applies to women. Jung and Jungians[7] who adopt this view often speak of the androgyne, who has fully actualized both masculine and feminine psychological potentialities, as offering us a privileged image of the integrated self. Human wholeness is here defined in contrasexual terms: the challenge of individuation for a man is establishing a conscious relation to his anima; for a woman, it is forming a conscious bond with her animus. One difficulty with this is, of course, that it confirms social stereotypes and accepts the notion that intellectual capacity, goal-directedness, creative energy, courage, and self-confidence are somehow inherently masculine, and other qualities, such as being in touch with one's feelings, are intrinsically feminine.

Another difficulty is that it assumes that the most important helpful inner figures will always be contrasexual. The opposite-sex images within the psyche are seen as soul guides because the most important same-sex figure included in Jung's description of the psyche, the shadow, is primarily defined in negative terms. But many of us, both heterosexual and homosexual, would testify to the positive role played by inner helpers that are the same sex as ourselves. This has led Mitchell Walker, a Jungian-oriented therapist and author of *Between Men: A Sex Guide and Consciousness Book*, to propose that there is a singularly important "soul figure" whom Jung failed to include: the *double*, which is distinguishable from both shadow and anima as a supportive same-sex partner or alter ego. His essay helps us remember the importance of not taking Jung's description of the psyche as definitive.

The last essay, by Jungian-oriented therapist and poet David DeBus, is a sensitive account of individuation—the process of engaging all these parts of the Self and moving toward some degree of wholeness and integration. Part I helps us see how an archetypal perspective on the Self issues in a *polycentric* view. We move beyond imagining that the other parts of the psyche—shadow, anima, animus, double—all simply orbit around a stable center, the ego. We discover, rather, that each of these figures within the self may from time to time occupy center stage.

C. G. Jung

The Ego:
The Conscious
Side of the
Personality

Although its bases are in themselves relatively unknown and unconscious, the ego is a conscious factor par excellence. It is even acquired, empirically speaking, during the individual's lifetime. It seems to arise in the first place from the collision between the somatic factor and the environment, and, once established as a subject, it goes on developing from further collisions with the outer world and the inner.

Despite the unlimited extent of its bases, the ego is never more and never less than consciousness as a whole. As a conscious factor the ego could, theoretically at least, be described completely. But this would never amount to more than a picture of the *conscious personality;* all those features which are unknown or unconscious to the subject would be missing. A total picture would have to include these. But a total description of the personality is, even in theory, absolutely impossible, because the unconscious portion of it cannot be grasped cognitively. This unconscious portion, as experience has abundantly shown, is by no means unimportant. On the contrary, the most decisive qualities in a person are often unconscious and can be perceived only by others, or have to be laboriously discovered with outside help.

Clearly, then, the personality as a total phenomenon does not coincide with the ego, that is, with the conscious personality, but forms an entity that has to be distinguished from the ego. Naturally the need to do this is incumbent only on a psychology that reckons with the fact of the unconscious, but for such a psychology the distinction is of paramount importance.

I have suggested calling the total personality which, though present, cannot be fully known, the self. The ego is, by definition, subordinate to the self and is related to it like a part to the whole. Inside the field of consciousness it has, as we say, free will. By this I do not mean anything philosophical, only the well-known psychological fact of "free choice," or rather the subjective feeling of freedom. But, just as our free will clashes with necessity in the outside world, so also it finds its limits outside the field of consciousness in the subjective inner world, where it comes into conflict with the facts of the self. And just as circumstances or outside events "happen" to us and limit our freedom, so the self acts upon the ego like an *objective occurrence* which free will can do very little to alter. It is, indeed, well known that the ego not only can do nothing against the self, but is sometimes actually assimilated by unconscious components of the personality that are in the process of development and is greatly altered by them.

It is, in the nature of the case, impossible to give any general description of the ego except a formal one. Any other mode of observation would have to take account of the *individuality* which attaches to the ego as one of its main characteristics. Although the numerous elements composing this complex factor are, in themselves, everywhere the same, they are infinitely varied as regards clarity, emotional colouring, and scope. The result of their combination—the ego—is therefore, so far as one can judge, individual and unique, and retains its identity up to a certain point. Its stability is relative, because far-reaching changes of personality can sometimes occur. Alterations of this kind need not always be pathological; they can also be developmental and hence fall within the scope of the normal.

Since it is the point of reference for the field of consciousness, the ego is the subject of all successful attempts at adaptation so far as these are achieved by the will. The ego therefore has a significant part to play in the psychic economy. Its position there is so important that there are good grounds for the prejudice that the ego is the centre of the personality, and that the field of consciousness is the psyche *per se*. If we discount certain suggestive ideas in Leibniz, Kant, Schelling, and Schopenhauer, and the philosophical excursions of Carus and von Hartmann, it is only since the end of the nineteenth century that modern psychology, with its inductive methods, has discovered the foundations of consciousness and proved empirically the existence of a psyche outside consciousness. With this discovery the position of the ego, till then absolute, became relativized; that is to say, though it retains its quality as the centre of the field of consciousness, it is questionable whether it is the centre of the personality. It is part of the personality but not the whole of it. As I have said, it is simply impossible to estimate how large or how small its share is; how free or how dependent it is on the qualities of this "extra-conscious" psyche. We can only say that its freedom is limited and its dependence proved in ways that are often decisive.

Edward C. Whitmont

The Persona: The Mask We Wear for the Game of Living

The term *persona*, taken from the Latin, refers to the ancient actor's mask which was worn in the solemn ritual plays. Jung uses the term to characterize the expressions of the archetypal drive toward an adaptation to external reality and collectivity. Our personas represent the roles we play on the worldly stage; they are the masks we carry throughout this game of living in external reality. The persona, as representational image of the adaptation archetype, appears in dreams in the images of clothes, uniforms and masks.

In childhood our roles are set by parental expectations. The child tends to behave in such a way as to win approval from his elders, and this is the first pattern of ego formation. This first persona pattern is made up of collective cultural codes of behavior and value judgments as they are expressed and transmitted through the parents; at this point parental demands and the demands of the outside world in general seem identical. In the course of adequate psychological development it is necessary for a differentiation between ego and persona to occur. This means that we have to become aware of ourselves as individuals apart from the external demands made upon us, we have to acquire a sense of responsibility and a capacity for judgment which are not necessarily identical with external collective expectations and standards, though of course these standards must be given due regard. We have to discover that we use our representational clothes for protection and appearance but that we can also change into something more comfortable when it is appropriate and can be naked at other times. If our clothes stick to us or seem to replace our skin we are likely to become ill.

We must learn to adapt to cultural and collective demands in accordance with our role in society—our occupation or profession and social position—and still be ourselves. We need to develop both an adequate persona mask and an ego. If this differentiation fails, a pseudoego is formed; the personality pattern is based on stereotyped imitation or on a merely dutiful performance of one's collectively assigned part in life. The pseudoego is a stereotyped precipitate of collective standards; one "is" the professor or judge or society matron rather than an individual who gives the role its proper due at the necessary times. Such a pseudoego is not only rigid but also extremely fragile and brittle; the necessary supportive psychic energy from the unconscious is not forthcoming but rather is in opposition to consciousness, since such an ego is completely split off from the intentions of the Self. The pseudoego is subject to constant pressure from within and has no means of adjusting its precarious balance; it often straddles the boundary of psychosis. The threatening elements of the opposing objective psyche are likely to be experienced in projection upon the outside world to the degree that paranoid delusions arise, and the pseudoego deals with these by retreating further into the protective role-identification; the vicious circle again.

An extreme example of the psychic dissociation that accompanies the persona-identified pseudoego is given by Bennet in his description of a girl who was haunted by a double.[1] As a child she felt she had to be perfect to make up for her dead sister's absence, and by the time she had reached her teens she had fallen into a depressive state marked by repeated suicidal attempts to get away from "Kathleen," her pseudoego. She saw herself as "a tiny, undeveloped baby, still living in the first moment of existence, unable to conceive of love and hate as coming from the same source." She was entirely selfish and love-hungry. "The socially-adapted Kathleen, on the other hand, was a nineteen-year-old student, fond of music and painting, a good teacher, keen on literature and with a knowledge of French and German—a false and empty creature."[2] The persona identification which was the source of her failure to develop a genuine ego (the tiny, undeveloped baby) is clearly described in a dream of hers which is taken from Bennet's description: "I am standing in a vast hall. It is very cold and I am . . . worried lest I had come to the wrong place. . . . I became frightened and turn to run away, but I could not get away. Before me was a large mirror in which I could see myself in fancy dress. I was wearing black silk pajamas. . . . I wanted to take off the pajamas, not from myself, but from my reflection in the mirror. . . . I tore off one jacket after another and there seemed to be no end to it all, for on removing one another was revealed."[3]

The dream depicts the cold, depersonalized world (the cold hall) in which she becomes frightened through her dim sense of being in the "wrong place," as indeed she is. She cannot get away because she cannot get hold of herself; she is not in touch with herself but only with her reflected image, hence the persona identification cannot be "taken off," cannot be overcome. Under each jacket is another jacket; the naked selfhood cannot be reached in the cold atmosphere of a mere reflected reality.

A person in such a state needs the impact of individual feeling, which develops a sense of one's own individual identity. But he will protect himself, with a formidable array of "clothing," against having his real skin touched, against precisely this feeling impact.

When individuality is thus confused with the social role, when the reality adaptation is not sufficiently individual but is wholly collective, the result may also often be a state of inflation. Its victim feels great and powerful because he is a fine public figure, but he fails to be a human being or even to make the first steps toward becoming human. Such an inflated overreliance upon the persona, or identity with it, results in rigidity and lack of genuine responsiveness. Such a person is nothing but the role, be it doctor, lawyer, administrator, mother, daughter or whatever part is so compulsively played. The example of Eichmann has shown how such a role-identified nonpersonality fails to develop a personal, moral responsibility; he has no ethical principles or personal feelings and values of his own but hides behind collective morality and prescribed manners. He has no conflicts of conscience because everything is settled beforehand in a stereotyped fashion.

It is hard for this kind of person, who usually thinks of himself as abiding by the highest principles, to realize that he is really immoral. It is rather shocking to discover that something deep within oneself may demand individual decision at the price of individual risk. There is such a universal human tendency to confuse one's clothing with one's skin that this differentiation becomes a crucial ethical problem.

At the opposite end of the spectrum, when persona formation is inadequate because of poor social training or rejection of the social forms as a result of feeling excluded in some way, one cannot play or refuses to play the assigned role successfully. Such a person will suffer from lack of poise, unnecessary defiance and overdefensiveness.

Personality development is thus interfered with at either extreme; an ill-formed persona is just as limiting as its opposite. An inadequate relationship to the persona archetype may range from a fixation in its purely collective aspect to a rebellious refusal or inability to accept any collective adaptation or demand. Examples of dreams that express the former condition are those of being unable to take off one's clothes, of being stuck in heavy armor, of being overdressed or of wearing heavy, overdecorated gaudy uniforms, of having an overly hard or tough skin. The opposite condition, the refusal of the collective, might be expressed in dreams of being at a party stark naked, of discovering suddenly while walking in the street that one has on a transparent gown, of appearing in filthy rags at a reception, of being an oyster without a shell or a flabby mass of jelly.

If the persona is too rigidly "stuck," if one lacks the necessary distinction between individual skin and collective clothes, one is in a precarious position; it is as if one's skin could not breathe. Actual skin diseases may even coincide with such difficulties. There was a young woman who had a severe skin eruption on her face, which resisted all attempts at treatment. She discovered in the course of analysis (which was undertaken for an entirely different reason) that she had a serious adaptational problem; she had always hidden the fact that she was Jewish when she applied for a job, in order to save face, as she expressed it. Psychologically speaking, it was as if she continually wore a mask on her face. The unconscious reaction to this failure to bare her face was expressed in the actual skin eruption, which ceased when she was able to risk exposure of her face psychologically.

Collectivity and individuality are a pair of polar opposites; hence there is an oppositional and compensatory relationship between persona and *shadow*. The brighter the persona, the darker the shadow. The more one is identified with one's glorified, wonderful social role, the less it is played and recognized as merely a role, the darker and more negative will be one's genuine individuality as a consequence of its being thus neglected. But on the other hand too much concern with the shadow, with one's "bad" side—overconcern with how one appears, with how unattractive and awkward one is—can make for a rather negative, defensive and miserable persona. This negative—that is, unadapted—persona will then express itself in stiffness, uncertainty or compulsive, primitive behavior.

Even though at first the ego finds itself in and through the persona, we have seen that the two are not meant to remain in a state of identity. We are performers in the social game, but we must also participate in another play. We are also meant to be our individual selves.

Robert Bly

The Shadow:
The Rejected
Self

When we were one or two years old we had what we might visualize as a 360-degree personality. Energy radiated out from all parts of our body and all parts of our psyche. A child running is a living globe of energy. We had a ball of energy, all right; but one day we noticed that our parents didn't like certain parts of that ball. They said things like: "Can't you be still?" Or "It isn't nice to try and kill your brother." Behind us we have an invisible bag, and the part of us our parents don't like, we, to keep our parents' love, put in the bag. By the time we go to school our bag is quite large. Then our teachers have their say: "Good children don't get angry over such little things." So we take our anger and put it in the bag. By the time my brother and I were twelve in Madison, Minnesota, we were known as "the nice Bly boys." Our bags were already a mile long.

Then we do a lot of bag-stuffing in high school. This time it's no longer the evil grownups that pressure us, but people our own age. So the student's paranoia about grownups can be misplaced. I lied all through high school automatically to try to be more like the basketball players. Any part of myself that was a little slow went into the bag. My sons are going through the process now; I watched my daughters, who were older, experience it. I noticed with dismay how much they put into the bag, but there was nothing their mother or I could do about it. Often my daughters seemed to make their decision on the issue of fashion and collective ideas of beauty, and they suffered as much damage from other girls as they did from men.

So I maintain that out of a round globe of energy the twenty-year-old ends up with a slice. We'll imagine a man who has a thin slice left—the rest is in the bag—and we'll imagine that he meets a woman; let's say they are both twenty-four. She has a thin, elegant slice left. They join each other in a ceremony, and this union of two slices is called marriage. Even together the two do not make up one person! Marriage when the bag is large entails loneliness during the honeymoon for that very reason. Of course we all lie about it. "How is your honeymoon?" "Wonderful, how's yours?"

Different cultures fill the bag with different contents. In Christian culture sexuality usually goes into the bag. With it goes much spontaneity. Marie Louise von Franz warns us, on the other hand, not to sentimentalize primitive cultures by assuming that they have no bag at all. She says in effect that they have a different but sometimes even larger bag. They may put individuality into the bag, or inventiveness. What anthropologists know as "participation mystique," or "a mysterious communal mind," sounds lovely, but it can mean that tribal members all know exactly the same thing and no one knows anything else. It's possible that bags for all human beings are about the same size.

We spend our life until we're twenty deciding what parts of ourself to put into the bag, and we spend the rest of our lives trying to get them out again. Sometimes retrieving them feels impossible, as if the bag were sealed. Suppose the bag remains sealed—what happens then? A great nineteenth-century story has an idea about that. One night Robert Louis Stevenson woke up and told his wife a bit of a dream he'd just had. She urged him to write it down; he did, and it became "Dr. Jekyll and Mr. Hyde." The nice side of the personality becomes, in our idealistic culture, nicer and nicer. The Western man may be a liberal doctor, for example, always thinking about the good of others. Morally and ethically he is wonderful. But the substance in the bag takes on a personality of its own; it can't be ignored. The story says that the substance locked in the bag appears one day *somewhere else* in the city. The substance in the bag feels angry, and when you see it, it is shaped like an ape, and moves like an ape.

The story says then that when we put a part of ourselves in the bag it regresses. It de-evolves toward barbarism. Suppose a young man seals a bag at twenty and then waits fifteen or twenty years before he opens it again. What will he find? Sadly, the sexuality, the wildness, the impulsiveness, the anger, the freedom he put in have all regressed; they are not only primitive in mood, they are hostile to the person who opens the bag. The man who opens his bag at forty-five or the woman who opens her bag rightly feels fear. She glances up and sees the shadow of an ape passing along the alley wall; anyone seeing that would be frightened.

Patricia Berry

The Shadow:
Agent Provocateur

I have always found the shadow the most difficult of psychological experiences, even though it is supposed to be the first and so presumably the easiest. The shadow is not difficult to understand conceptually. The idea is based on a model of opposites and Jung's notion of the one-sidedness of conscious functioning. What is easy to understand theoretically is practically and experientially more difficult. Part of the difficulty for me, I thought, had to do with my generation of the fifties and sixties in which conscious identifications were uncertain, since consciousness itself was uncertain. The generation Jung addressed appeared more solid, still a bit Victorian in its convictions. In that generation, there seemed a clear distinction between what the ego embraced and the shadow undid. There was a light and a darkness of the light. There really were Dr. Jekylls and Mr. Hydes.

In my generation we were "on the road" with Kerouac, wailing with Elvis, Fats Domino, Little Richard; we also embraced the virtues of science (there was a space race, and LSD was a chemical compound); we were idealistic (we marched for racial integration and burnt draft cards).

Now all of this confused emotionality (beatnik, scientific, idealistic) makes of the shadow a complicated entity. First, there is not *a* shadow but many (as there is not one conscious standpoint but many—all equally serious, depending upon the mood and the moment). Structures of awareness shift. What is relatively conscious at one moment is not at the next. As the source of light shifts, as position or situation changes (as a different light is cast on things), so the shadow wanders.

The shadow must threaten awareness, and nothing *in general* is really threatening. Only the specific and the unexpected hit us hard. The specific is intimate (close, small, near), and the unexpected is simply the unconscious itself. So the shadow comes in specific and unexpected moments—in the moment I am baring my soul and also manipulating for sympathy; or when I am feeling love and genuine warmth for my analysand—then realize it is *my* need, and that I am also binding the analysand to me; or when I predict a marriage is breaking up—and realize my prediction is playing a role in the disaster, scheming it along; or, in the realm of thought, when I'm speaking intellectually and suddenly realize I am lost in my own abstraction.

There seems a certain masochistic enjoyment in shadow awareness. We must like this suffering, else why do it? Something in us must delight as our ground collapses. Maybe this painful enjoyment of losing certainty is an aesthetic pleasure—like the enjoyment of a good play or novel that upsets, turns round the way we have viewed things and, through the tensions it creates, forces on us another vision.

So we come to tension. Shadow awareness proceeds through tension, and again we find that the more specific or close our focus on shades of difference, the more the tension. It is the pink that clashes with the red, because they are so close. Blue does not clash with red so much as it compensates or balances it, preventing the intimate tension that makes for specific shadow awareness.

As an example of these tensions: a woman I work with in analysis is wildly libidinous, irrational, and "liberated" in her night life; whereas in her day life, she is rational, considered, responsible. These red and blue opposites stand side by side, balancing each other in a way that does not move and makes psychic work difficult. Although the red and blue sides of her personality are large-scale opposites, they are not effective shadows. They do not create tension, nor would they make an interesting painting. A psychologically working tension, a moving tension, would be between her softly pink sentimental notions of love and her red hot-tin-roof nights. Then her pink and red would be in tension.

This aesthetic emphasis on the particular is like Jung's insistence on the individual—the unique against which he posited the collective.

Edward C. Whitmont

Anima: The Inner Woman

As a numinous image, namely as an affective image spontaneously produced by the objective psyche, the anima represents the eternal feminine—in any and all of her four possible aspects and their variants and combinations as Mother, Hetaira, Amazon and Medium. She appears as the goddess of nature, *Dea Natura*, and the Great Goddess of Moon and Earth who is mother, sister, beloved, destroyer, beautiful enchantress, ugly witch, life and death, and in one person or in various aspects of the one; thus she appears in innumerable images of enchanting, frightening, friendly, helpful or dangerous feminine figures, or even in animal figures as we have seen—foremost as cat, snake, horse, cow, dove, owl—which mythology assigns to certain feminine deities. She appears as seductress, harlot, nymph, muse, saint, martyr, maiden in distress, gypsy, peasant woman, the lady next door, or as the Queen of Heaven, the Holy Virgin, to mention but a few examples. These are some of the many facets in which feminine nature, the Yin element, has ever been experienced by men.

As a pattern of behavior, the archetype of the anima represents those drive elements which are related to life as life, as an unpremeditated, spontaneous, natural phenomenon, to the life of the instincts, the life of the flesh, the life of concreteness, of earth, of emotionality, directed toward people and things. It is the drive toward involvement, the instinctual connectedness to other people and the containing community or group. Whereas separate individuality is personified as a male element, connectedness—the "containing" unconscious, the group and the community—is experienced and personified as a feminine entity.

As a pattern of emotion the anima consists of the man's unconscious urges, his moods, emotional aspirations, anxieties, fears, inflations and depressions, as well as his potential for emotion and relationship. Whenever a man acts in identity with his anima—unconscious of the moods that "pull" him—he acts like a second-rate woman. In this form the anima represents a man's relatively unadapted, hence inferior, world of nature and emotional involvement, loves and hates. Consequently the objective psyche presents itself to the man at first as a totally irrational, dangerously primitive, chaotic temptation, as an enchanting seduction.

Since what we are speaking of constitutes a level of operativeness which has not yet been in consciousness and to a great extent is not capable of ever being completely realized consciously, yet which at the same time demands awareness and confrontation, the process of gaining even partial awareness of the anima constitutes an indispensable means of approach to the nonpersonal dimension of the objective psyche.

As long as the anima remains in an unconscious state, like all unconscious elements, her means of expression are compulsively primitive—through identity, inflation and projection.

Identity with the anima manifests itself in all sorts of *compulsive* moodiness, self-pity, sentimentality, depression, brooding withdrawal, fits of passion, morbid oversensitivity or effeminacy—namely in emotional and behavior patterns that cause the man to act like an inferior woman.

Inflation by the anima is a state in which ambitions, hopes and desires are confused with accomplished facts and realities. A minister who was fanatically impressed by the urgency of his particular mission had the following dream: "I heard a voice as if from the depths of space. It said that if Suzy did not leave the parsonage I would have to." Of such a voice from afar, with such a strong sense of authority, we might say that it was like the voice of the Self. His associations to "Suzy" were that she was no particular friend of his. Indeed he suspected that she did not care too much for him as a person. She admired him, even fancied herself in love with him, not because of himself but because he was a "man of God." His dream then says something like: There is an emotional personality aspect of you which is in love with the halo—with being the great "man of God." But unless that attitude leaves, unless you can gain some distance from it, you will fail as a minister (have to leave the parsonage yourself). For the inflation, the being in love with our own greatness, deprives us of our sense of human limitations. Then we become unrealistically exacting of ourselves and intolerant of others.

The inflationary aspect of the anima is most difficult to deal with because it tends to be so pleasantly convincing. Her illusion appears as obvious truth; one feels rather self-righteous and good about it. But, as we have seen by this time, just when we are most ardently convinced of an issue we are most likely to be in the grip of an unconscious power—hence most likely deceived.

The anima *in projection* is responsible for man's state of being in love or in hate. One has now met one's soul image, the ideal and only woman, or conversely an absolutely unbearable bitch. Both reactions are found to be fascinating and irresistible. In such situations there tends to be a compulsive involvement which we can neither deal with nor let alone. Were it simply the fact that the woman is so wonderful or so awful, we could either love her or leave her. But if we can do neither, then we are under the arresting spell of the archetype.

Relationships to the other sex are almost bound to be initiated by anima or animus projections. But true relatedness requires that we reach past the projections to the reality of the other person. For the actual reality of the other person is likely to be quite at variance with the projected expectations, hence while the projections continue to prevail one feels disappointed and let down by the partner when he or she fails to conform to the image. Actual relatedness between one person and another, namely a meeting of "I" with "Thou," is therefore impossible unless the most unrealistic anima or animus projections have been dissolved—no small matter to accomplish. As long as only the anima projection determines the relationship, it tends to produce rather a pseudo-relatedness—between illusion and illusion—in the form of mutual fascinations and/or explosive resentments and flight reactions when the negative projections appear (the Puritan ghost, vampire, etc.). But remember that projections and the relations or pseudo-relations which they engender are states in which we find ourselves; they occur of themselves and cannot be avoided by will or good intentions. Our only chance lies in developing an awareness of when they happen and of the projected qualities involved.

The man's anima projection always offers a great temptation to the woman. She will tend to identify with his expectation and hence play-act, pretend to incorporate the man's ideal or his real or imagined needs. As an "anima woman" she may become all things to all men, a flirt or even a wise wife or inspiring muse, anticipating all of her husband's or lover's needs and aspirations, thereby making him so dependent on her that he falls in with all her plans and does what is expected of him. The wise wife, for instance, skillfully manages her husband and the whole situation between them. But, in Harding's terms, such a woman always refers to *her* husband, *her* marriage . . . with emphasis on the possessive pronoun.[1] It is her instinctive power-er drive and possessiveness or her need to seek security in identifying with a conventional persona or inspiring angel ideal that may induce the woman to act out such a role—and may make her lose her own soul, her own real identity, in the process.

In order to become a full person—not merely a cipher in a social role, or a male animal—or indeed sometimes in order to hold onto his manhood, a man must confront his anima and try to establish a living, growing relationship with her. This is of course essential for his relationships with other people also. When consciousness is held in thrall by the power of the archetype, the complex, which is formed around the archetype's nuclear core, and its projection make it next to impossible to come near to the reality of the other person. Jung describes what can happen when there is no confrontation by the man's ego of the "other" within:

> Very often the ego experiences a vague feeling of moral defeat and then behaves all the more defensively, defiantly, and self-righteously, thus setting up a vicious circle which only increases its feeling of inferiority. The bottom is then knocked out of the human relationship, for, like megalomania, a feeling of inferiority makes mutual recognition impossible, and without this there is no relationship.[2]

Confrontation of the anima, or for that matter of any unconscious autonomous complex or drive, requires awareness of the nature of its autonomous expectations and personal response patterns. It requires the establishment of a relationship to the complex as an autonomous entity like an inner "Thou," allowing for and consciously adapting to its urges and needs, channeling its impulses whenever and wherever possible into expressions compatible with external reality and the ethical dictates of one's innermost conscience; thus not only taking into account one's own accustomed habits and the demands of one's family and community responsibilities but also serving the needs of that which wants to come to life.

It is never a simple matter to meet the anima, however; she tends to appear with reflex-like speed, as an emotional reaction, before one has a chance to take heed, and by the time the ground has been surveyed she is gone, the feeling has vanished. An additional difficulty lies in the fact that the archetypes as such—the sources of all these reactions—cannot ever be integrated with any finality but continue to express themselves in ever new forms. Only their manifestations can be integrated, to the extent that one gets to know them, but the archetypes themselves are the

> foundation stones of the psychic structure, which in its totality exceeds the limits of consciousness and therefore can never become the object of direct cognition. Though the effects of anima and animus can be made conscious, they themselves are factors transcending consciousness and beyond the reach of perception and volition. Hence they remain autonomous despite the integration of their contents, and for this reason they should be borne constantly in mind.[3]

A fundamental fact we easily tend to lose sight of is that anima and animus are not subject to will and conscious control. We can never tame or eliminate them; we always have to be on the lookout for new tricks and surprises. Every intense affect indicates that anima or animus is at work. Unless we realize this we will always fall victim to the illusion that we have mastered it, and just when we feel self-righteous about this mastery we are already in the inflation which sets the next trap.

James Hillman

Anima:
Guide to
the Soul

The first notion of anima as the contrasexual side of man is conceived within a fantasy of opposites.[1] Men and women are opposites, conscious and unconscious are opposites, conscious masculinity and unconscious femininity are opposites. These oppositions are qualified further by others: a youthful consciousness has an elderly anima figure; an adult pairs with a *soror* image near his own age; senile consciousness finds correspondence in a girl child. Then, too, a social factor enters into the contrasexual definition. In several passages "anima" refers to the contrasocial, inferior personality. There is an opposition between the external role one plays in social life and the interior, less conscious life of the soul. This less conscious aspect which is turned inward and experienced as one's personal interiority is the anima as "soul-image."

The more a man identifies with his biological and social role as man (persona), the more will the anima dominate inwardly. As the persona presides over adaptation to collective consciousness, so the anima rules the inner world of the collective unconscious. As male psychology, according to Jung, shifts after mid-life toward its female opposite, so there is a physiological and social softening and weakening toward "the feminine," all of which are occasioned by the anima.

No doubt experience does confirm this first notion of the anima which holds her to be the inferior distaff side of men. Indeed, she is

ANIMA: GUIDE TO THE SOUL

first encountered through the dream figures, emotions, symptomatic complaints, obsessive fantasies and projections of Western men. Anima is "the glamorous, possessive, moody, and sentimental seductress in a man."[2]

Today the notions of "masculine" and "feminine" are in dispute. This dispute has helped differentiate gender roles from social ones, and even to differentiate kinds of gender identity, i.e., whether based on primary or secondary, manifest or genetic, physical or psychic gender characteristics. It has become difficult to speak of the anima as inferior femininity since we are no longer certain just what we mean with "femininity," let alone "inferior" femininity. Moreover, archetypal psychology has placed the very notion of the ego in doubt.[3] Ego-identity is not just one thing, but in a polytheistic psychology "ego" reflects any of several archetypes and enacts various mythologems. It may as well be influenced by a Goddess as by a God or Hero, and it may as well display "feminine" styles in behavior without this indicating either ego-weakness or incipient ego-loss.

Because the fantasy of opposites keeps the anima in a social tandem with either the persona or the shadow and in a gender tandem with masculinity, we neglect her phenomenology per se and so find it difficult to understand her except in distinction to these other notions (masculinity, shadow, animus, persona). We are always regarding anima phenomenology from within a harness or from the opposite arm of a balance. Our notions are drawn in compensation to something else to which she is always yoked.

That we conceive anima in tandems is already given by her phenomenology. So, we think of her in notions of attachment with body or with spirit, or in the mother–daughter mystery, in the masculine–feminine pairings, or in compensation with the persona, in collusion with the shadow, or as guide to the self.

In these pairs, like in the mythological imagery, anima is the reflective partner; she it is who provides the moment of reflection in the midst of what is naturally given. She is the psychic factor in nature, an idea formulated in the last century as "animism." We feel this moment of reflection in the contrary emotions that anima phenomena constellate: the fascination plus danger, the awe plus desire, the submission to her as fate plus suspicion, the intense awareness that this way lie both my life and my death. Without these soul-stirring emotions, there would be no significance in the natural places and human affairs to which she is attached. But, life, fate, and death cannot become "conscious," so that with her is constellated a consciousness of our fundamental unconsciousness. In other words, consciousness of this archetypal structure is never far from unconsciousness. Its primary attachment is to the state of nature, to all things that simply are—life, fate, death—and which can only be reflected but never separated from their impenetrable opacity. Anima stays close to this field of the natural unconscious mind.

Demaris Wehr

Animus:
The Inner Man

Jung understood the anima concept better than the animus concept because he experienced it from within, whereas he only deduced that an animus was operating within women, since he could not, by definition, experience it from within. His descriptions of the animus are from the outside, a man's experience of a woman in a certain frame of mind, rather than what she feels like inside herself.

Jung admitted the androcentric nature of the model as well as the prior nature of the concept of the anima and derivative nature of the animus.[1] In his autobiography, Jung tells us that he formed his concept of the anima out of his living experience of her during the period of confrontation with the unconscious. He named her "Salome," and found that she was always in the company of Philemon (a Wise Old Man). He understood their pairing later. The derivative nature of the animus may explain partly why women never quite resonate to the animus concept in the way men do the anima. Jung tells us in several places that, whereas men always understand fairly easily what is meant by the anima, women have trouble grasping what the animus is (*Two Essays, Aion*, "Marriage as a Psychological Relationship," and others). This is interesting. One major reason for this must be that the concept is androcentric—i.e., generated out of a male experience of women. Although we have tried for centuries, women are increasingly having trouble squeezing ourselves into molds made by others. Jung, himself, was aware of the problem of a male-made model of looking at women. He said in "Marriage as a Psychological Relationship":

> ... most of what men say about feminine eroticism, and particularly about the emotional life of women, is derived from their own anima projections and distorted accordingly. (Vol. 17, p. 198)

Similarly, in *Mysterium Coniunctionis*, Jung says:

> Statements by men on the subject of female psychology suffer principally from the fact that the projection of unconscious femininity is always strongest where critical judgment is most needed, that is, where a man is most involved emotionally. (Vol. 14, p. 278)

Yet, Jung fell into the trap he criticized.

NATURE AND MISOGYNY IN THE MODEL

Other factors besides androcentrism may account for the more problematic aspect of the animus, such as pure misogyny. The earliest theoretical formulations of the anima/animus theory are built on the notion that women, by definition, think in an inferior way, and that men, by definition, are deficient in emotional-personal relatedness. Early statements about the animus link his function to the deplorable state of women's thinking when he is unintegrated. The following statement from *Two Essays* is from the conclusion of the essay on "Anima and Animus" where Jung discusses the fact that the general means more to men than the personal. He says:

> ... his world consists of a multitude of co-ordinated factors, whereas her world, outside her husband, terminates in a sort of cosmic mist. (p. 210)

The task of the animus, then, at this early stage (and for many later theorists as well) is to lead a woman out of this cosmic mist into a differentiated and discriminating consciousness, something she sorely needs.

In this early discussion, too, a woman's inferior thinking and a man's inferior emotional relatedness are clearly implied by the following:

> If I were to attempt to put into a nutshell the difference between man
> and woman in this respect, i.e., what it is that characterizes the ani-
> mus as opposed to the anima, I could only say this: as the anima
> produces *moods*, so the animus produces opinions. (p. 206)

This is the classic understanding of the animus, and both anima and
animus are compensatory for what is lacking in consciousness in
both sexes.

Besides this fundamental difference in the characteristics of men
and women, and in the anima and animus, Jung's early and late
thought about the animus was that it was plural, whereas the anima
was singular. This fact is accounted for in at least two ways. The first
is that it reverses the conscious social situation in which men are
polygamously inclined, at least in their desires, and therefore are
monogamously inclined in their unconscious, focused on one woman. The opposite is true for women.

The anima/animus model is undergirded by several other assumptions as well. One is that biology provides a good analogy for
psychology, as though men's thinking were characterized by a penetrating, clean, incisive quality and as though women's consciousness were characterized by receptivity, generativity, passivity. The
biological analogy is carried to its furthest extreme, as far as I know,
by Hilde Binswanger. In an essay entitled "The Positive Animus,"
in *Spring*, 1963, she further corroborates the difference between animus and anima because it takes many sperms to reach one ovum.
On the biological level she finds evidence that the masculine principle would be plural and the feminine principle would be singular
(pp. 90-91). Although Jung did not use this particular analogy, he
did speak of the genetic imprint of the opposite sex in everyone. The
other assumptions on which the model is built are elaborated in *Two
Essays.*[2]

Often, Jung, when discussing the anima in men, refers to the
possibility that women did not have souls. He refers to it briefly in
Two Essays: "We have the testimony of art from all ages, and besides
that, the famous question '*Habet mulier animam?*' ("Does woman
have a soul?")."

In "Marriage as a Psychological Relationship," written in 1925,
Jung poses the question in all seriousness. He says, in discussing the
anima concept in men,

I have called this image the anima, and I find the scholastic question, *Habet mulier animam?* especially interesting, since in my view it is an intelligent one inasmuch as the doubt seems justified. Woman has no anima, no soul, but she has an animus. The anima has an erotic, emotional character, the animus a rationalizing one. (Vol. 17, p. 198)

In another essay, entitled "Mind and Earth," (Vol. 10), Jung says:

If we carefully examine the uncontrolled emotions of a man and try to reconstruct the probable personality underlying them, we soon arrive at a feminine figure which I call, as I said, the anima. On the same ground the ancients conceived of a feminine soul, a "psyche" or "anima," and not without good psychological reasons did the ecclesiastics of the Middle Ages propound the question, *Habet mulier animam?* (p. 41)

Besides the androcentric mold of the animus theory, another reason the animus concept did not seem to fit women's experiences as neatly as the anima concept did that of men's may be due to the repeated questions about whether or not women have souls. Even though Jung is always careful to state that he does not mean *soul* in the theological sense, the word carries that connotation, and the question *Habet mulier animam?* which Jung was so fond of quoting was a theological question.

JUNG'S FOLLOWERS

Jung's followers varied in the degree to which they followed in his footsteps with this theory. Many of his female followers picked it up and parroted Jung, describing the animus in terms of what it looked like from the outside—i.e., they adopted a male perspective themselves, looking at women from the outside. The description of the opinionated woman became well-known. Interestingly, Jung's wife, Emma Jung, did the first and, in my opinion, best job of describing the animus from the inside, from woman's *own* perspective and experience of herself. In her book *Animus and Anima*, the masculine principle is represented by four possibilities: the Word, Power, Meaning, and the Deed. These are remarkably on target in terms of the capacities which women need to claim for ourselves. Emma Jung was the first to describe the "negative animus" from the inside, which she describes as a self-devaluating voice, which, after devastating the woman, sometimes switches to exaggerated self-praise. She says,

> First, we hear from it a critical, usually negative comment on every movement, an exact examination of all motives and intentions, which naturally always causes feelings of inferiority, and tends to nip in the bud all initiative and every wish for self-expression. From time to time, this same voice may also dispense exaggerated praise, and the result of these extremes of judgment is that one oscillates to and fro between the consciousness of complete futility and a blown-up sense of one's own value and importance. (p. 20)

My guess is that Emma Jung's description resonates better with women's experiences of ourselves than Jung's own, primarily because it came from her own experience, and thus it is a touchstone for the experience of other women. It is more compassionate, too, in its understanding of the woman dominated by the "negative animus." Jung, himself, in his later years had changed somewhat in his use of the two concepts. In *Aion*, for example, he spoke of the two, anima and animus, much more often in conjunction with each other than he had in his earlier years. In his later years he emphasized the syzygy in both sexes more than the contrasexual element by itself. However, in *Aion*, he still spoke of the rather more difficult-to-grasp nature of the animus: "It is not quite so easy to recognize the woman's animus, for his name is legion" (p. 267).

THE MODEL OF BALANCE

Jung's model of contrasexuality was founded on the idea that what was the conscious experience of one sex was necessarily the unconscious component of the other; or that a man's experience of femininity in the unconscious is the same thing as a woman's conscious experience of femininity. For example, in *Mysterium Coniunctionis*, Jung says:

> In the metaphorical descriptions of the alchemists, Luna is primarily a reflection of a man's unconscious femininity, but she is also the principle of the feminine psyche, in the sense that Sol is the principle of a man's. . . . If then Luna characterizes the feminine psyche and Sol

the masculine, consciousness would be an exclusively masculine affair, which is obviously not the case since woman possesses consciousness too. But as we have previously identified Sol with consciousness
and Luna with the unconscious, we would now be driven to the conclusion that a woman cannot possess a consciousness. (pp. 178–179)

To rectify this situation, Jung suggests that the moon characterizes
the unconscious of a man whereas it characterizes the consciousness
of a woman. "Her consciousness has a lunar rather than a solar character. Its light is the 'mild' light of the moon, which merges things
together rather than separates them" (p. 179). Many Jungians have
picked this up as a description of woman's consciousness, as well as
the character of the feminine in general. Yet, in other places, as we
have seen, Jung knows that men's experiences of and descriptions of
women cannot but be distorted, since they are seen through a veil of
projections. Ann Ulanov, in her recent book *Receiving Woman*, states
this issue clearly, as have other recent theorists. She says, "Just as the
anima's femininity differs from that of actual women, so the masculine qualities of the animus differ from those of actual men" (p. 129).

Ulanov's statement makes clear that the unconscious femininity of the man is *not* the same thing as the conscious femininity of the
woman, and vice versa for the animus and men's consciousness.
Drawing out the implications of Ulanov's statement, we have a warn-
ing against creating a psychology for women out of men's anima
projections.

Jung's model assumes that women are the reverse—the opposite of men—both biologically and psychologically. It also assumes
that the opposite sexed parent carries an infant's first projections.
He says in *Aion*, "Just as the mother seems to be the first carrier of
the projection-making factor for the son, so is the father for the
daughter" (p. 14).

Recent scholarship in psychology and anthropology indicates
that this is not true. The mother is the first object of the infant's
projections, in both sexes. This fact no doubt endows the "feminine"
with numinosity for both men and women. The fact of the mother
being the first object of projections for both sexes has implications
for the concept of the animus as well as the anima. As Dorothy
Dinnerstein has suggested in *The Mermaid and the Minotaur*, if fathers take as active a role in the early parenting of infants, then per-

haps the infantile projections (needs), which now go unshared toward the mother, will be directed toward the father as well, and will change our attitudes toward men and women. Some people are moving in this direction, but we have by no means seen a generation of children who have experienced early parenting by men as much as by women. Women are still the major need-meeters of that early, intense, infantile phase. This is another reason why the anima theory "works" better than the animus one. If women are the first objects of projections for members of both sexes, then in a very real sense, both sexes can resonate to Jung's concept of the anima—particularly in her maternal and goddess form.

The archetype of the feminine has numinosity for both sexes because both men and women have been carried in the womb of a woman, and with the exception of cases of severe deprivation, have been nurtured, cared for, fed primarily by women during the first years of life. Very seldom is the father the first or primary object of projections for the daughter, although he becomes the object of her affections and projections later on. This fact may also help explain the emphasis in literature on anima images, as opposed to animus images. The experience of the mother is basic, primary and numinous because of its essential nature, no matter what sex we are. Both sexes have trouble de-numinizing women, coming to terms with women (i.e., withdrawing the projections) because of this fact.

THE NEGATIVE ANIMUS

The animus is an archetype.[3] The way in which we understand what an archetype is has something to do with our application of the animus theory to our lives. Is an archetype an instinct, the instinct's image of itself, or a metaphor, or an *a priori* category? How the archetype is conceived makes a difference, I think, in terms of how "divine" the animus is thought to be. If, for example, the contrasexual archetype is our gateway to the divine, we are in danger of giving a peculiarly Jungian religious sanction to internalized images of a hierarchical, patriarchal society which is oppressive to women. There is enough evidence in Jung's works to support this view of the archetype; i.e., that it is a manifestation of the "Divine" in human life.

If an archetype is an image of our contrasexual other, this is a somewhat different matter, although there is still potential for blaming the victim for her own victimization with this view, if we locate the source of her victimization archetypally "within her" as a "negative animus" of a certain sort. Most of us women are so hard on ourselves, living in a patriarchal society where female values are not valued, that we are inclined to blame ourselves once again if we are told that we have an inner self-devaluing mechanism, rather than understanding that we have internalized a patriarchal society's sexism. This is a fundamental point on which I am in disagreement with most if not all Jungians, for from the Jungian perspective "devaluation of the feminine" is also archetypal, represented by the negative animus in women and the negative anima in men or the archetype of the Terrible Mother in both. Jungians certainly believe that this is something we have to come to grips with, but it is considered collectively *archetypal* in origin, and not social (except inasmuch as the social *is* archetypal). Jungians would not consider "devaluation of the feminine" as primarily a function of male experience projected onto women.

Also, there is not much room within most Jungian theory for considering that the collective unconscious replicates society's images of men and women.[4] Jung speaks to that issue rather pointedly. The collective unconscious exists *a priori*. Yet, on the other hand, there is a lot of latitude within archetypal theory for interpreting psychological images and society's images in relationship within each other, leaving the *a priori* aspect on the level of empty form, or predisposing tendency, with no particular determined content. Jung's and Jungians' descriptions of archetypes and archetypal images vary tremendously on this score.

THE "INNER FORM": SELF-DEVALUATION

I believe that if a woman is the victim of a "negative animus," speaking from the inside, a self-devaluing voice such as Emma Jung described, it is more helpful to her to see that her inner self–putting-down voice (a voice which can be male or female by the way) is an internalization of society's views of women, rather than some terrible voice of her own making. The latter may well be the way she hears it if you tell her, "It exists in your unconscious." If she hears, for example, "you're stupid," "you don't think straight," "you don't argue logically," and so on, ringing in her own head whenever she undertakes an intellectual project, she will, by entertaining such thoughts, bring about a self-fulfilling prophecy, and secondly she is buying into our society's view of women. What she needs to do is buy out of those fundamental assumptions, not into them. She needs to buy out of them in a way which challenges society's definitions—a difficult task, admittedly. And here is where I differ from traditional Jungians. They would agree that a woman must differentiate herself from the negative animus, that is, not identify with his voice. But they would not add the element of sociological awareness, i.e., social origins of the so-called "negative animus," which I am suggesting here.

We are doing woman a service if we help her to see that she has bought into the prevailing definition of women, given to us by a society which does not properly value women. This society also claims that logical thought belongs to men and the masculine mode of being and values it highly. We are not serving woman well if we encourage her to think that she has an internal mechanism for putting herself down (negative animus)—even if we go on from there to help her stop it, or worse, if we try to get her to adapt to her incapacities. The reason it is important to call self-denigration by another name than negative animus, is that seeing through what has been going on is the first step toward liberation. It has been crucial in liberation thinking to realize that internalized oppression operates in the psyches of all non–culture-creating groups, otherwise known as minorities. In finding liberation, it is essential to step out of alienating and depotentiating categories of thought, rather than claiming them as one's own in the sense of arising out of one's own experience. For truly, they are not one's own if one is a member of a subordinate group in a given society, rather than a member of the culture-creating group. Thus, de-alienation—a seeing-through of false categories—is the first step toward becoming liberated. I wish to underscore this. Male-created categories of thought are not women's own categories—they represent the male experience of women, which may be quite different from women's experiences of ourselves, particularly as women gain access to our own voices and hence our own experience. So this one aspect of the negative animus, then, that of self-devaluation, I find important to name another name—internalized oppression, rather than claiming it as an intrinsic or universal aspect of the female psyche. It is, unfortunately, an aspect of the female psyche in a patriarchal society, but one which can be shed, and I believe will be shed, as misogynist society learns painfully that it must value women, and as women learn to value themselves. I hope it is obvious that I am not advocating lack of self-criticism in women, or what is called "inflation" by Jungians, or arrogance. I am suggesting that the crippling, paralyzing inner voice termed "negative animus" by Jungians be seen as an internalization in women of patriarchy's misogyny. My hope is that once this voice is exposed for what it is, women's energies will be freed.

THE "OUTER FORM": BITCHINESS

There is another form of a typical negative animus which deserves to be seen in the context of culture, rather than being seen as an internal, archetypal propensity existing in the psyches of women. That form is well known to us: it is the "bitchy woman" (Freud's "castrating female," called in Jungian circles by the name "animus dominated," "animus possessed" or "animus ridden"). This term is definitely an abuse of Jung's psychology for women.[5] A woman who is found arguing in a most irritatingly illogical manner ("irritating to whom?" Mary Daly would have us ask), holding on to an irrelevant opinion like a dog with a bone, is probably suffering from the first form of the "negative animus" just described; the inner self-denigrating voice, telling her that she can't think well, and so on. She is, in short, suffering from an internalization of sexism. Thus, believing that she is short on thinking power, when she does think, she lacks confidence in her thoughts and claims an outside authority for them rather than her own. Besides that, she tends to be defensive in her presentation of them, since she fears that they are inadequate. Furthermore, the fear she feels functions to distort the message she would like to communicate, so it comes out "irrelevant." She has bungled her own case because of her fear of inadequacy, and perhaps, indeed, in Jung's day she was not very well educated.

This, to me, is a descriptive account of what very often goes on in the case of the "animus dominated" woman. She fears to claim her own thought-power and authority and so she does it in a way which is not authoritative, but defensive, because of her felt lack. This is no doubt due, at least in part, to the experience of "punishment" she may have had, or may fear, from the patriarchy if she does assert herself. This is a double-bind for women well documented by the

Brovermans.[6] As with the case of the first form of the negative animus, and they are related, with one being the "outer" description and the other being the "inner" feelings producing the "outer" behavior, this form too is better understood when rendered in relationship to the society which surrounds the "animus ridden" women, rather than seen as archetypal, *if* archetypal means filled with numinosity and giving us access to the "realm of the gods."

For all these reasons, and particularly because of the preponderance of pejorative descriptions of the "animus-possessed woman," my recommendation is that Jungians drop that term altogether. It is an abuse of Jung's psychology for women. Its *function*, if not its intent, is to keep women "feminine" in the traditional sense and to keep them from effectively challenging exclusively male authority, privilege, and status. The term is also an easy dodge for men and patriarchal women, who then do not have to come to terms with the content of what an "animus-possessed woman" is saying. Most of the focus is on the style of her behavior and the irritating effect it has on the "poor man." "Poor man" is a term used frequently in a film I recently saw, "The Way of the Dream," produced by Frazer Boa, showing Marie Louise Von-Franz interpreting dreams. On one occasion, Von-Franz spoke of the "poor man" who had to contend with his wife's "negative animus" (the wife was speaking "like a lawyer, not like a woman") as she reacted in an "unadapted way" to hearing of her husband's affair. No attention was paid to the fact that it was the "poor man" who was having the affair, and that the woman's recourse to a "lawyer-like style" was no doubt a defense against the hurt and vulnerability she felt. What was Von-Franz's recommendation for the woman's behavior? Unclear, since in other parts of the film, Von-Franz was hard on women for whining and crying, characterizing this as "manipulative behavior."

If archetypal means merely "image" or "metaphor," there is less danger of lending sacred legitimation to internalized oppression than when we link archetype to numinosity. Still even an "image" gains in clarity when rendered as an internalization of culture. Obviously, we all have an innate predisposition to create mental images of things. The content of the images is at least culturally related—a view of images which is coordinate with Jung's view, theoretically. One may ask, "where does culture come from? Surely it comes from psyche." And the answer is, "Yes, but it has come from the male psyche primarily." Feminists, especially Carol Christ, Mary Daly, and Elizabeth Dodson-Gray, have pointed out that women have not been the creators of culture, institutions, and myth-systems, but the internalizers of them. Women may also have been the possessors of and creators of an alternative culture—an oral tradition—but, unfortunately, it was never written down. Our mainstream culture, as we know it, is a male construct.

Actually, the numinosity of the archetypal images is well known and it is hard to think of archetypes without something of the numinous about them. *Numinosity* comes from the Latin *numen*, which means "sacred" or "holy." Anything which is numinous is awesome, holy, sacred. It holds the human psyche in fascinated suspense, and as Jung has so often pointed out, numinous archetypal images often have us in their grip rather than our having them. This is part of Jung's understanding of the collective unconscious and its images as autonomous. It functions as though it had autonomous power. We are powerless to control it; but we can come into better acquaintance and relationship to it.

Now, I do not discredit sacred images. The history of religion, both eastern and western, abounds in them. I do, however, take issue with assigning such numinous power to internalized oppression—oppressive images of women given to us by patriarchy. The reason for my wishing to remove the element of the sacred from these particular images is that I believe that by divinizing them, seeing them as numinous, we are giving them more legitimation than they deserve—and a sacred, holy sort of legitimation at that.

POSITIVE ANIMUS

The Jungian descriptions of the "positive animus" run the gamut from a guiding spirit, a *logos* capacity, or ability to think clearly, to a mediator to the unconscious in much the same way that the anima is reputed to be the mediatrix to the unconscious for men. The idea of the anima being the mediatrix to the unconscious makes a lot more sense than the other way around. If men are the producers of culture, then what has gone underground is "female" and "feminine." Thus, real women as well as images of women function to help men get in touch with that part of their natures which they have diverted underground, and possibly perform the same function for women. Since women have been made to carry and represent that which is emotional and frightening in our human natures, then it is logical to assume that it is through women that men can come to reclaim this part of themselves. They can either fail or succeed at this. They fail if they continue to project their image of what it means to be female or of the "feminine" onto women. They also do women a disservice, since their assumptions about what it means to be female are probably inaccurate and we women continue in a kind of inauthenticity by picking up and carrying the projections. They succeed if they realize that they have been seeing women through a grid, a filter, in their own psyches, which they need desperately to claim as their own. The animus as a useful construct, however, cannot exist as merely the counterpart in the psyches of women of the anima in the psyches of men because of the different status accorded to men and women in our society.

Women and feminine images are the gateway to the unconscious in a male-dominated society—for both sexes. James Hillman's work on the anima (*Spring* 1973 and 1974) has made a strong case for that. The implications for women are that we have a subculture, an underground culture, waiting to be discovered. It does not mean, however, that the animus will take us there. Uncovering women's tales, building women's rituals, and basically celebrating the female dimension of living and being will take us there.

How about "guiding spirit," as animus? Again we are on shaky ground. The problem with this image of the "masculine" or the "animus" is that it reinforces the power relationship between men and women in society, as Carol Christ has pointed out.[7] If the "animus" is our "guiding spirit," this is the spiritual reconstitution of the male in society, who also guides us, tells us who we are, and makes the rules. I will not speak here of female domination of men, which can also happen, but usually in a different mode. Women tend to "dominate" by manipulation—the trick of an underdog; not the domination of one who has been raised to rule. (See Jean Baker Miller's book *Toward New Psychology of Women* for corroboration and elaboration of this point.) It is certainly true that the animus as spiritual guide brings women closer to a sense of their own authority than in the pre-individuated state, since the animus is conceptualized as part of the female psyche. The problem, however, is with the socio-cultural implications of the gender of the image, if it still reinforces the powerlessness of the woman in society. We need empowering images of women, and we need to release overreliance on male figures, even the animus, inasmuch as that replicates our already under-developed sense of female authority and spirituality.

The notion of animus as *logos* in the sense of capacity for rational thought is similarly problematical. This is because it replicates society's view of the male thinker, even though this time it is the inner male in the woman. Conceptualizing the animus this way was a very important halfway step in the liberation of women from powerlessness and inferior thinking. Jungians saw the need for women to actualize the so-called "masculine" side, the power, authority and rational thought heretofore accorded to the male. But they did not take the next step, which it is up to us to take, which is to legitimate female thinking, power and authority in its own right, and not as the contrasexual other.

It is crucial that we women recognize our society's validation of male thinking, authority, and power and the potential for inauthenticity in using a male symbol to legitimate our own power. If we do not find female images of empowerment and thinking, we dodge the issue of our society's fear and avoidance of women's power, authority, and rationality.

There is no doubt that we need male as well as female images nurturing and strengthening us. I am not suggesting rejecting all male images as women. I am suggesting that we not use male images as a fraudulent way of gaining female power and legitimating female thinking. Replicating a power situation which exists in society is not a liberating use of the animus. All potential for reinforcing sexism must be removed from the images in order to make analytical psychology congruent with the guideline cited in the beginning of this paper, which is that for a therapy to be freeing for a woman, it must recognize sexism as a fact and oppose it in an unrelenting way.

So, if these forms of the animus are problematic, what is the usefulness of the concept? My recommendation is that the animus concept needs to be deontologized and seen as culture-specific. The concept can be helpful if we realize that psyche internalizes images as well as projects them. Psyche and culture exist in dialectical relationship with each other. That means that psyche is not only the producer of images as Jungians suggest, but also the consumer of them. It is especially important for us women to realize that we are consuming images of the feminine—including the animus (an aspect of the feminine)—which have been projected by the male psyche onto our western culture. Thus seen, the concept can be useful.

Each woman can examine her own animus images which would be represented by male figures in dreams, men she's attached to, and her feelings and perceptions about typically "male" institutions and see the way in which she has internalized society's definitions—to her own detriment or to her own benefit. Animus (and anima for that matter) can be used as ingenious devices for seeing the way in which our psyches wrestle with the internalized demons of a sexist culture. That's what I mean by "de-ontologized." A part of Jung's genius lay in uncovering the imaginal aspect of our collective psyche and of our individual psyches. Because of his genius in that area, the concept has great usefulness, if it is put specifically into cultural context, because it demonstrates psyche at work image-making and image-processing.

The animus is useful also if it is used by women to uncover our own unconscious views of men and the kinds of relationships we tend to form with men. Dialoguing with male images in our dreams and fantasies in the way Jungians suggest can give us self-knowledge in the area of what we expect from men, as well as aiding us in claiming capacities for ourselves which we project onto others (men), thus strengthening us. One use of the animus at this point is to see it as giving us insight into the ways we have internalized sexism (i.e., learned to oppress ourselves). Animus is also a symbol of a woman's unlived life,[8] as shown in our expectations of men and our possible idealization, or contrarily, our hatred or blaming of them.

And finally, our animus images understood shed light on the mystery of why we fall in love with the men we do if we are heterosexual. The animus, integrated, can help us stop falling in love in a powerless way so that we become free, finally, to love as equals.

Mitchell Walker

The Double: Same-Sex Inner Helper

Jung never intended that his conceptualizations were final, or that he was always correct. Rather, he hoped that his tentative interpretations would be developed and revised. In this light, I would like to propose an archetypal concept, the "double," to cover a soul figure with all the erotic and spiritual significances attached to anima/us, but of the same sex, and yet not a shadow. This figure has mythological examples, and is felt in psychological experience. It is lost if named either shadow or anima/us.

The double is that set of characteristics which give rise, ultimately, to our conscious awareness of identified sex role, although the double is much more than our paltry social idea of manness or womanness, and is entirely lacking in sexist connotations (these are added on later). The double and the anima/us are equal and complementary, and form a whole, androgynous in nature. For example, the anima contains the archetypal images of mother, daughter, sister, lover. The male double, then, contains those of father, son, brother, lover. Just as a woman can serve for projection of the anima, so a man can serve for projection of the male double, and vice versa for women. The double, as well as the anima/us, can be part of a transcendent function.

Anima/us and double are equal in all process mechanisms. Psychically, both can serve as "soul guides." Both appear in literature, mythology, etc., and are involved in the process of individuation.

Double is revealed in mythology in such hero-pairs as David and Jonathan, Achilles and Patroklos, and Gilgamesh and Enkidu.

The double often appears with an aura of beauty, youth, and perfection or near-perfection. Unfortunately, it is apt to be mistaken simply as a symbol of the ego (which it partially is, the ego resting on the double), or a symbol of the shadow or of the self, all of which it may also be. This haziness is due to the fact that the contents of the collective unconscious are not distinct and separate, but merge into each other, and may be difficult to fix definitively. But psychologists have exploited this characteristic to hide realization of the double from themselves and others.

ASPECTS OF THE DOUBLE

Let me illustrate a few of the qualities and functions that I see in the double. It is one's deeper support, one's partner, leading on, helping. We see this in many stories, such as the *Iliad* for example. Achilles would not have raised his weapons for the Greeks, had not Patroklos fought Hector and been slain by him. The Trojans would have been victorious, but that Achilles, as explained by Phaedrus in the *Symposium*, "bravely chose to go and rescue his lover Patroclos, avenged him, and sought death not merely in his behalf but in haste to be joined with him whom death had taken."[1] In the same vein, in the Bible Saul would have killed David, but for Jonathan: ". . . my brother Jonathan: very pleasant hast thou been unto me: thy love to me was wonderful, passing the love of woman."[2]

As these myths suggest, the double is a soul-mate of intense warmth and closeness. Love between men and love between women, as a psychic experience, is often rooted in projection of the double, just as anima/us is projected in love between the different sexes.[3] And as with anima/us, such love may occur within or without the heroic quest. Furthermore, since the double is a soul figure, the sexual instinct may or may not become involved. That is, the double motif may include a tendency to homosexuality, but is not necessarily a homosexual archetype. Rather the double embodies the *spirit* of love between those of the same sex. And the spirit of love in the double is what I see as the supportive ground of the ego.

Double fuses the fate of two into one. We see this in Tolkien's *The Return of the King*, in which Frodo could never have made his great and epic trek to Mount Doom without Sam, his faithful servant: " 'So that was the job I felt I had to do when I started,' thought Sam: 'to help Mr. Frodo to the last step . . .' "[4] In *Robinson Crusoe*, the hero would not have survived the cannibals without his companion Friday. Mark Twain several times focused on this double motif. For example, in his *The Adventures of Huckleberry Finn*, it is Huck and Jim, the black slave, whose fates and affections are bound together towards freedom on the great river. In *The Prince and the Pauper*, the plot hinges on the interacting destiny of two identical boys.

In this way, the double is facilitative of *rapport*. It creates an atmosphere between the friends of profound equality and deep familiarity, a mysterious, joyful sharing of feelings and needs, a dynamic, intuitive understanding. Such a pleasurable camaraderie easily extends to a sharing of purpose or goal through which difficult tasks are undertaken and fulfilled.

If, as I suggest, the double is the root of ego identity, it may lead one to significant self-realizations. This is the symbolic meaning of its presence in the hero myth. For many the double can unlock creative processes. I believe this was the case in certain famous collaborations, for example, between Gilbert and Sullivan, Picasso and Braque, and Marx and Engels. As a source of strength and inspiration, the double can be a great driving force in a person, and collectively in the growth of arts and sciences. As Lamb explains in his introduction to Plato's *Symposium*, "Love is here treated with a sense of its universal importance," of how "we may pass with ever wakening and widening powers to the best and freest activity of our faculties, the contemplation of invisible, eternal verity."[5] In ancient Athens it was believed that two lovers, Harmodius and Aristogiton, sparked the flame of Democracy.[6] In modern times the work of many artists, such as Gertrude Stein, Oscar Wilde, Andre Gide, and so on, may be regarded as the product of self-growth stimulated by the double.

As is to be expected, however, such growth occurs only to those who recognize the inner urgings of the double and allow themselves to follow in this direction. In order to grow through the double, one must be open to its function as inner soul-guide.

DARK ASPECTS OF THE DOUBLE

Every archetype has its destructive features. The double, being a multifaceted archetype (or a group of closely interrelated archetypes, just as the anima includes the great mother and the feminine soul-guide), has several dark aspects. One of these involves the puer aeternus. Another is the shadow. That is, aspects of the double, such as a tendency toward homosexual expression, may be rejected by the ego and fall into the shadow personality. This is due to the similarity of the double and the shadow in relation to the ego; each is a source deeper than the conscious personality. While the double is typically the fount of conscious ego-identity, the shadow is typically that of morally inferior ego-identity. Therefore it is to be expected that rejected aspects of the double will tend to collect in the shadow-unconscious.

The negative side of the partner is the "competitor," the mythical figure of the same stature as the partner, but who is committed against the hero's success. Whereas the partner strives to enhance the ego, the competitor desires to supplant it. An example of the competitor is Hector in the *Iliad*. Just as Achilles and Patroklos are bound together in love and guidance, so Achilles and Hector are united in hatred and vengeance. As Achilles says to Hector at their fateful meeting, "Lions and men make no truce, wolves and lambs have no friendship—they hate each other forever. So there can be no love between you and me; and there shall be no truce for us, until one of the two shall fall and glut Ares with his blood."[7]

The negative archetype always contains the force of the positive, including the drive toward individuation. The competitor presents a challenge to overcome, and thus provides an image of oneself to grow into. However, the image is posed in a negative context, as a threat. Because of this, it is often easily projected, and can become a major factor in stimulating interpersonal aggression and competition. Furthermore, in a society such as ours, in which aggression and competition are encouraged among men, negative-partner projection will be thereby stimulated. This can lead to hostility and resentment, either overt or covert, toward men in general. We might call such a situation a competitor-complex. Or, since often the prime competitor is a man's father, we could in such cases place this phenomenon under the Jungian heading of father-complex, but rather for the son than for the daughter. One can see this complex on the collective level as stimulating such manly pursuits as war. And further, fixation on the competitor archetype can help block the constructive impulses inherent in the double motif. For the person who blindly spurns the love-overtures of the double, the rebuffed archetype may take revenge through transformation into this negative.

In conclusion, awareness of the double expands our understanding of diverse human phenomena such as "homosexuality," group bonding, and war. Recognition of the double simultaneously enriches and simplifies our vision of the psyche. We can see the field of anima/us and double as containing the source of sex-role identities, projections, and complexes. It is the center of this field, then, which gives rise to the significant archetype of the androgyne, and it is this androgyne which in turn may lead us to a more differentiated vision of the entire psyche.

Just as the anima/us appears to us as a mysterious source, so too does the double. Yet it is this double which has been, and continues to be, a significant factor in social and cultural phenomena. If we are to continue elaborating consciousness into more subtle awareness, we must give this archetype its rightful due, and learn to see its potentials for individual and society.

David DeBus

The Self Is a Moving Target: The Archetype of Individuation

The Self impresses its wholeness on our psychological lives as we develop. It represents itself to us as the psychological image of the divine. And as such, it partakes of the qualities of a transcendent goal, a moving target toward which we travel.[1]

Our first glimpses of the Self come to us imbedded in general displays of psychological energy rather than as events or images we can identify as specifically from the Self. The first glimpses that Carl Jung had of the Self led him to reduce signs of its presence to "libido." Later, clinical experience and theoretical necessity forced him to propose an "archetype of the Self" distinct from general displays of psychological energy. Through the decades his writings seem to undergo an individuation process as he comes to describe the Self increasingly as the organizer of the other archetypes and of personal lives in his case studies. Like us, he could not at first distinguish the young child's unconscious immersion in the unity of the Self from the maturing adult's conscious meeting with symbols of the Self.

The Self cannot be reduced to infant consciousness. It should instead be known as what contained us in our beginnings. As circle or sphere, primal waters, or garden, the Self surrounded and infused us. When we were one with our unconscious, our bodies, our mothers and fathers, and the universe, our time-sense gives us a bone-deep knowing about the kind of time in which the Self has its being. I call this time "aeonic time" to distinguish it from a religious notion of God's eternity, and from secular clock-time. Aeonic time resembles the time in mystical vision, artistic inspiration, dreams, fairy tales and myths which start with "Once upon a time." It resembles the time-sense surrounding meaningful coincidences and parasympathetic nervous system experiences such as heightened sexuality. When we remember the unconscious unity of the world and our psyches in the aeonic time of origins, we remember an experience of the Self's presence without conscious differentiation. Our first unity is unconscious. It has not moved through the One to the Two to the Many; it has not passed through what the Chinese call "the ten thousand things."

Sometimes Jung emphasizes the reciprocal relation of Self and consciousness, but often he emphasizes the subordinate role of the personal consciousness which he designates as "ego":

> The term "self" seemed to me a suitable one for this unconscious substrate, whose actual exponent in consciousness is the ego. The ego stands to the self as the moved to the mover, or as object to subject, because the determining factors which radiate out from the self surround the ego on all sides and are therefore superordinate to it. . . . It is not I who create myself, rather I happen to myself.[2]

Whether the Self's relation to the personality is as a reciprocal equal or as a superordinate container, a most difficult succession of paradoxes applies: the Self both contains and is the content of the complete person; the Self is both what we came from and what we aim for; the Self includes ego, yet the Self and the ego can undertake dialogue as representatives of the complete person and the more limited conscious personality; the Self is hidden but loves to be known; the Self has a supreme value like a psychological "pearl of great price" but is present in the midst of ordinary life, "in the straw and manure," as the alchemists put it. All archetypes have this double nature, and for this archetype that affects all the others, this double nature takes on the character of paradoxical extremes. Indeed, the Self contains personal and transpersonal polarities like good and evil, female and male, point and circle, harmony and dissonance, order and chaos, complexity and simplicity.

Yet it would be wrong to draw from this a kind of pseudo-Oriental philosophy. The German term *Selbstverwirklung*, which Jung uses to mean "Self-realization," suggests the presence of an acting, making, urge-laden trajectory of movement, not a thinning out into diffuse consciousness. By contrast to Eastern accounts of psycho-spiritual development, Jung's account of the personality's movement toward the Self does not end in the dissolution or disappearance of the ego.

The critique in spiritual literature of the desiring ego contrasts with the valuing in modern psychology of the psychological ego. Jung uses "the ego" to suggest a receiver of conscious experience counterpoised to and compensated by the unconscious. Without the psychological ego, no one is present to live life or experience the Self. Jung's ego is one of many complexes to which feelings and thoughts happen. It retains the illusion of originating feelings and thoughts, and the illusion that it stands at the center, until the Self "dethrones" it during the process of individuation.

Individuation, as the name implies, means coming to accord with our true natures. Individuation challenges the ego to move into an unknown condition rather than remain captive to habit and familiarity. A personal life into which the Self as a transpersonal factor does not intrude runs the risk of stagnating. If the Self challenges our personal lives with individuation, we usually begin with a feeling of discomfort and a sense of loss. This process requires a considerable enlargement of our personalities. Our personal lives come to be governed increasingly by a center of gravity and organization that includes transpersonal and unconscious realities. Even as the Self's governance becomes established, its ways of governing our personal lives change as we undergo individuation.

We can see how the governance of the Self begins in our lives by examining the modes of exerting power, being in relationship, and asserting the importance of the Self from the throne of the ego.

Our power over people, nature, and things habituates us to an illusion of control. When this apparent control fails—when our children become more independent and defy us, when a garden we plant gets frostbitten, when our cars break down, or when someone we count on dies—our misplaced sense of control-oriented identity fails too. In extreme instances, we feel as if we are dying, impotent, or unworthy. The Self may even push particularly grandiose and puffed-up control identities into failing, as happened to Oedipus and King Lear, as if the Self means to put us in a suitably surrendered and receptive state. Sometimes the Self makes its appearance only when we have been brought to desolation.

When we have the attitude that relationships can bear the ultimate value and meaning in our lives, we practice a kind of idolatry. The Self tends to break this idolatry open by various means, including steering us toward seeing that the other person does not match our most intimate and ultimate soul-image. Jung names the "anima" and "animus"—archetypes for the most prominent unconscious opposites—after the Latin words for "soul." In heterosexual and some same-sex–preferring people, these soul-images of the opposite sex within the unconscious are projected upon another person. These projections contain some of the psychological force that later flows to the Self.

Furthermore, the Self stands for a union of inwardly reconciled opposites. So long as we search the world for this opposite within us, we may receive healing and knowledge of what lives within us but fail to turn our seeking inward. These images, when projected upon another person in a relationship, carry instinctive, sexual, erotic, affiliative, and spiritual possibilities. Some people seem to discover their inner opposite *through* relationship, while others must abandon idolatrous levels of relating and turn directly inward. Eventually the Self demands new ways of being in relationship based on greater inner contact with the opposite.

When we allow the Self to influence our old ways of relating, we forego or modify projections for the sake of maturing. We may climb what Plato calls "the ladder of love," following our yearning for the Self, originally mislocated in personal relationship. First we engage in physical attraction, then love for another's soul, and finally, through education in love, a coming home to the reality of our own souls. In contrast to maturing *through* relationship, we may instead withdraw our projection upon another person with an effort that increases consciousness. The charged images we have projected do not match the real human being in either pattern, and the "honeymoon" phase—in romantic relationships or even in friendships—ends. Like an adult version of a young child's movement into either increased dependence or increased autonomy, we give ourselves away or we grow.

The governance of the Self, to which individuation gradually turns our consciousness, seeks to advance our maturity by undermining old ways of using power and engaging in relationships. The Self acts behind our uses of power, for its power consists in giving pattern, harmonizing us with the nature of the cosmos in right proportion, and seeking to incarnate a paradox-laden truth of reconciled opposites. And the Self acts behind our yearning in relationships, for it contains in its potentiality the inner marriage.

But the third surrender to the Self's governance concerns the sacrifice of everything we thought we were. The Self moves from the periphery of our psychological life to the center. One guru told me that when the skull bones at the top of a baby's head close up, God cannot enter, and so the ego thinks it is God. For most people the Self begins to exert its centering, individuating effect on both conscious and unconscious realms in the middle of life. Forming our personalities and committing our psychological energy to developing our personal lives through skills, work, and relationships limits our access to the unconscious with its creative, spiritual, and disorganizing influences. The Self becomes the center of the conscious and unconscious psyche, and the other archetypes, such as the anima or animus, subordinate themselves to it. But the Self plays other roles as well. As witness, the Self watches our personalities undergo and integrate experience, like the two birds in this passage from the *Manduka Upanishad:* "Two birds, companions always united, cling to the self-same tree. Of these two, the one eats the sweet fruit and the other looks on without eating." While the Self is the tree, it is also the bird witnessing our personalities' experiences.

Our personalities sometimes begin the process of individuation without sufficient preparation in our connection to the body, the earth, and engagement with our lives. Jung gives an account of a woman who passively experiences individuation as "sight-seeing through the country in an express train." Of this woman he says,

> Individuation can only take place if you first return to the body, to your earth, only then does it become true. . . . She must go back to the earth, into the body, into her own uniqueness and separateness; otherwise she is in the stream of life, she is the whole river; and nothing has happened because nobody has realized it. . . . Individuation can only happen when it is realized, when somebody is there who notices it; otherwise it is the eternal melody of the wind in the desert.[3]

At times the Self seems like a destroyer to our accustomed identities. But viewed through the lens of its purposes, it acts to make our involvement complete. The alchemists said that their transformational work requires the whole person, and the Self demands the same. Usually this demand falls most heavily on our least-developed functions, our weakest links, which we have ignored during the first half of our lives.

Jung emphasizes that the Self can represent God in our psyches, that it is "the psychological image" of God in our psyches. But he notes that as a matter of empirical experience, contrasted to belief,

> we are unable to distinguish whether these actions emanate from God or from the unconscious. We cannot tell whether God and the unconscious are two different entities. . . . But there is in the unconscious an archetype of wholeness which manifests itself spontaneously in dreams, etc., and a tendency, independent of the conscious will, to relate other archetypes to this center.[4]

In Jung's writings the experiences of God recorded in scriptures and in the accounts of mystics receive treatment as psychological facts rather than religiously known realities. Especially in Jung's essay, "Answer to Job," the psychological image of God in the Western psyche seems itself to be individuating. Specifically, Jung sees the psychological image of God in the Western psyche as growing toward an inclusion of dark and feminine qualities. For Jung the nature of the Self in the human psyche corresponds with an image of God that includes the suppressed and repressed sides of Western civilization in a union of reconciled opposites, a wholeness beyond a good God or a masculine Trinity. To one commentator, Murray Stein, it almost seems as if Jung were performing analytical work with Christianity as the analysand.[5]

Although the Self enlarges our personalities, often by moving them to develop less-developed functions and attitudes, and although the Self surrounds the personality on all sides to embrace both conscious and unconscious life in a larger totality, we experience the Self as if it dwells in the unconscious. As a two-million-year-old "person," it is usually nonverbal, expressing itself instead through pictures, sound, and feeling. It may also guide us through our experience of the outer world, pulling us toward its fulfillment in compensating our one-sided conscious standpoints. When we stop painting pictures, stop talking, and stop pretending that we originate feeling from the ego, we can see its pictures, hear its sound and music, and participate in feeling that comes from beyond our limited conscious knowing.

As individuation begins, our personalities as well as our unconscious lives undergo reorganization. The Self begins to exert influence on personal and collective unconscious energies. As the unconscious life undergoes reorganization, it expresses both itself and the changed role of the Self in symbols. Symbols point beyond themselves, and their meanings never succumb to rational formulations entirely. Often they compress many layers of meaning and trajectories of development. We experience symbols in dreams and visions and must bring our half of the relationship to them. This is our conscious side of the dialogue with the unconscious and with the Self via the unconscious. Together, conscious and unconscious halves of the coin restore a broken totality. When our conscious orientation moves, the unconscious moves also. The Self seems to move responsively to our movement, even though the Self often brings about our conscious movement.

Our tendency to turn such dynamic realities as the Self into motionless things or into disembodied mental furniture mirrors our immobilized images of spiritual and psychological realities. But all such realities come to us as both doing and being. As William Butler Yeats asks, "How can we know the dancer from the dance?" The Self's ceaseless activity in our developing consciousness means that stopping places are booby prizes. One Buddhist saying advises, "When you reach the top of the mountain, keep climbing."

Our glimpses of the Self seem to reveal something static but instead develop into a moving and complex reality when we take the long view, looking at sequences of dreams, years of alchemical works, and the trajectories of conscious and unconscious life in dialogue over a decade, as if a kind of glacial movement could be discerned through the psychological equivalent of time-lapse photography. Arthur Schopenhauer spoke of the way that our lives can appear to have been planned even though apparent detours and disruptions have wrecked our conscious intentions. Only by looking back on our lives for the shaping influence of these deeper intentions can we see that our personalities have grown toward the Self's plan for our lives.

The Self gives symbolic form and utterance to its constant activity and structuring effect on our lives—in dreams, in works of art, in integrations of the spiritual into our personal lives, and in sequences like those Jung studied showing transpersonal and unconscious life projected onto matter by alchemists. But even these deeper symbolic communications come to us as still-life paintings and verbal descriptions of a moment in the time of the Self. By their discrete occurrence, they can obscure the continuous reality of the Self. And since the Self acts as our implicit individuality, our pictures of it as separate and different from us are partly false. If we consider that our personalities express in a limited way what originates, contains, guides, and acts as symbol of mature completion for them, we come to understand ourselves as an operational identity, or personality, and as a cosmic identity, or soul.

What practical advantage might this disquieting, risky, and change-laden relationship with the Self bring as we become more individual? The political philosopher John Stuart Mill articulated one social value of becoming more individual when he wrote: "It is not by wearing down into uniformity all that is individual in themselves, but by cultivating it, and calling it forth, within the limits imposed by the rights and interests of others, that human beings become a noble and beautiful object of contemplation . . . therefore capable of being more valuable to others."[6]

Mill did not have in mind the relation to unconscious life that coming into a subordinate connection to the Self implies, but he understood "individuality" to mean a development of human potential that advances humanity as a whole. This is in accordance with Jung's essential insight. But in his work Mill also anticipates the social friction that arises from people becoming individual, for such people cease to harmonize themselves so adaptively to institutions, communities, families, and the implicit rules of marriage. He argues that all societies impoverish themselves when they do not permit individual development. Real individuals disturb tyrants. Genuine "autonomy" or "law unto one's self" means that social methods of control lose their hold. The desiring ego hears rumors of this free-seeming autonomy, and in the name of the Self it can rationalize license through opportunistic pretense to individuating. Superficially, what arises from obedience to awareness when the Self comes into view can look like license. As a Bob Dylan song puts it, "To live outside the law you must be honest." Jung repeatedly stresses the grave ethical responsibilities we take on when we depart from collective norms as a result of this obedience.

Our personalities will never have the stature, comprehensive and aeonic existence, or future-oriented developmental wisdom of the Self. No matter how extensive our travel toward the moving target Self, we shall always be right between stone and angel, between grinding daily struggles and the cosmos. Fortunately for the true proportion of our personal identities, when we are puffed up, or "inflated" as Jung puts it, by the Self, life usually knocks the wind out of us. Any archetype from the unconscious can inflate our personalities, but when the archetype of the Self inflates us, specific forms of spiritual pride result. We are led into glamor-laden sojourns by superhuman attitudes of inferiority or superiority; by a particular blindness to our bodily, emotional, intellectual, or spiritual limits; or by a misapplication of qualities such as those coming from an oceanically loving heart that erases personal boundaries inappropriately. We return to ourselves knowing how ordinary we are. What Jung calls "the compensatory function of the unconscious" acts as a wise and sober friend, even if it feels to our inflated personalities like a killjoy.

The original meaning of "sin" in Greek implies "missing the target." Jung understands the Greek word for *repentance* to mean "becoming more conscious." When we do not aim at the target of the Self accurately, it can mean that our consciousness, maturity, and vision need fundamental revision. The inflation that leads us away from our aim also leads us to imagine we are most on target. The consummate value of a truth-seeking dialogue with the unconscious shows its strategic importance in correcting this self-deception. Humility results from becoming more conscious of our personal limits and the guidance of the Self, and this humility has no exaggerations. It renders our personalities receptive and "poor in spirit." Since our personalities do not own the Self, only what Jung calls "a religious attitude" can loosen our arrogant certitude and reverse the situation. Jung likens the Self to the Chinese Tao, which cannot be owned even in words or concepts.

Jung takes the serpentine movement, rather than the straight line between our personalities and the Self, to betoken an essential quality of the process of individuation and the accompanying rounding out of our personalities. "This rounding out," he says, "may be the goal of any psychotherapy that claims to be more than a mere cure of symptoms."[7]

The pain and danger in the process of individuation are equaled only by its felt necessity. Gaining something means sacrifice. Jung says, "Any higher development of consciousness is tremendously dangerous. We are generally inclined to think that it is ideal and desirable to develop toward a higher condition, but we forget that it is dangerous, because the development usually means sacrifice."[8]

Spatial metaphors for the Self and the personality's enlargement during the process of individuation (what Jung calls "the scope of integration" as it aims toward the Self) include descent as well as ascent, elaborated and enlarged circle and sphere, spiral-like motion, and the spatial equivalent of Bach's music. It means an inclusive wholeness rather than a single-pointed perfection.

The resulting simplicity of our personalities when the Self has been a moving target for our development does not come from a Procrustean amputation of inconvenient or unacceptable aspects of who we are. Rather, it seems to derive from the terrible and beautiful task of self-acceptance and a movement that integrates and accepts the diversity of the "ten thousand things" because of a felt sense of the Tao abiding through them. In this simplicity, what is known, what is unknown, and what is knowing continue their folding movement, better tuned to our essential natures.

II

The
Archetypal
Family

Even before Jung developed his theory of the collective unconscious and archetypes, he was intrigued by the powerful symbolic role played by the mother in psychology, particularly male psychology. Jung's break with Freud was in large measure occasioned by his insistence in the 1913 book, *The Psychology of the Unconscious*, that what the son's incestuous longing for the mother *really* means is his longing to reestablish contact with the source of psychological renewal—not with the literal mother but with the symbolic one. Later, as Jung elaborated his theory, he stated even more emphatically that the mother archetype is not a derivative of our experiences with our personal biological mothers; rather, we cannot help but see our mothers through the archetype.

> "Mother," as our psyches imagine her, is associated with maternal solicitude and sympathy; the magic authority of the female; the wisdom and spiritual exaltation that transcend reason; any helpful instinct, all that is benign, all that cherishes and sustains, that fosters growth and fertility. The place of magic transformation and rebirth, together with the underworld and its inhabitants, are presided over by the mother. On the negative side the mother archetype may connote anything secret, hidden, dark; the abyss, the world of the dead, anything that devours, seduces and poisons, that is terrifying and inescapable like fate.[1]

Little wonder that Jung expresses his sympathy for the women who are "the accidental carriers" of the archetype.

Although in Jung's psychology and, Hillman has suggested, in depth psychology generally, the focus has fallen on the mother archetype, there is also recognition that other family figures dwell in our psyches as imposing archetypes: father, son and daughter, husband and wife, sister and brother. All these figures live in us in ways not entirely determined by our literal experience (and, of course, not entirely independent of it, for we are speaking in this book of archetypal images, not of archetypes *per se*). These archetypal images influence how we respond to those "accidental carriers" of the archetypes who are our actual parents, spouses, or siblings. We project assumptions and feelings derived from the archetypes onto nonfamilial others as though in some way they were (or should be) our mothers, our fathers, our children. This may enrich relationships, adding resonance and meaning, but may also (and perhaps more often) damage them by falsifying who the other really is and how that other is ready to relate to us.

All of us, whether we know it or not, thus may be said to have an invisible yet powerful archetypal family, in addition to the one we usually admit to having; indeed, the two are almost inextricably entangled with each other. The father or mother who appears in our dreams is, for example, usually a confusing admixture of the archetypal and the personal parent.

As we noted in Part 1, archetypes are always in linkage with other archetypes. Usually they appear in pairs, but not always paired with the same other archetype—and this makes a difference. It also makes a difference which archetype we are looking *through* and which we are looking *at*. Thus the father–son bond will look different if we focus on the son's perspective than if we focus on the father's. Opening this section, professor of religious studies T. Mark Ledbetter looks at how the son's journey toward maturity is shaped by his ambivalent relation to both the personal and the archetypal father. Ledbetter turns to contemporary literature for "amplification" of this theme, as other writers influenced by Jung often turn to mythology or folklore.

Jungian analyst Murray Stein, author of *Midlife*, takes the more traditional approach as he explores how Greek myths illumine our experience of the father archetype. Stein is not interested in how archetypal images affect how sons view their fathers or how fathers view their sons. What concerns him is how a devouring inner father stifles our creative impulses, as Kronos, according to legend, swallowed his children immediately after birth. Zeus provides us with the image of a more tolerant, flexible inner father who thwarts only those revolutionary changes that truly threaten psychic order and harmony. Stein's essay suggests that there can be development within the archetype: we are not necessarily stuck with the version of the father archetype that first appears.

In her discussion of the archetypal dimensions of the mother–daughter bond, Helen M. Luke, founder of the therapeutic community Apple Farm, also turns to Greek mythology. Her reading of the Demeter–Persephone story helps us see the pertinence of this myth to the self-understanding of women. In each of us there lives a daughter who must break away from containment by her mother; in each of us there also lives a mother who wants to protect the daughter and grieves when she cannot. Women long to grow *and* resist change. Through the myth we discover that time spent in the underworld is a necessary part of all human life, but also that psychic renewal remains a possibility at every age.

Jungian analyst and former philosophy professor Linda Schierse Leonard helps us see how differently the archetypal father figures in the lives of daughters than of sons. Her vivid, personal account shows an adult daughter struggling to work through her relationship to the historical and archetypal father in order to heal her wounded relationship to herself, as well as to make possible a reconciliation with her actual father. David DeBus's poem, written to a daughter not yet born, expresses all the tenderness and hope evoked in a father who is imagining what having a daughter will mean to him.

The mother and father archetypes play so powerful a role in our psyches that we often feel overwhelmed by them. In contrast, grandmother and grandfather may be associated with many of the same attributes and powers but in a less formidable, less fearsome way. In his contribution, professor of religious studies David L. Miller writes about why this is so. Novelist and essayist Jane Rule, writing in a more personal vein, how her childhood experiences with her grandmothers have shaped her feelings about aging and her understanding of love. Poet Alma Luz Villanueva's lyric lines express how profoundly empowering the image of the grandmother can be. And Jungian-oriented therapist River Malcolm celebrates the particular encouragements only a grandfather can provide.

Mothers and fathers are also sons and daughters and often wives and husbands. The view of ourselves we gain when looking at our lives through the marriage archetype is very different from that provided by the parental one. But we may discover how difficult it is to disentangle these archetypes because no actual relationships are influenced by a single archetypal image alone. In my essay on marriage I suggest that we view our marital partners through many archetypes. Our husbands constellate the husband archetype but also those of father, son, brother, lover, and perhaps even mother! I also consider the problems involved in expecting the carrier of any of these archetypes to fulfill us and in expecting to become whole through relationship.

The archetypal family also includes sisters and brothers, which my essay explores in general terms. Adrienne Rich's poem explores the intense feelings of closeness and distance that characterize her relationship with her sister; Galway Kinnell's poem expresses the sadness of brothers who have no real way of communicating with each other. Psychologist Howard Teich writes about the archetypal significance of the closest of all sibling ties, the one between twins.

I also wanted to include family members often disregarded when we first reflect on the archetypal family but who nonetheless figure as members—often as unrecognized or disowned members. So I have included both an excerpt from Eileen Simpson's *Orphans* and a poem by Olga Cabral on the spinster. Essays by Jungian-oriented therapist Robert H. Hopcke, author of *Jung, Jungians and Homosexuality*, and Jungian analyst Caroline T. Stevens give us personal accounts of how gay couples and lesbian families are influenced by traditional archetypal images of the family and how they might deepen and expand our understanding of what the archetype of the family encompasses. These essays help us see once again how intimately the archetypal and the personal are interfused. Reflection on personal experience helps us see the archetypes at work in our lives; at the same time, attunement to the archetypal realm opens us to deeper dimensions of our personal lives, so that our outer relationships may bring inner growth.

T. Mark Ledbetter

Sons and Fathers:
Or Why Son Is a Verb

Who is this character, in life's narrative, called the "son"? Is he best understood in the epic tale *The Odyssey*, a story of a father whose life is adventurous and exciting and of a son, Telemachus, who must form his identity while deprived of the presence of a father? Do we know the son best in the murderous act of Oedipus? Or perhaps those of us who are sons see our reflection in the disturbingly romanticized story of the sacrificed Isaac. Perhaps any attempt to choose a definitive image of the son is futile. Maybe we can only describe him as a pilgrim, a male child seeking identity in a world that makes unreasonable demands of him.

The journey of the son from birth to adulthood is fascinating, empowering, and tragic. The maturation of a son embodies fantasy and failure, and perhaps most important, is profoundly influenced by his relationship to his father, his first male friend and his first model for the male endeavor.

A rather common feature of an adolescent son's life is unbridled fantasy. Sons dream incessantly of becoming one of life's "leading men." Sons assume, at an early age, that they will ascend to a place of honor.

Ironically, the son's first role model is the father who is very unlikely to be one of life's "leading men." Few of us, as sons, have fathers who are in society's limelight. Yet for a small child, "it is what a father can do and not what he can't that seems to matter."[1] Fathers are heroes in their own right, providing food, shelter, and, if possible, some luxuries. Yet more important to the son, fathers model strength and control, physically and emotionally, and assure their sons that an inheritance awaits them, an ascendancy to the hero's role in society. Thus, sons' lives, particularly the early years, are expectant and burdensome. Expectation is empowering; it can also be debilitating.

How does a son develop his own identity in light of such tension? I am convinced that a son's maturation, his psychological and emotional development, depends on his unique relationship with his father. Yet beneath the surface of individual relationships there appears a common journey that connects all father–son relationships. This journey and its three developmental stages are the framework of my essay.

THE FIRST STAGE

Fathers can do no wrong in the eyes of their sons, at least for a while. In turn, the young adolescent son is content, encouraged, and safe. *Safe* is the important word here. Fantasies occupy day and night dreams; some are of fame and importance, others are altruistic. Fathers protect sons from the simple though possible devastating fact that the early fantasies of a son are, most likely, childlike illusions. And sons encourage their fathers to perpetuate such lies. Sons enjoy the friendship born of fathers' encouragement. At this stage, fathers often call their young sons "buddy," "bud," or "best friend."

In many ways, this intimate relationship allows for and even encourages what Ernest Becker calls the "vital lie," an important, perhaps necessary, but often psychologically injurious part of a child's life. We do not tell young children that they may develop a terminal illness, nor do we suggest to them that life is haphazard and holds in store for them, at any moment, the chance of physical or emotional harm. We assume that children will encounter these negative dimensions of life soon enough. And so, while all around them men, either by choice or because of failure, are not fulfilling their fathers' or society's definitions of maleness, many young sons live with a vital illusion that success, by tradition's definition, awaits them.

For the son, the adolescent years are safe. Six-year-old Rufus, in James Agee's *A Death in the Family*, feels safe with his father. The young boy describes an evening out with his father. On the walk home after seeing a movie, they stop and sit on a large rock. Agee's description of their relationship reflects the early stage of a son's development:

> He was not in a hurry to get home, Rufus realized; and, far more important, it was clear that he liked to spend these few minutes with Rufus. . . . Rufus had come recently to feel, during the ten to twenty minutes they sat on the rock, a particular kind of contentment, unlike any other that he knew. He did not know what this was, in words or ideas, or what the reason was; it was simply all that he saw and felt. It was, mainly, knowing that his father, too, felt a particular kind of contentment, here, unlike any other, and that their kinds of content- ment were much alike, and depended on each other.[2]

Agee has captured an important dimension of what it means to be a young son. In fathers, sons find someone who provides gender awareness, who nurtures the most farfetched dreams a son might have, and who encourages, even expects, the son to assume his role as a male in society. And the son, for the sake of comfort, security, and, to use Agee's word, *contentment*, eagerly accepts his father's traditional values and embraces his expectations. The relationship is mutually beneficial. Through his son, the father is promised im- mortality. In his father, the son sees the successful man whom he will become.

THE SECOND STAGE

Fathers soon lose the talent to do no wrong; rather, as sons grow out of adolescence, fathers can do no right. Sons rather systematically reject all those traditional values that they and their fathers held in common. While to the father such rejection is unexpected, for the son the rejection is inevitable. The son feels betrayed. These unbri- dled fantasies of childhood have failed to come true, and the son holds the father responsible. Of course, this betrayal is not perni- cious; rather, it is tragic. The father is convinced that he is doing all the right things for his son. His goals are sincere: to initiate the son into the male world and to make the transition from boyhood to manhood easier. Yet a father's good intentions may only deepen a son's sense of betrayal if he fails his father's initiatory process or stumbles in the transition from childhood to adulthood. The expectations a father has for his son and the reasons the son fails to live up to them vary from family to family and often reflect the experiences of the father's childhood. The son fails because he is not as good an athlete as his father was. Or maybe the son gets poor grades while his father was the school "whiz kid."

For whatever reasons, the father's betrayal of his son and the son's rejection of his father are tragic because they both do the right things by each other. The father makes childhood less frightening for his son, but only by defining the son in the father's own image. The son has to reject the father in order to become his own person. Sons decide, soon after their adolescent years, that they cannot become their fathers; furthermore, sons decide that they do not *want* to become their fathers.

Perhaps it is competition between father and son that allows the son to see his father's weaknesses and foibles. Is the competition Oedipal? Maybe. To a greater extent, I suspect that the competition is a consequence of years of intimacy, of sons and fathers defining themselves in relation to each other. And I resist the Freudian notion that sons wish to slay and devour their fathers. I do believe that sons find reasons to deny their fathers' influences on their lives. The son moving from the adolescent stage seeks to distort the image of his father and make him into a buffoon, a larger-than-life satire on the role of male in society.

A fascinating example of the father as comic figure and as an embarrassment to his son is found in Robert Penn Warren's *A Place To Come To*. The novel begins with a son's description of the death of his father. The narrator of the passage is the son. The "I" of the narrative impresses on us the sad state of the father–son relationship and gives the passage its power. The son is in control of his father's description and is not very sympathetic toward him:

> I was the only boy, or girl either, in the public school of the town of Dugton, Claxford County, Alabama, whose father had ever got killed in the middle of the night standing up in the front of his wagon to piss on the hindquarters of one of a span of mules and, being drunk, pitching forward on his head, still hanging on to his dong, and hitting the pike in such a position and condition that both the left front and the left rear wheels of the wagon rolled, with perfect precision, over his unconscious neck, his having passed out being, no doubt, the reason he took the fatal plunge in the first place. Throughout, he was still holding on to his dong.[3]

I am not suggesting that sons hate their fathers, though I am certain such feelings arise. Sons mock and satirize their fathers out of fear of being like their fathers. If, in some way, a son can portray his father as an unattractive and repulsive person, he can get about the task of forming his own identity over against that of the father. Jed Tewksbury, the son in Warren's narrative, spends much of his early adult life telling, over and over again, the story of his father's death, a story that never fails to elicit laughter from his friends, therefore assuring Jed that he is not the buffoonish character he makes his father out to be.

For a son to see his father as weak and vulnerable, even once, is to never see his father in the same light again. And the story of *The Emperor's New Clothes* is an appropriate metaphor for the relationship of sons to fathers because the father, in an attempt to please and be all things to his son, has been deceived and betrayed, too. Society has urged him to create a son in his own image, strong and impregnable, emotionally and physically, to life's vicissitude.

A father's willingness to accept society's characterization of what the father "ought to be" is an act of self-deception, an unwillingness to know himself, to admit to personal weaknesses and shortcomings. He creates a fantasy of the "invulnerable self." Sadly, a son learns to practice this self-deception. Men must accept responsibility for this personal lie. No person is an "invulnerable self," though patriarchy has often suggested otherwise. Fathers and sons must abrogate their postures of authority, their fantasies of power, if they are to ever discover emotional and physical liberation.

The father works at "creating" a son and takes the task to heart. Of course, the father's imposition is under the guise of "wanting more" for the son's life than he had in his own, a seemingly sacrificial act on the part of the father. Still, such action serves only to create a wider chasm between the imposing father and the son, who is seeking to develop an identity over against that of his father.[4]

The irony of this stage of the son's journey is that, on the one hand, the son seeks to exaggerate the father's weaknesses in order to justify his rejection of him. Yet, on the other hand, this deliberate attempt at exposing the father as the buffoon can lead to rather unexpected results in the father–son relationship. Once the son sees his father as vulnerable to or perhaps frightened by failure, old age, and death, a reconnection may take place. A final stage of a son's development is the embracing of his father, whom he now sees as another son.

THE THIRD STAGE

Sons return to fathers when they see their own reflections in their fathers' faces. Perhaps failure unites the two. The father fails to make life easy for the son. The son fails to achieve the seemingly fantastic life promised by his father. Therein lies the connection. While both men may never be fathers, both men are sons. I am convinced that it becomes incumbent for the son to see himself in his father; the father is often too busy to make this observation. The father is consumed with making life better for his son, better than it was for him as a son.

So I complain about what my father failed to do for me, and I fret that I will fail my son in the same fashion. But I must remember that my father did for me the things he did because he assumed that his father had failed him. Perhaps, then, the journey is not so much about fathers and sons but simply about being and discovering sons. Warren's character in *A Place To Come To* makes such a discovery. Jed has grown older and now has a son of his own. He walks into his son's nursery and, looking at his child, reflects for a moment about his own father:

> Had there been a time, before the panther-piss took hold, when Old Buck Tewksbury—then young Buck Tewksbury, with the biggest dong in Claxford County, and the glossiest head of black hair so stiff it needed a curry comb . . . and the lovingest little wife in the county, to boot—had there been a time when Young Buck crept at night into a darkened room and stood to look down at a black-haired male infant, in an improvised cradle, sucking, no doubt, at its thumb or a sugar-tit? . . . I finally approached the expensive antique crib and leaned to kiss the upturned, rose-down cheek and let the tears just come.[5]

Tradition suggests that sons become like their fathers. I am convinced that the reverse is true, at least from the perspective of the son. *Son* is a verb, the seeing, knowing, and discovering of ourselves in our fathers. Sons mend fences with their fathers when they see themselves in their fathers. As a father, then, I do not worry about my son's future because my father worried about my future. I worry about my son's future and, in a moment of self-reflection as a son, realize that my father had the same worries about me. Because I am so attuned to my fears and weaknesses, I become aware that my father, too, made his decisions about his son in fear and trembling. By our fear, then, we become one, sons who are discovering sons.

Murray Stein

The
Devouring
Father

Greek mythology, in the figures of Ouranos, Kronos and Zeus, offers a differentiated picture of the archetypal background of father-devoured consciousness. All three are gods, but not merely ordinary gods: they are dominant gods, kings, undisputed rulers. All three, too, are not only fathers, but devouring fathers.

Each of these three instances of the devouring father presents a different nuance in the archetypal pattern. Ouranos is perhaps the most malicious, certainly the most archaic and ferocious of the three. He does not, however, devour his children directly, but pushes them back into their mother, Gaia, *materia*, and imprisons them there. Ouranos, the sky, defends his position by keeping his young unconscious, mother-bound, encapsulated in dull day-in, day-out *materia*.

Consciousness dominated by Ouranos results in conventionality through gross unconsciousness: "this is the way it's always been done," "this is what I was taught as a child." The subject is unconscious of his attitudes and presuppositions and displays a nearly total lack of self-awareness and poverty of insight into his psychic background. Convention, tradition, collective values are unconsciously assimilated, and the new, the child, the creative future development, remains locked in the mother.

In the bloody victory of Kronos over his sky-father, and the subsequent emergence of a new order, we must note a central motif in the mythologem of the devouring father: change comes through the revolutionary act of the son. Puer leaps high and tears down senex. One of Ouranos' sons finds release and brutally castrates the father.

Freud placed the fear of castration in the son. Our myth would place it more properly on the side of the father: not son but father is the victim of castration. If the threat to the son (Kronos) is repression and imprisonment, the threat to the father is castration.

Castration is the ultimate act of unmanning and humiliation. It is also deprivation of the masculine ability to fertilize and impregnate; it is sterilization of the spirit.

If Kronos is at first puer and carrier of new spirit, he quickly himself turns to devouring father. From his parents he learns that one of his children is destined to overcome him. At this he digs in his heels and through the stratagem of eating his children tries to resist the law of life that sons bury their fathers. The mythologem of the devouring father rests on a principle of eternal revolution, son replacing father, puer overthrowing senex, new destroying old. It is a myth of changes. Kronos, as the puer who comes to power, knows the treachery and energy of the young and is determined to resist their dynamic advance. Whereas the strategy of Ouranos is to keep his potential rivals, his children, unconscious through repression in *materia*, the strategy of Kronos is to incorporate them and thus to spiritualize or psychologize them, thereby severing them from their instinctual origins. Through this process of spiritualization the children are deprived of their radical transformative power.

Under Kronos, consciousness is finely tuned to the prevailing values and attitudes of an outer collective, be it secular society at large, a church group, a political party, or whatnot. It is threatened by stirrings in the unconscious, by "infantile" impulses, "crazy" thoughts, "childish" reactions. It either rejects these unwanted children out of hand or more often tries to find in them a positive spiritual content, "child*like*" reactions, "interesting" ideas, "creative" movements of the soul. This act of splitting positive and negative, spiritual and instinctual, creative and destructive is Kronos swallowing his children. For the future most often lies with the dark children, who naturally pose a threat to the established order of things: "a man's destiny is always shaped at the point where his fear lies."[1]

But Kronos can be tricked. He is deceived, however, not by one of his clever children, but by Rhea, who in this instance performs the role of the Great Mother in her aspect as protector of children. Rhea deceives Kronos with a blanket-covered stone and delivers the real child, Zeus, to a protected cave in Crete where he is raised by three Dictaean Ash-nymphs.[2] Through the agency of Rhea the dynamic movement toward change through the revolutionary son takes a new leap forward. The cycle is again put into motion, but as Kronos is different in nuance from Ouranos so Zeus is different from Kronos. The development within this archetype is not therefore purely cyclic but more in the nature of a spiral which with each turn acquires new characteristics.

Zeus leads to power the Olympian gods, and the old Titanic pantheon is locked away in Tartarus. But Zeus, too, betrays traces of the devouring father. His first consort is Metis, daughter of the Titans, Okeanos and Tethys. Warned by Gaia and Ouranos of the danger posed by a future son of this union, Zeus tricks the pregnant Metis into entering his stomach and keeps her there. He thereby devours his *potential* children. This strategy seems effective, for Zeus maintains his power to the end of the mythological age. He himself bears Metis' child, Athene; in some accounts she springs fully armed from his head. She later becomes his wisest and most trusted counselor.

In contradistinction to Ouranos and Kronos, Zeus bears many children whom he does not devour. Generally he is fond of his children and takes care to look after them. But the myth of Zeus ingesting Metis shows that he, too, like his fathers before him, seeks to stabilize the revolutionary cycle with himself in the dominant position.

Under Zeus, consciousness attains to a much greater degree of flexibility than under Kronos. Looking at the children of Zeus who are allowed to live, one can see what a really remarkable tolerance for opposites the Olympian world has: Apollo and Dionysos, Athene and Ares, Artemis and Helen. The *Iliad* tells of the deep-going strains on Olympus; Zeus rules but his hand is relatively light. Under Zeus, consciousness is flexible enough to integrate all but the truly revolutionary ideas and forces. One sees emerging the Greek ideal of exercising creativity within a framework of balanced order and harmony. Such impulses and urges as cannot be integrated, the truly revolutionary children, are kept dormant and merely potential in their encapsulated mother; they are kept contained in the belly of Zeus.

Under Zeus, consciousness is able to contain and tolerate and let live to a far greater degree than under Kronos where all the children have to be incorporated in spirit. But if the rule of Zeus produces stability, it does so at a certain price: through cancellation of the possibility for revolutionary change, destructive though it may appear at the time, a creative future is also lost. So, in the internal development of this archetype, the more or less tolerant, flexible, reflective senex wins out. This is a gain, and a loss.

Helen M. Luke

Mothers and Daughters: A Mythological Perspective

In his essay on the Kore[1] (the primordial maiden) Jung has said,

> Demeter and Kore, mother and daughter, extend the feminine consciousness upwards and downwards—and widen out the narrowly conscious mind bound in space and time, giving it intimations of a greater and more comprehensive personality which has a share in the eternal course of things . . . It seems clear enough that the man's anima found projection in the Demeter cult . . . For a man, anima experiences are of immense and abiding significance. But the Demeter–Kore myth is far too feminine to have been merely the result of an anima projection . . . Demeter–Kore exists on the plane of mother–daughter experience which is alien to man and shuts him out.

There is an immense difference between the mother–son and the mother–daughter experience. On the archetypal level the son carries for the mother the image of her inner quest, but the daughter is the extension of her very self, carrying her back into the past and her own youth and forward to the promise of her own rebirth into a new personality, into the awareness of the Self. In the natural pattern of development the boy will feel his separateness from his mother by reason of his masculinity much sooner than the girl and will begin his striving for achievement. Everywhere, however, before the twentieth century, the growing girl remained at home contained in the orbit of her mother until the time came for her to become a mother herself and so reverse her role. Thus she would grow naturally from the passive state of being protected into the vital passivity of opening herself to receive the seed, the transition point being marked actually or symbolically by the violent breaking of her virginity.

In ancient Greece the Eleusinian mysteries of Demeter bear witness to this overwhelming need of woman in her already growing separation from the natural pattern of the primitive feminine—the need for the Goddess to teach her the *meaning* of the deep transformation of her being from daughter to mother to daughter again. How much greater is that need today, when so often the woman lives almost like a man in the outer world and must find the whole meaning of her motherhood inwardly instead of physically, and when so many of those who do bear children are simply playing at "mothers and babies," never having allowed themselves to experience consciously the violent end of their daughter identification.

Persephone is playing with her companions in the eternal Spring, completely contained in her carefree belief that nothing can change this happy state of youth and beauty. Underneath, however, the urge to consciousness is stirring, and "the maiden not to be named," strays away from her fellows, and, intoxicated by the scent of a narcissus, she stoops to pick it and in so doing opens the door through which the Lord of the Underworld rushes up to seize her. We may notice here that Gaia, mother earth, is clearly distinguished from Demeter in this myth. She is Zeus's fellow conspirator as it were! Kerényi says, "From the Earth Mother's point of view, neither seduction nor death is the least bit tragic or even dramatic."

It is through the father that the daughter first becomes conscious of her self. When there is no adequate father-image in a girl's life, the identity of daughter and mother can assume a tremendous intensity, or else when the father-image is very negative and frightening, the daughter may unconsciously take on the mother's problem in a peculiarly deep way, sometimes carrying it all her life, long after the mother's death, and so remaining crippled in her effort to face her own fate in freedom. Normally the girl begins to detach from the mother, and to become conscious of her own potential motherhood through love of the father. Thus she is ready for the intoxicating moment of finding the narcissus—seeing *herself* as a person (as Narcissus saw his own face in the water), and the inevitable rape will follow.

The moment of breakthrough for a woman is always symbolically a rape—a necessity—something which takes hold with overmastering power and brooks no resistance. The Lord of the Underworld is he who arises, bursts forth from the unconscious with all the tremendous power of instinct. He comes "with his immortal horses" and sweeps the maiden (the anima in a man) from the surface life of her childish paradise into the depths, into the kingdom of the dead—for a woman's total giving of her heart, of herself, in her experience of her instincts is a kind of death.

Persephone cries out in fear and protest as the cord of her tie to her mother, to her unconscious youthfulness, is violently cut. Demeter, the mother, hears and knows that the daughter is lost but not how. For nine days she wanders over the earth in fear and sorrow, searching for her daughter but not *understanding*. She is wholly identified with her grief, swallowed by it, even her body forgotten so that she does not eat or wash. It is the beginning of the unspeakably painful struggle of a woman to separate from her possessive emotions, the struggle which alone can give birth to love.

The loss of the daughter in older women is the loss of the young and carefree part of oneself, the opportunity for the discoveries of meaning which are the task of the second half of life: it is the change from the life of outer projection to the detachment, the turning inward, which leads to the "immediate experience of being outside time" in Jung's words. In the language of this myth Death rises up and takes away the woman's belief in everlasting spring. The great majority of women today, having no contact at all with the Demeter mystery, have extreme difficulty in giving up this unconscious clinging to youth, their partial identification with man's anima image, the unraped Persephone eternally picking flowers in blissful unconsciousness of the dark world below her. To such women the menopause brings long drawn-out disturbances of the body and the psyche as the conflict grows more acute and remains unresolved.

Kerényi has written, "To enter into the figure of Demeter means to be pursued, to be robbed, to be raped" (as Persephone), "to rage and grieve, to fail to understand" (as Demeter), "and then to get everything back and be born again" (as Demeter and Persephone—the twofold single reality of Demeter–Kore). There can be no shortcuts in this experience.

Only when Hades the Lord of Death, Zeus's dark brother, will cooperate can the answer come. It is he who gives Persephone the seed of the pomegranate to eat—and she, who has hitherto rejected all food (refused to assimilate the experience), now in the moment when she is full of joy at the thought of not having to accept it, takes the pomegranate seed involuntarily, but voluntarily swallows it. In spite of her protests, she really has no intention of regressing to identification with her mother again. This is an image of how the saving thing can happen in the unconscious before the conscious mind can grasp at all what is going on. There are many dreams in which the dreamer tries to return to an old thing or situation but finds, for example, the doors barred or the telephone broken. The ego still yearns for the status quo, but further down the price has been paid, and we *can't* go back. Hence the great value of dreams in making us aware of these movements below. Even Demeter in her conscious planning, still half yearns for her daughter to return as before; but her questioning is quite perfunctory. As soon as she knows the seed has been eaten, there is no more said on the subject—all is joy. Persephone has eaten the food of Hades, has taken the seed of the dark into herself and can now give birth to her own new personality. So also can her mother. They have both passed through death to the renewal of a new spring—the inward renewal which age need never lose—and have accepted the equal necessity of winter and life in the darkness of the underworld.

Linda Schierse Leonard

Redeeming the Father

In my own life, redeeming the father has been a long process. It started when I went into Jungian analysis. With the help of a kind and supportive woman analyst who provided a warm, protective container for the emerging energies, I entered into a new realm—the symbolic world of dreams. There I encountered sides of myself I never knew existed. I also discovered my father there—the father I had long ago rejected. There was in myself, I discovered, not only the personal father I remembered. There were a variety of paternal figures, images of an archetypal Father. This father had more faces that I had ever imagined, and that realization was awesome. It terrified me and it also gave me hope. My ego-identity, my notions about who I was, crumbled. There was in me a power stronger than my consciously acknowledged self. This power rolled over my attempts to control my life and events around me, as an avalanche changes the face of a mountain. From then on, my life required that I learn to relate to this greater power.

In rejecting my father, I had been refusing my power, for the rejection of my father entailed refusing all of his positive qualities as well as the negative ones. So, along with the irresponsibility and irrational dimension that I had denied, I lost access to my creativity, spontaneity, and feminine feeling. My dreams kept pointing this out. One dream said that my father was very rich and owned a great palatial Tibetan temple. Another said he was a Spanish king. This contradicted the poor, degraded man I knew as "father." As far as my own powers went, my dreams showed that I was refusing them too. In one dream a magic dog gave me the power to make magic opals. I made the opals and had them in my hand, but then I gave them away and didn't keep any for myself. In another dream, a meditation teacher said, "You are beautiful but you don't recognize it." And a voice said to me in still another dream, "You have the key to medial knowledge and you must take it." But I woke up screaming in terror that I didn't want the responsibility. The irony was that although I criticized and hated my father for being so irresponsible and letting his potentialities go down the drain, I was doing the very same thing. I wasn't really valuing myself and what I had to offer. Instead I alternated between the unconfident, fragile pleasing puella and the dutiful, achieving armored Amazon.

Because of my rejection of my father, my life was split into a number of unintegrated and conflicting figures, each trying to keep control. Ultimately this leads to an explosive situation. For a long time I was unable to accept the death of these individual identities for the greater unknown unity that could ground my magic—the mysterious ground of my being, which I later found to be the source of healing. And so I experienced this powerful ground of my being in the form of anxiety attacks. Because I would not let go willingly and open up to the greater powers, they overwhelmed me and showed me their threatening face. They struck me suddenly and repeatedly in the core of my being, shocking me out of my controlling patterns like lightning jolts open a closed and clutching hand. Now I knew how little help my defenses really were. Suddenly I was face to face with the void. I wondered if this was what my father had experienced too, and whether his drinking was an attempt to ward this off. Perhaps "the spirits" of alcohol that ruled his being were a substitute for the greater spirits, and perhaps even a defense against them because they were so close. Since I had denied any value to my father after he "drowned" in the irrational Dionysian realm, I needed to learn to value that rejected area by letting go of the need to control. But this required experiencing the negative side, being plunged into the uncontrollable chaos of feelings and impulses, into the dark depths where the unknown treasure was hidden. Ultimately, to redeem the father required that I enter the underworld, that I value that rejected area in myself. And that led to honoring the spirits.

About a year after I started really facing my father, I had the following dream:

I saw some beautiful poppies, glowing with red, orange, and yellow colors and I wished my mother-analyst were there with me to see them. I went through the field of poppies and crossed a stream. Suddenly I was in the underworld at a banquet table with many men. Red wine was flowing and I decided to take another glass. As I did, the men raised their wine glasses in salute to my health, and I felt warm and glowing with their affectionate tribute.

The dream marked my initiation into the underworld. I had passed from the bright world of the mother into the realm of the dark father-lover. But there I was saluted as well. This was of course an incestuous situation and yet a necessary one for me. Part of the father's role, according to Kohut, is to let himself be idealized by the daughter and then gradually allow her to detect his realistic limitations without withdrawing from her.[1] And of course with the ideal projection goes deep love. In my own development the love turned to hate, so that the previous ideals associated with my father were rejected. I had to learn to love my father again so I could reconnect with his positive side. I had to learn to value my father's playful, spontaneous, magic side, but also to see its limits, as well as how the positive aspects could be actualized in my life. Loving the Father-ideal allowed me to love my own ideal and to realize that ideal in myself. This entailed first seeing my father's value and then realizing that that belonged to me. This broke the unconscious incestuous bond and freed me for my own relation to the transcendent powers in my Self.

For wounded daughters who are in poor relation to other sides of the father, the details of the redemption may be different, but the central issue will be the same. To redeem the father requires seeing the hidden value the father has to offer. For example, those daughters who have reacted against the too authoritarian father are likely to have problems accepting their own authority. Such women tend to adapt or react rebelliously. They need to see the value in their own responsibility, in accepting their own power and strength. They need to value limit, to go up to it and see the edges, but know when too much is too much. They need to know when to say no and when to say yes. This means having realistic ideals and knowing their own limits and the limits of the situation. To put it in Freudian terms, they need to get a positive relation to the "super-ego," the inner voice of valuation and responsible judgment and decision-making.

This voice, when it is constructive, is neither too critical and severe nor too indulgent, so that they can see and hear objectively what is there. One woman expressed it this way: "I need to hear the voice of the father inside tell me in a kind way when I'm doing a good job, but also when I'm off the mark." Redemption of this aspect of the father means the transformation of the critical judge, who proclaims one constantly "guilty," and the defense lawyer, who responds with self-justification. Instead will be found a kindly, objective arbiter. It means having one's own inner sense of valuation, rather than looking outside for approval. Instead of falling prey to the cultural collective projections that don't fit, it means knowing who one is and actualizing genuine possibilities. On the cultural level, it means valuing the feminine enough to stand up for it against the collective view of what the feminine is "supposed" to be.

Daughters who have had "too positive" a relation to their father have still another aspect of the father to redeem. If the relation to the father is too positive, the daughters are likely to be bound to the father by over-idealizing him and by allowing their own inner father strength to remain projected outward on the father. Quite often their relationships to men are constricted because no man can match the father. In this case they are bound to the father in a similar way to women who are bound to an imaginary "ghostly lover." (Often an idealized relation to the father is built up unconsciously when the father is missing.) The too positive relationship to the father can cut them off from a real relationship to men and quite often from their own professional potentialities. Because the outer father is seen so idealistically, they can't see the value of their own contribution to the world. To redeem the father in themselves, they need to acknowledge his negative side. They need to experience their father as human and not as an idealized figure in order to internalize the father principle in themselves.

Ultimately, redeeming the father entails reshaping the masculine within, fathering that side of oneself. Instead of the "perverted old man" and the "angry, rebellious boy," women need to find "the man with heart," the inner man with a good relation to the feminine.

The cultural task of women today involves the same process. The value of the father principle needs to be seen and its limits need to be recognized as well. Part of this task involves sorting out what is essential to the father and what has been imposed artificially by the culture. Most often the father principle has been split into two conflicting opposites—the rigid, old authoritarian ruler and the playful but irresponsible eternal boy. In Western culture the authoritarian side of the father has been consciously valued and accepted, and the playful, boyish side repressed or consciously devalued. Culturally, this has resulted in the kind of situation found in *Iphigenia in Aulis*. The authoritarian power side makes the decisions (Agamemnon) and sacrifices the daughter, but the initiating cause of the sacrifice comes from the jealousy of the boyish brother (Menelaus). These two sides are at odds on the conscious level, but unconsciously, through their possessiveness, they collude in the sacrifice of the daughter, i.e., the young, emerging feminine. Women today need to confront this split in the father principle and contribute to its healing. In this sense, redeeming the father may entail "re-dreaming" the father, i.e., a feminine fantasy about what the father could be and do. My disappointment with Iphigenia was that finally she went willingly to her death. Even though the outer situation of her sacrifice caused by the trap into which her father had fallen seemed inevitable, she could have spoken out of her feminine instinct and wisdom and told her father what could have been possible. And this might have produced a change in masculine consciousness. Women are just beginning to do this today—they are beginning to share their feelings and fantasies and bring them out in public. Women need to tell their stories. They need to tell men what they expect of them. They need to say it out of their gut and not try to justify their feelings on masculine grounds. But they also need to tell about themselves in the spirit of compassion and not out of bitter defeat. Many women remain trapped in the facticity of their lives, not seeing their own possibility. This leads to bitterness and cynicism. Here is where the value of the puella is redeeming, for its deep connection with the realm of possibility and imagination can lead to new ways of seeing and doing things and to a new valuation of the feminine. When this creative vision is combined with the strength and focus of the Amazon woman, a new understanding and feeling for the father may emerge.

Recently, I asked one of my classes to write down their fantasy of a good father. The class consisted mostly of women in their twenties and early thirties, but there were also a few men. Here is their composite fantasy of a father: Father is a man who is strong, stable, dependable, firm, active, adventurous; yet he is warm, loving, compassionate, tender, nurturing, caring, and involved. Their fantasy of the father was as an androgynous person, i.e., someone who has integrated both the masculine and feminine elements in himself.

A major theme that kept recurring was that the father should provide guidance, both in the outer and inner worlds but without lecturing or demanding. "Guide and teach, not push and preach" was the way they thought the father should help them to form their own limits, principles, and values and to balance discipline and pleasure. Their emphasis was that the father lead by example and *be* a model of adult confidence, honesty, competence, authority, courage, faith, love, compassion, understanding, and generosity in the areas of work, creativity, social, ethical, and love commitment. At the same time, he would clearly own his values as his own neither imposing them on his daughter nor representing them as "the only right way." As a guide he would provide both nurturance and advice, yet encourage his daughter to be independent and explore things on her own. On the practical level he would encourage and teach financial management and support any aspirations she might have toward professional work. Believing in her strength, beauty, intelligence, and ability, he would be proud of her. But he would not project his own unfulfilled wishes on his daughter and be dependent or overly protective of her. Rather, he would affirm his daughter's unique and individual way of being, respecting and valuing her personhood, yet not expecting responsibilities beyond her years. He would be sensitive and emotionally available when she needed him throughout the course of her development. And with this good timing and intuitive sense of his daughter, he could offer the protection and guidance she needed at the right time. But when she was ready to become an adult, he would also sense this and withdraw from the role of father to mutual friendship with the necessary respect and love. So he would want and be able to learn from her too. Ultimately, the father and daughter would be able to talk and listen to each other, sharing life experiences and learning from one another.

David DeBus

Fathers and Their Daughters: Walking Our Street

You walk with me through the streets
like a little gust of wind
at my hand

past the new Nectar fruitjuice bar
and the Old Bicycle Shoppe just opened
past the natural grocery and its owner
who says to me, "Tanks to God,
and money is not so important"

past the frontyard gardens and through
the clouds of wind-drift when the surf
is up

past the laundromat's chunk-chunking
concerto, and the ocean sotto voce,
the dizzy high school kids
in their pomp and bomp stylishness
at the AM/PM Minimarket gas/food
just hanging and just looking
through their rock 'n' roll sunglasses

past where Sylvia died of cancer,
under where Jane took her old
and frightened life,
and outside of where Terry died
when the streetdrugs finally
got this man of heart's heart

and you walk with me through
the poems and songs and paintings,
through the walks and kisses and candles
that got you here through us,
through the pages of her book
on children and their monsters,

and my book on Whitman, and all
of the money-panics and times when
I had two potatoes and a cup of rice

under the bower and by the jasmine
I think that you already smell, and petting
the cat Thomas, imagining when you
first meet Thomas, and wondering
if you will fall in love with Thomas'
friend Christopher who wants you
to be a girl because boys are too violent

David L. Miller

Great Mothers and Grand Mothers

Why has the most common name for archetypal images of the goddess been "Great Mother"? Why, for example, has it not been "Grand Mother"? After all, "Great Mother" and "Grand Mother" are at least linguistically equivalent expressions and both would have translated the Latin phrase *Magna Mater* equally well. Yet there is surely a difference, as our ear and our experience immediately tell.

Imagining mother and mothering to be "great" may be the wish of children and mothers for a sort of social security. But grand-mothers, having already suffered through the mothering business and its negative and positive inflations, and knowing how it comes out or does not come out, see through it and know better. They are mothers-in-law as well as mothers! That is, they are not attached by virtue simply of a history of unconscious and biological dependen-cies; rather, they are attached due to the historical accident of a mar-riage. These mothers-in-law, who see through great-mother pre-tension, are no longer great but are now in some simple and uninflated way just grand, which may be why they, unlike great mothers, are a fertile source for a sense of humor.

Theorists have somehow unwittingly obscured this family ex-perience by a witless use of terminology. The pluralistic myths and possibilities of the feminine somehow become reduced in the act of idealization. The theoretical discourse constructs a sort of academic fairy tale that is not true to experiences of the feminine sources.[1] But it may be an informative trope concerning the ways we have been unknowingly initiated into thinking and feeling about mother and mothering. For within the archetypal image of the great mother resides many grand myths, many grand mothers, each of which offers plural possibilities for imagining the female source and its resourcefulness. Rhea, a grand mother of Greek gods and goddesses, is one example.

It is to Dionysos, and to Persephone, too, that Rhea especially serves as grand mother. Immediately following his birth, Dionysos met with trouble due to the nagging jealousy of the great mother Hera. The latter sent Titans (great ones) to tear the infant into a myriad of pieces. This may be what the titanic (the great) does to one psychologically. But it was grand mother Rhea who picked up the pieces, following the manner of the Egyptian Isis, and boiled them in a cauldron. In the essence of the vapor the many pieces of Dionysian madness discovered their own life.[2]

Similarly, Persephone found herself in hell. The bottom had fallen out of her innocence. She felt swallowed by the abysmal. For the first time she suffered depth. Two great brothers and a sister fought over the situation, but the sibling rivalry of the greats came to nothing. Zeus, the great father, was quite literally caught between Demeter, the great mother of Persephone, and the great deep, Hades. Persephone was lost in all this greatness. Rhea interceded and negotiated the fertile compromise, giving the breadth of grandeur to all: innocence of the maiden variety will spend a quarter of its time in the depths and three-quarters of its time in the light.[3]

Now the archetypal complexity of the grand mother can be sensed. Rhea is associated with Hermes because, like him, she is grand enough to be associated with Dionysian craziness and Persephonic hell. She has the breadth of the "wide wandering" Eurynome and the depth of the "moon snake" Ophion. She participates in an earthy way in many stories and brings them back down to earth.

One handbook of mythology ends its account of Rhea by saying simply that "the Romans identified her with *Magna Mater*," who came to be called "the Great Mother."[4] But this marks the decease of Rhea, who is a grand mother. The openness of "grand" is lost in the closure implied by fantasies of "great." Mother thereupon is idealized. The feminine is inflated, to be sure; but at the same time she is reduced to nothing since the inflation, like that of current economy, is in the mode of a heroic male fantasy articulated in the fairy-tale rhetoric of ego-greatness.

Fundamentally, the mythic way of the grand mother is imaginal rather than behavioral, perspectival rather than programmatic, and psychological rather than political, but through Rhea's imagination, through the grandeur of her deep perspective, social behaviors and political programs are transformed. It happens in the affirming of the many, the tasting the fullness of the deeps, and more resembles Persephone, stuck with the taste of all those tiny pomegranate seeds, than it does Demeter's motherliness.

Jane Rule

Loving
Grandmothers

I think it's probably a "masculine trait" to practice dying from a very young age. Anyway, it's always the boy children I invent who shoot themselves with their own bow ties, grab their arrow-pierced stomachs and fall to the ground; and most of the real hypochondriacs I've known have been men who at the first twinge of headache are convinced of spinal meningitis; at the gentlest fart, terminal cancer. I also have a hunch that fatherhood is a way men practice dying. Women don't seem as often to need to invent melo-dramatic premonitions of death, the house of the body so much a way station for other life that even those of us who do not give birth acknowledge the wasted blood, the monthly murder of some new soul for the sake of our own lives. Our bodies seem to practice dying for us without aid of our imaginations. It is only when women have imposed on them men's fear of dying that they are caught up in the vanity of pretending not to age, contemplate suicide at my age for a lost womb, a second chin, bifocals.

I loved all my grandparents, but I loved the *bodies* of my grand-mothers, both of whom suffered from arthritis as I do now. They were fragile and deliberate in the way they moved, and from the time I was tall and sturdy enough to be some aid, they used my body as brace or hoist. They taught me early how to touch pain and to comfort, because they were at the candid mercy of my love. From them, far more than from my marvelously ample-bodied and com-petent mother, I learned the close intimacy of flesh. When, as an adolescent, I was physically shy with my mother, I always had sweet excuse to touch my grandmothers, to brush their hair, to help them dress, to choose among their rings which would still traverse the swollen joints of what were to me their beautiful hands, accurate still with needle and thread, with cards, with flowers, accurate with requests. I found their faces lovelier than any others of my childhood because they were *made,* could be understood as the bland faces of other children could not, as even those of my parents could not, since they did not yet know themselves and masked their ignorance as best they could. My mother has that wondrous face now.

To become an old woman has always been my ambition, and it may be that my life span is to be short enough to make a speeding up of the process necessary. I have had a long apprenticeship as lover; and in the way I can, I will still carry out those patterns of courtship, but I am coming into a time when I must be the beloved of children and the young, who will measure their confidence in terms of my growing needs. As my grandmothers taught me the real lessons of erotic love with their beautifully requiring flesh and speaking faces, so I would wish to teach the children I love that they are capable of tenderness and of strength, capable of knowledge because of what they can see in my face, clear in pain and wonder, intent on practicing life as long as it lasts.

Alma Luz Villanueva

Song of the Self: The Grandmother

Surrounded by my shields, am
I:
Surrounded by my children, am
I:
Surrounded by the void, am
I:
I am the void.
I am the womb of remembrance.
I am the flowering darkness.
I am the flower, first flesh.

Utter darkness I inhabit—
There, I watch creation unfold—
There, I know we begin and end—
Only to begin, again, and again—
Again. In this darkness, I am
Turning, turning toward a birth:
My own—a newborn grandmother
Am I, suckling light. Rainbow
Serpent covers me, head to foot,
In endless circles—covers me,
That I may live forever, in this
Form or another. The skin she
Leaves behind glitters with
The question, with the answer,

With the promise:
"Do you remember yourself?"
"I am always woman."
"Flesh is flower, forever."

I enter darkness, to enter birth,
To wear the Rainbow, to hear her
Hissing loudly, clearly, in my
Inner ear: love.

I am spiralling, I am spinning,
I am singing this Grandmother's Song.
I am remembering forever, where we
Belong.

River Malcolm

The Grandfather Archetype: His Kingdom for a Hand

As I summon my own experience with the grandfather archetype, I find it elusive and out of my reach. Strange, since my personal grandfathers were so important, so shaping in my girl-hood. Yet that personal experience involves a conjunction of family roles: the granddaughter and the grandfather. The granddaughter herself is a conjunction of puella, puer, and ego—for I was at the same time puella to my grandfather's gentlemanly courtship and crown prince to his kingdom, which, as it seemed to me, my parents had so miserably failed to inherit. To this succession I saw gender as no real barrier.

My grandfathers were men of power, important men of the world. They were writers, tellers of stories. They had power and importance in the world of letters, scrapbooks, and stories, not the ordinary world my parents labored in. My grandfathers, whose post-retirement time curved back to the shape of my childhood time, joined me outside of the urgency of schedules and goals. In our shared and mythical world, they were kings. In my childhood dream life, my father was culpable. The atom bomb fell in my dream: my father and his colleagues were meeting and couldn't reach an agreement. My grandfather was not culpable, even in dreams. He held out his hand to me. When I read his palm, it was covered with symbols and hieroglyphs from literature and mythology: his warm welcome, invitation to a rich cultural heritage. My parents, carrying the archetypes of father and mother, were conjunct with the world; they carried the blame for its limitations.

My grandfathers joined me outside time. There, the dichotomy between male and female, young and old, seemed fluid and bridgeable. The place where the granddaughter and grandfather meet is so distant to me now. As a middle-aged woman, I taste the ways I cannot inherit my grandfather's kingdom. I taste the double-binds of gender in a culture of gender confusion, a culture in which women's lives are shaped by men's dominating and conflicting needs.

How hard it is to imagine the complete trust and identification of that girl-child who stood as crown prince on the threshold of her grandfather's kingdom. Yet perhaps she has lessons for me. Perhaps there are things she accepted as birthright to which I have lost my access as I faced and embraced the ordinary world of middle age, the world of choices and culpability. Perhaps in wrestling free my identity as woman, free from men's fears and their longings, wrestling with the female as over against the male, I have lost her easy trusting access to the grandfather. I have lost her access to a part of my heritage that I need not experience as toxic, that I need not subject to the tests of middle-aged life. She is my link back to grandfather–granddaughter time, where the grandfather archetype lives on in me, a time of androgyny, a time in which young and old were conjunct, a world in which only middle age was truly alien. How far from my orbit that archetype now seems.

I reach back in memory. I am seven. I sit in Grandpa's study, once a stable. Floor, walls, and ceiling are wood. He sits on a rocking chair, wire-rimmed glasses, fine white hair, reading a newspaper. I sit on a couch, playing a game of peg solitaire. It is quiet between us. We sit in a still pool of time, my child time, innocent of the urgencies of middle-aged life, his post-urgency elder time. Surrounded by dozens of antique clocks, the fruit of a lifetime's collecting, all of them ticking, we sit quietly together.

Or, I am on the veranda with him, my grandmother angry over some practical matter. My grandfather and I fade into a world of humor and fantasy. We become invisible to her. He holds out his hand full of birdseed. Wild birds perch on his hands and feed. Their trust and mine are complete.

Or, I am three thousand miles away in the California sunshine reading his letter, in which he spins memories: a story of a young rural school superintendent, setting out with his horse and buggy to visit schools in the deep snow of Massachusetts winter. He is me and not me, kin and other; I commune through him, through the mysteries of shared blood and shared story, with another gender, another geography, another generation.

My other grandfather stands in his study. The passionate Pacific is framed in his large picture window—rock cliff, sand beach, enormous breakers. The smell of leather, high-backed, armed leather chairs, the leather binding of his scrapbooks. He stands, elegantly dressed, perfectly erect. He tells me the story of his business success, his power, how he made his own choices, how he defied everyone and succeeded. He talks and talks and talks. I listen. My eyes burn, my heart burns. We burn with shared courage, my grandfather and I. He hands me the torch. Like him, I will have the courage to make my own choices. We argue, we have debates. He delights when I oppose him, he delights in the muscle and determination of my young mind. How few men, after him, will wrestle me mind-to-mind for pure joy, unthreatened by my native strength and swiftness. How few men will I meet whose battles are over and won. How few whose identity, united by blood and story with mine, transcend the polarities of age and gender.

It hurts to remember him. I know there are many reasons that crown prince myth did not manifest in ordinary reality. My choices were shaped by the mystery of gender and by my need in order to be true to my grandfather, to find my own truth. As I grew older, I knew that had to include the truth of my body, to find in my life a meaning for living in a female body—a body with breasts, womb, and vagina—and living in this body in a culture dominated by men's way of being. I could not follow a simple succession to my grandfather's life and ignore the text of my body. Instead, for much of young adulthood, I turned my back on the patriarchal world in which he could succeed as himself, but I could not discover how, as myself, to succeed. I now know some women, many women—even myself on a smaller scale—have done so. I did not know how then.

Memory pulls me to young adulthood. I have not yet turned away from patriarchy. I am a graduate student at a major university, immersed in the life of the mind. I sit by my grandfather's bed. He is in a coma, stroke-smitten, almost certainly soon to be dead. This room has a different window, a more distant view of the blue Pacific. It is a quiet view; the vast horizon dominates. Red brick roofs and white stucco punctuate the blue expanse of sky and ocean. My grandfather and I cannot talk; he is silenced. The last words I hear him speak are my name and his surprise at my arrival: "Why, Mary Malcolm, I had no idea." Self-conscious before his silence, I pour out my story. I tell him I am in graduate school, will be a university professor, am leading the life he always wanted to lead. He had an eighth-grade education, succeeded in business, was self-educated, a genuine lover of knowledge. As I tell my eager story to my silent listener, I recognize how much my life is not my own, but his dream living on in my body. My words trail off. In my vigil at the silent brink of death, we communicate for the first time wordlessly, for the first time *not* mind to mind. We communicate through the body. I take his hand. I am afraid of his dying. I sing an improvised song, cheeks streaming with tears: "I sing because I'm afraid." Out of his coma, his surpassing love for me reaches, gives my frightened hand a strong and reassuring squeeze.

My last memory of him lingers, tactile, imprinted in skin, in the life of my body. And so the grandfather archetype for me is paradoxical, an archetype that seems to bridge the dichotomies of male and female, old and young, to transcend the limitations of the workaday middle-aged world. And also an archetype that introduces death, limitation, the call to the truth of the body. For that handclasp with my grandfather and with his dying challenges the entire structure of myth and story in which granddaughter and grandfather once lived. I leave his death knowing that my living must change, must learn to honor the mysteries of death and the body.

I suppose I have not turned away from my grandfather nor from the archetypal depths he touched in me. I suppose I am following my grandfather still. The archetype finds its deepest meaning in this ordinary world it both transcends and demands participation in. Neither being a crown prince nor being myself has turned out to be quite what I thought it would.

Christine Downing

Coming to Terms with Marriage: A Mythological Perspective

After having been married for more than twenty-five years, I was about to be divorced. My husband and I had been separated for several years; the divorce felt right to each of us but I knew that for me some ritual observance of the ending was essential. The intuition led me to recognize that what I wanted to do was to come to terms as wholly as I could with what "wifeness" had meant to me. My way of doing that was to turn to the Greek mythological representation of wifeness, the figure of Hera, and ask what role she had played in my life.

As wife to Zeus, king of the gods, and as the only goddess centrally defined by her marital role, Hera is *the* wife of the Olympian pantheon. The most accessible classical accounts of her tension-filled relationship with Zeus suggest that being wife is singularly unfulfilling. This coming to terms seemed to provide me with a way of understanding myself more fully, more consciously, and more symbolically than I had before—at a point in my life where in an outward literal sense I was no longer to be defined by my relation to her. I hoped that in this way I might now become more aware of the life I had lived and what it meant, not to wish it away nor to get free of it through understanding it. It was not that I felt my life should have been different, but that I wished to know it better.

I spent most of a winter weekend lying on my bed, propped up by pillows, surrounded by books and half-emptied coffee cups, writing about Hera, about me, about our connection. I had imagined this as a kind of ritual farewell to Hera—and so it was—but it became a kind of greeting as well.

As we turn to Hera, we begin where we must, with Hera as wife, yet also with Hera as maiden and widow, for it is an essential part of her relation to wifeness that marriage never quite contains her. Indeed, the very ambivalence toward wifeness suggested by her triple status may lead toward an appreciation that marriage is in its very essence something to which women are both pulled and resistant.

This central ambivalence, the double message associated with Hera, was, I have come to realize, clearly present in the image of Hera first conveyed to me by my mother. "I have chosen Hera as my goddess," she seemed to be saying all through my childhood, "but she asks too much; I will protect you from her. This goddess demands total allegiance. If one is wife, that is all one gets to be."

Hera's absolute commitment and fidelity are at the very heart of her self-image. In the myths this is represented by the violence with which she rejects those men who dare to try to seduce her. Her faithfulness is a provocation to Zeus because it encompasses the demand that she should be loved for what she has sacrificed. In return for her renunciation, she expects absolute fidelity and is inevitably jealous of any other who receives his attention. Hera, as so many of the myths represent her, is a wife who always expects as her due a more total commitment from her husband than she will ever get. Her jealousy is most virulently evoked by Zeus's sexual involvements with other females, but Hera-women may be just as jealous of their spouse's devotion to parents or children, job or hobby. Truly to understand the Olympian Hera is to realize that Zeus's promiscuity is not her bad luck, not something that could have been different. That she experiences him as betraying her is the inevitable correlate of her own obsessive fidelity; it is a necessary part of being Hera so long as we see Hera, or she sees herself, only as woman defined by being wife.

Thus, although Zeus and Hera are supposed to represent the ideal patriarchal family, they seem to represent instead the tensions which undermine its stability. The relation between Hera and Zeus has in it elements that express the pull in any marriage to escape differentiation and also elements that pertain to the longing for participation in a match between two self-fulfilled persons—but primarily it reflects the struggle that ensues when both partners are confusedly and contradictorily trying to realize both aims. Their relationship also illustrates how this struggle is exacerbated in a patriarchally determined marriage where the wife will almost inevitably become pathologically possessive and jealous.

Though provoked by Zeus, Hera's jealousy is most actively directed into persecution of his mistresses and their children. The Hera of Olympus does not like women—or being a woman—at all. She is singularly without any positive relation to other females—except for the two daughters whom she completely dominates. Hera's obsession with the other women in Zeus's life may reflect a subliminal recognition of how important they are to her, how in some way they represent otherwise unknown aspects of her own being.

We are more interested in what Hera's jealousy tells us about her (and about us) than in what it may reveal about Zeus. Much of its passion derives from the intensity with which she has repressed direct expression of her own sexuality: she projects onto Zeus the fulfillment of her own denied desires. Her jealousy may also include penis envy not just in the narrow sense of envy of Zeus's genital potency but its deeper meaning as resentment of his unrestrained freedom and aggressive power. In a sense her jealousy is an overt expression of her otherwise repudiated masculinity since in it she moves from feminine passivity to forceful activity. Her jealousy is a kind of fantasy activity that both expresses and disguises her deepest wishes and fears.

Freud refers often to the importance of the "third" in provoking psychic life. The dyad, whether it unites mother and infant or husband and wife, tends to be static. It is often characterized more by fusion than by genuine relating; the arrival of the third (father or mistress) forces differentiation, change, movement. Perhaps this is why the relationship between Hera and Zeus seems most alive when she is stirred to jealousy. It is her jealousy that provokes her to creative activity in the form of parthenogenetic procreation; it is also her jealousy that finally leads her to leave Zeus—not for another lover but for her own self-renewal, the re-creation of her virginity, her in-one-self-ness. In his essay "Marriage as a Psychological Relationship," Jung says:

> Seldom or never does a marriage develop into an individual relationship smoothly or without crisis. There is no birth of conscious-

ness without pain. . . . Disunity with oneself begets discontent, and since one is not conscious of the real state of things, one generally projects the reasons for it upon one's partner. A critical atmosphere thus develops, the necessary prelude to conscious realization.[1]

From this perspective Hera's jealousy is a painful initiation into the realization that Zeus cannot bring her to fulfillment after all, that she has projected onto him her own unlived masculinity, her animus (and thence, Jung would say, stems the "animosity" between them). Murray Stein speaks of Hera in terms of a "mating instinct" and asserts that "the *telos* of Hera is *gamos*."[2] Though his language does not feel quite right to me, I agree with Stein that what pulls Hera to Zeus is not really sexual longing. The longing has a political element which represents Hera's hope for a matching of power. (We should remember that Hera's promise to Paris is sovereignty and wealth.) She wants to be fully met, matched, mated— sexually, yes, but more importantly, psychologically. I am half-embarrassed to recall now how ripe I was for marriage when I was a bride, how though I had gone to college as Athene, I left, to my own surprise, as Hera. Yet it seems important to remember and acknowledge that: to feel again what it was like to need to live being wife *now* as an imperative as impelling as is orgasm when one is at its brink, to recall the certainty of that conviction: "I am living exactly what I was created to live."

To understand this longing is to understand Hera from within. We are introduced here to marriage not as something imposed by patriarchy but as something fulfilling a deep longing of women themselves. This understanding of marriage underlies the fact that in Greek cultic life the *gamos,* the wedding, was part of the Hera cult, not part of the Zeus religion.

Hera represents that moment of transition between matriarchy and patriarchy when both mother-right and father-right are honored. This is a moment the myths never catch; in a sense it is a moment that never happens except in Hera's fantasy. Because all that is every visible is the move from one exclusive claim to the other, in the myths Hera is represented as the goddess who has capitulated. Somehow even in the myths both Heras are present: the one connected to patriarchy and the archaic one. Both are present in the myths—and in us: the one who chooses marriage and the one who works to undermine it. Inevitably this is confusing, to Hera *and* to Zeus, to husband and to wife. The fantasies of swallowing him and making his power her own or of losing herself in him are inevitably intermingled with the fantasy of being truly met. This does not mean that the first are somehow "realistic" fantasies and the latter pure illusion.

I see Hera as representing the transition from virginal in-one-self-ness to *hieros gamos,* in response to a vision of a *coniunctio* that is neither dissolution nor battle. She is never just Hera Teleia but is also Hera Parthenos; the two belong together not as subsequent stages but as coexistent, mutually illuminating aspects of who Hera *is.* The narrative temporality of myth necessarily obscures this. Focusing on the married-to-Zeus aspect of Hera's life without recognizing how she is still also the virginal Hera misrepresents her. Cult with its recognition that the transition from one phase to the other happens repeatedly opens us to a deeper understanding. Ritually Hera renews her virginity annually when she immerses herself in the spring of Kanathos near Nauplion; ritually Hera is never only the Hera of Olympus but the pre-Olympian Hera as well.

Hera represents that in virginity which longs for conjunction as part of its own nature and that in *coniunctio* which looks back nostalgically toward in-one-self-ness as part of its own nature.

Hera's pathos is that after her marriage she finds that Zeus is not Zeus after all, is not the fully equal other, the perfectly matched other, she had imagined him to be. As Stein puts it: "Zeus thwarts Hera in a specific way, i.e, he will not allow her to find her 'perfection' and fulfillment in *gamos.* He will not be married to her in more than a token way, nor allow her to be deeply married to him."[3] The Hera-Zeus struggle appears inevitable, and yet one also feels that both really know better, both really mean something else, want something different. Reflection on their union brings us to an appreciation of the "dialectical content" of marriage, of its "progressive as well as regressive aspects, helps us see monogamy not simply as human oppression but as the attempt at a sustained relation between two people."[4]

It was only as I came to understand this that I began also to comprehend why there are not just two Heras but three. All coexist and mutually define one another. Hera is not only Parthenos and Teleia; there is also Hera Chera, Hera the solitary, unbound, widowed or divorced, no longer married. Hera represents not only the transition to marriage but the transition beyond. Here my reading of Hera (perhaps because I am a woman) is radically different from Stein's who sees Hera Chera as representing the ugly, unhappy phase of Hera's life. Though of course I agree with Kerényi that this is its most dangerous phase—dangerous to men, that is, and to patriarchy. It is dangerous also to women as any phase that implies radical transformation must be, but many women would want to reinvoke "the increased religious valuation of this lowest phase"[5] which Kerényi describes as occurring in the late classical period. Stein's interpretation seems to proceed from an entirely negative view of Hera's jealousy and possessiveness, which no longer seems adequate to me, and to issue in a therapy which would aim at making Hera content in her marriage. I have come to see journeys into dark places in a different way.

The mythological version of Hera's separation from Zeus says that, when she could take his infidelities no longer, she left him and returned to her birthplace in Euboea. I understand her departure as providing the distance between them that might allow each to rediscover the fantasy, the hope that had brought them together in the first place. Perhaps Hera had only really discovered her essential aloneness *within* the relationship, and could only learn what genuine relationship might be in solitude. The separation can be understood as the necessary prelude to what Jung would call a genuinely psychological marriage. The divorce is thus an integral part of the shared history and, even more important, an essential aspect of Hera's being. According to the myth, Zeus and Hera come together again afterward. When he is unable to persuade her to return, he approaches Mount Cithaeron in the company of a veiled female statue and it is announced that he is about to marry a local princess. When Hera discovers the ruse, she is amused and reconciled to him. That smiling acceptance of him and of herself shows that something significant has changed between them.

Of course, such a return to marriage might not on the human level necessarily mean remarriage to the original spouse or remarriage at all. It may simply represent a recognition of how the pull to what Stein calls "deep marriage" continues to be important. On the other side of patriarchal marriage, the longing for a fully mutual and sustained primary relationship persists. It might lead toward a remarriage in which the partners can now truly accept and enjoy one another, or into a new marriage or deep love affair. It might lead into a genuinely fulfilling relationship with a woman rather than a man, or into an acceptance that something for which one deeply longs may not be granted. What Hera means is the strength not to pretend that some lesser gift is the fulfillment nor to deny the longing. Her in-one-self-ness on the far side of marriage is different from the maiden's innocent self-absorption and immersion in her fantasies—it is an aloneness that includes within it being-with as both memory and hope.

Christine Downing

Sisters and Brothers

For a woman the sister is the other most like ourselves of any creature in the world. She is of the same gender and generation, of the same biological and social heritage. We have the same parents; we grew up in the same family, were exposed to the same values, assumptions, patterns of interaction. (Of course, I know that the probability is that we share only half our genes and that no two children ever have quite the same parents—we experience them somewhat differently and evoke different responses from them. Nevertheless there is no other with whom we share so much.) The sibling relationship is among the most enduring of all human ties, beginning with birth and ending only with the death of one of the siblings. Although our culture seems to allow us the freedom to leave sibling relationships behind, to walk away from them, we tend to return to them in moments of celebration—marriages and births— as well as at times of crisis—divorces and deaths. At such moments we often discover to our surprise how quickly the patterns of childhood interaction and the intensity of childhood resentment and appreciation reappear.

Yet this other so like myself is, ineluctably, *other*. She, more than any other, serves as the one over against whom I define myself. (Research suggests that children are aware of the distinct otherness of siblings well before they have fully separated from the mother.) Likeness and difference, intimacy and otherness—neither can be overcome. That paradox, that tension, lies at the very heart of the relationship.

Same-sex siblings seem to be for one another, paradoxically, both ideal self and what Jung calls "shadow." They are engaged in a uniquely reciprocal, mutual process of self-definition. Although daughters create mothers as much as mothers create daughters, the relationship is not symmetrical as the one between sisters is. Of course, even between sisters there is some asymmetry, some hierarchy; birth order, relative age, does make a difference. But unlike the overwhelming, somehow sacred difference that separates mother and infant child, the differences between sisters are subtle, relative, on a profane scale. The differences between siblings can be negotiated, worked on, redefined by the siblings themselves. The work of mutual self-definition seems typically to proceed by way of a polarization that half-consciously exaggerates perceived differences and divides up attributes between the sisters ("I'm the bright one, and she's the pretty one"). Often, too, sisters seem to divide up their parents between them ("I'm Daddy's girl, and you're Mommy's"). I am who she is not. She is both what I would most aspire to be but feel I never can be *and* what I am most proud *not* to be but fearful of becoming.

The sister is different from even the closest peer friend (though such a friend may often serve as a sister surrogate), for sisterhood is an ascribed not chosen relationship. We are stuck with our particular sister as we never are with a friend. John Bowlby says that the most important thing about siblings is their *familiarity*—siblings easily become secondary attachment figures to whom we turn when tired, hungry, ill, alarmed, or insecure. Siblings may also serve as playmates, but the role is different: we seek out a playmate when in good spirits and confident and what we want is, precisely, play. The relationship to a sibling is permanent, lifelong, one from which it is almost impossible entirely to disengage. (One can divorce a mate much more finally than a sibling.) Because that permanence helps make it the safest relationship in which to express hostility and aggression (safer than with our parents because we are never so dependent on a sibling as we are in infancy—and in imagination always—on our mother and father), the bond between same-sex siblings is very likely the most stressful, volatile, ambivalent one we will ever know.

I have discovered that the longing for relationship with the sister is felt even by women without biological sisters, and that all of us search for "her" in many surrogates throughout our lives.

The Sister and the Brother are what Jung would call archetypes, as present in our psychic life irrespective of literal experience as are the Mother or the Father. (It is easy for me to speak of "the" sister since I have only one. When there are several the archetype is likely to be divided among them in oft-shifting ways. Our relation to each has its own specific valence and significance, yet together they carry the complexity of the archetype.) Like all archetypes the Sister keeps reappearing in projected or "transference" form and has an inner aspect. Sorting through the meaning of sisterhood in our lives requires attending to all three modes: that of the literal sister(s), the surrogate sisters, and the sister within, the archetype.

I am who she is not. The inner sister—my ideal self and shadow self as strangely one—figures so significantly in the process of individuation that she is there whether I have a literal sister or not. Yet like all archetypes she demands actualization and particularization, demands to be brought into the outer world of distinct images. When there is no actual sister, there seem always to be imaginary sisters or surrogate sisters. Even when there is an actual sister, there are often fantasy figures or substitutes, as if the real sister were not quite adequate fully to carry the archetype, and yet the archetype needed nevertheless to be imaged, personified. The Sister appears with the particular face of a friend or a dream figure, of a character in a novel or a mythological heroine.

That the Sister is indeed one of those primal fantasies that Freud saw as active in our psychic life independent of historical experience has been confirmed for me by how frequently unsistered women have come to the workshops on sisters that I have led, knowing they, too, needed to work on the meaning of this relationship in their lives. The first time this happened, I wondered: "What do I have to say to them? What do I know of what it is like never to have had a biological sister?" Then I remembered: "Probably quite a bit." For I have a mother who was an only child and a daughter who has only brothers. My mother has told me how ardently she looked forward to my growing up, so that she might at last have a sister, and I know that as subtle counterpoint to the mother-daughter bond that relates me to my daughter there is a sister-sister one.

I realize also how my mother's understanding of sisterhood is colored by her not having had a sister as a child. She idealizes the relationship; she sees as sisterly only our intimacy not our rivalry; nor could she see anything of value in the stressful moments of interaction between my sister and myself when we were young. For over fifty years the encounters between her and her sister-in-law have been contaminated by a mutually obsessive jealousy, yet it would not occur to her that theirs is a sisterly relationship. My daughter's lack of a biological sister shows differently: since she grew up with brothers, men carry little mystery to her; she turns to women as lovers—and as sisters.

To call the Sister an archetype helps express my sense that there is a transpersonal, extrarational, *religious* dimension to sisterhood that endows all the actual figures upon whom we "transfer" the archetype with a numinously daemonic or divine aura. Yet I do not mean that there exists some universal, ahistorical essence of sister-hood. The trigger for an archetype is always particular experience; the degree to which such experiences are shared, recurrent, evoca-tive of similar responses, is always to be explored not assumed. I have also been deeply impressed by Freud's observation that though we have made something sacred of parent–child love we have left that between brothers and sisters profane. I, too, experience the Sister archetype as less overwhelmingly numinous than that of the Mother. The Sister's sanctity is somehow commensurate with that which characterizes my own soul: she is woman not goddess. The engagement with mortal Psyche occurs in a different dimension from the one with Persephone, the goddess with whom I began my search of Her.

My particular interest lies with sister-sister relationships, but it seems obvious that fully to understand their uniqueness requires attending also to sister-brother and brother-brother relationships. I wanted to perceive more clearly how being a sister to a brother differs from sistering a sister. It seemed important to explore my intuition that brother-brother relations and sister-sister relations are not symmetrical. Because the first primary relationship in the lives of female children is to a same-sex other, the mother, same-sex bonding would, I suspected, have greater salience in the lives of women than in the lives of men, and sisters would figure more powerfully in women's psychology than brothers in men's.

When I first came in touch with my pull to explore the meaning of sisterly relationships, I probably imagined this as primarily refer-ring to my relationship to my actual sister—may have thought in terms of sorting through the years of shared history and working toward a deeper connection in the present. That understanding sisterhood mostly has to do with *her,* mostly has to do with fixing things, is a perspective I left behind long ago. And I do remember that even at the beginning it was not so much she as my dying sister-in-law who seemed to be calling me to this task. This meant that the point was not changing things between us but coming to appreciate how the long-established patterns of sisterly interaction enter into the primary relationships of my ongoing life. The point was also somehow connected to a coming to terms with death.

Wanting a perfect relationship with that other in the world most like myself—one's same-sex sibling—may be an ineradicable fantasy. Yet I have come to believe that giving it up (except as fantasy) is among the deepest lessons that honest engagement with the meaning of this relationship has to teach: That relationships aren't perfect. That the sister so like me is *other*. That the particular, subtle, inexpungible ways in which we are intimate and distant, alike and different, are precisely what our sisterhood is all about. Coming to accept that we are not identical and won't be, that our differences don't add up to make one beautifully balanced whole, that somehow they aren't the "right" differences for that seems to be part of what we come to discover and accept. In a sense we always have the wrong sister—and that's just what makes her right, just what makes us aware of the reality of otherness, of what is involved in seeing another as other, in letting her be herself. It may also be just how she helps me discover who I really am.

In the beginning, we seem to look to our sister to fulfill a longing for another just like ourselves, as we look to our mother to fulfill a longing to dissolve all otherness. We end by discovering in our relation to our sister what is required of us in accepting that she truly is *another*. I have been signally aware of a particular dimension of that acceptance throughout the composition of this book. My own sister is not comfortable with the degree of self-disclosure I risked in my book on the Greek goddesses. Honoring her sense of privacy has meant that this book had to be written in a different way.

This is at the heart of what I have learned from Psyche and her sisters—that, though not the sisters she would have chosen, they are *her* sisters, the ones that start her on the journey to herself.

Wanting to change the relationship, to fix it, to deepen it, to make it more central in our lives is often, I've come to believe, really wanting to change her, to be in control, to make her part of me. Jung helps us to understand that this is a misplaced longing, that what it really signifies is a longing to change myself, to claim as my own aspects of my own potentiality that I long ago saw as belonging to her rather than to myself. The "deidentification" that was appropriate in childhood becomes anachronistic; we do not forever have to divide the world into her sphere and my sphere.

It seems that one of the dimensions on which such polarization often occurs is precisely that of intimacy; one sister wants more, the other resists her attempts as invasive. So often one sister wants the relationship to be different, better, more intense; but when she says, "I want to know you better," the other replies, "That just shows you don't want to know *me!*" Paradoxically, backing off, communicating, "I no longer want to change you, no longer need you to be 'my' sister," can sometimes open the way to a more spontaneously flowing, mutually enjoyable relationship.

But I have come to believe that we don't really want the "fixing" anyway, that that's a surrogate for something else. I've certainly discovered that sisters matter terribly to adult women, that the relationship feels focal, vital, often painful—and most especially *untold.* Whenever I have mentioned my interest in sisters, even casually, women have wanted to tell me their story—urgently, fully, intimately— often as though they had never before realized how *much* they wanted to tell it.

When we seize the chance to tell our story, we seem to know that its beauty and power come from its being *our* story, a never- before-told story. We are released from the illusion that there is one right version of the story, one normative pattern of sisterly experi- ence, to which ours should conform. We take it for granted that there are many different patterns, each with its own pains, its own gifts.

Relationships between sisters seem to be more intense and emotionally intimate than between brothers, which means that it may also be harder for us to tolerate differences without experienc- ing them as betrayal. The myths and fairy tales represent brothers as engaging together in adventures in the outer world, whereas sisters share feelings and inner experience. My sense is that our sisterhood might be strengthened were we to incorporate some more "brotherly" support of one another, were we to commit ourselves to arousing one another to the full exercise of our powers in the world, the outer world of work and creativity. But the "heart" of sisterhood is truly different from this fraternal kind of bonding.

The tales about sister-brother relationships suggest the deep meaning this bond has in the inner lives of men; "sister" seems to signify that which connects them to the realm of feeling, to their own inner depths, their soul, and what enables them to turn trustingly toward death. The sister represents a relation to what men seem truly to experience as their own inner but often inaccessible and mysterious "femininity"—a relation to that femininity that is life-bringing rather than death-dealing, less frightening than the otherness represented by the mother. For men this contra-sexual relationship carries tremendous power. For women, the brother, the contra-sexual other, seems to mean less than the same-sex other, the sister.

For us, too, the sister carries the soul-meaning that the sister carries for men. For us, too, she embodies that same connection to the source of our lives, the source of meaning, that the mother originally embodies—but less fearfully.

I see "sisterhood" as the right name for close relationships among adult women because it communicates a real intimacy that is based on an early experience of mutual giving and receiving. The actual sisters of childhood are in some sense our first mother surrogates, but we never expected from them the absolute love that at first we associate with our mothers. To speak of later women intimates as "sisters" is to acknowledge that this process of substitution goes on, that the point was never to remain forever within the original constellation. Coming to understand the meaning of sisterhood means learning about what happens in families and how this is passed down from one generation to the next—and how it is passed from the familial relationships of childhood into the relationships we form as adults.

If we can remember that we are here to sister one another, not to mother or be mothered, the possibility of another kind of relationship is opened to us. The turn from mothers to sisters is, as Freud saw, like the turn from goddesses to human women, the transition from a sacred to a profane relationship. Between sisters there is the possibility of a genuinely mutual, reciprocal relationship; each is giver and receiver. We can know the other as a flawed and needy human woman—like ourselves. When we do not expect her to be able to answer all our needs, to be all-good, we do not feel betrayed when she does not and is not. The moments of fusion when they occur can be celebrated—because we know they are *moments*, transformative but evanescent. We remember how intensely ambivalent and volatile those early interactions with our actual sister may have been and are not terrified when closeness temporarily disappears, when unexpected differences are suddenly revealed.

Though we may not be "blood" sisters, may not literally be born of the same womb, I believe women may discover their sisteredness to be just as much a *given* in their lives. What a gift to know that a relationship will endure despite its ebbing and flowing, despite times when the other's otherness leaves us feeling unbearably alone. Recollection of early sisterly experience reminds us that relationships have their dark side—and that this is part of what makes them life-giving, tranformative. There is space within sisterhood for likeness and difference, for the subtle differences that challenge and delight; there is space for disappointment—and suprise.

Adrienne Rich

Sibling Mysteries

(FOR C. R.)

1.
Remind me how we walked
trying the planetary rock
for foothold

testing the rims of canyons
fields of sheer
ice in the midnight sun

smelling the rains before they came
feeling the fullness of the moon
before moonrise

unbalanced by the life
moving in us, then lightened
yet weighted still

by children on our backs
at our hips, as we made fire
scooped clay   lifted water

Remind me how the stream
wetted the clay between our palms
and how the flame

licked it to mineral colors
how we traced our signs by torchlight
in the deep chambers of the caves

and how we drew the quills
of porcupines between our teeth
to a keen thinness

and brushed the twisted raffia into velvet
and bled our lunar knowledge thirteen times
upon the furrows

I know by heart, and still
I need to have you tell me,
hold me, remind me

2.
Remind me how we loved our mother's body
our mouths drawing the first
thin sweetness from her nipples

our faces dreaming hour on hour
in the salt smell of her lap   Remind me
how her touch melted childgrief

how she floated great and tender in our dark
or stood guard over us
against our willing

and how we thought she loved
the strange male body first
that took, that took, whose taking seemed a law

and how she sent us weeping
into that law
how we remet her in our childbirth visions

erect, enthroned, above
a spiral stair
and crawled and panted toward her

I know, I remember, but
hold me, remind me
of how her woman's flesh was made taboo to us

3.
And how beneath the veil
black gauze or white, the dragging
bangles, the amulets, we dreamed   *And how beneath*

the strange male bodies
we sank in terror or in resignation
and how we taught them tenderness—

the holding-back, the play,
the floating of a finger
the secrets of the nipple

And how we ate and drank
their leavings, how we served them
in silence, how we told

among ourselves our secrets, wept and laughed
passed bark and root and berry
from hand to hand, whispering each one's power

washing the bodies of the dead
making celebrations of doing laundry
piecing our lore in quilted galaxies

how we dwelt in two worlds
the daughters and the mothers
in the kingdom of the sons

4.
Tell me again because I need to hear
how we bore our mother-secrets
straight to the end
tied in unlawful rags
between our breasts
muttered in blood

in looks exchanged at the feast
where the fathers sucked the bones
and struck their bargains

in the open square when noon
battered our shaven heads
and the flames curled transparent in the sun

in boats of skin on the ice-floe
—the pregnant set to drift,
too many mouths for feeding—

how sister gazed at sister
reaching through mirrored pupils
back to the mother

5.
C. had a son on June 18th . . . I feel acutely that we are strangers, my sister and I; we don't get through to each other, or say what we really feel. This depressed me violently on that occasion, when I wanted to have only generous and simple feelings towards her, of pleasure in her joy, affection for all that was hers. But we are not really friends, and act the part of sisters. I don't know what really gives her pain or joy, nor does she know how I am happy or how I suffer.

(1963)

There were years you and I
hardly spoke to each other
then one whole night
our father dying upstairs

we burned our childhood, reams of paper,
talking till the birds sang

Your face across a table now: *dark*
with illumination
This face I have watched changing
for forty years

has watched me changing
this mind has wrenched my thought

121

I feel the separateness
of cells in us, split-second choice

of one ovum for one sperm?
We have seized different weapons

our hair has fallen long
or short at different times

worlds flash from you I never thought of
we are translations into different dialects

of a text still being written
in the original

yet our eyes drink from each other
our lives were driven down the same dark canal

6.
We have returned so far
that house of childhood seems absurd

its secrets a fallen hair, a grain of dust
on the photographic plate

we are eternally exposing to the universe
I call you from another planet

to tell a dream
Light-years away, you weep with me

The daughters never were
true brides of the father
the daughters were to begin with
brides of the mother

then brides of each other
under a different law

Let me hold and tell you

1976

Galway Kinnell

The Sadness
of Brothers

But no, that's fear's reading.
We embrace in the doorway,
in the frailty of large,
fifty-odd-year-old bodies
of brothers only one of whom has imagined
those we love, who go away,
among them this brother,
stopping suddenly
as a feeling comes over them
that just now we remember
and miss them, and then turning
as though to make their own
even more vivid memories
known across to us—if it's true,
of love, only what
the flesh can bear surrenders to time.

Past all that, we stand
in the memory that came to me this day
of a man twenty-one years strange to me,
tired, vulnerable, half the world old; and in large,
fat-gathering bodies, with sore, well or badly spent,
but spent, hearts, we hold each other, friends to reality,
knowing the ordinary sadness of brothers.

Howard Teich

The Twins:
An Archetypal
Perspective

In the cosmogony of many archaic cultures, the fundamental duality of life is associated with the two primary sources of light, the sun and the moon. Each exercising dominion over its separate sky, yet joined in a daily round of death and rebirth, Sun and Moon historically represent the central organizing principles around which many creation myths and religious motifs assemble.[1]

However, since the Greek and Roman traditions have come to dominate our mythology, the primary "solar" and "lunar" polarity has in Western culture usually been represented as "masculine" and "feminine." Those qualities associated with "solar psychology"—clarity, willfulness, competitiveness, endurance—have been labeled "masculine." The "lunar" qualities—tenderness, receptivity, intuitiveness, compassion, emotional availability—have been conversely designated "feminine." Interestingly, prior to the ascendancy of patriarchal traditions, most mythologies considered the solar principle feminine and the lunar principle masculine.

Both solar and lunar principles emerge in the same-sex archetype of male Twins. The Twins archetype functions to acknowledge the lunar principle as masculine and to personalize "solar/lunar" psychological and behavioral principles in the male psyche. Our recorded mythologies feature an extraordinary number of twin boys. Instances of female twinship are much less common, prompting us to consider the significance of the Twins first within the context of male psychology.

The solar/lunar male Twins serve to make us conscious of the psyche's tendency to "pull" in two seemingly contrary directions. Seeing these paradoxical forces as solar/lunar Twins, rather than as masculine and feminine "opposites," allows us to understand their symmetrical nature. The solar/lunar Twins represent an integral masculine unity which, like the sun and the moon, reveals itself in a cyclical fashion, showing first one variance, then the other.

The special dual perspective the Twins bring allows us a fresh look at the solar/lunar axis that defines the core structures of each and every archetype without restrictive cultural and gender distortions. For example, Egyptian myth depicts this essential twin-perspective in Horus the hawk, whose final transformation gives him a sun-eye and a moon-eye. When we can look at the raw material of an archetype through this dual solar/lunar lens, our ability to take inventory of its energetic potential expands dramatically. An awareness of its fundamental two-sided nature allows us to see not only the outer functions of the archetype (that is, how it reacts and responds in relationship to outer stimuli), but also the interplay of inner dynamics that generate the archetype's own unique energetic charge.

The birth of male Twins demands special notice, particularly since, in the archetypal family as in life, there is no obvious "reason" or "need" for Twins to be born. Within the Self, the Twins occupy a unique position. Unlike other members of the archetypal family, the Twins are not always among the central characters in the family drama. Their presence, therefore, invariably conveys an aura of the unusual, the odd, the immanent. Traditionally, Twins are at once honored and feared, their coming eagerly anticipated or anxiously dreaded, their arrival either joyously proclaimed amid much fanfare or surreptitiously swept under the rug and forgotten.

The antiquity and wide diffusion of Twin myths and their influence on religions and cultures throughout history present a tempting opportunity for long and satisfying study to those of us foraging for cross-cultural evidence of universal archetypes. Perhaps the first male twins that spring to mind are the Gemini twins of the Zodiac, Castor and Pollux. We are also quickly reminded of the twin founders of Rome, Romulus and Remus, and of the biblical pair of hostile twin brothers, Jacob and Esau. But even slight investigation of the historical Twins makes it immediately apparent that we are dealing with a phenomenon that occurs much earlier than its inscription in familiar myths. In fact, their position amid the stars of the Zodiac may be among the very last of homages paid the archaic Twins.

Historically, biological Twins of all three gender combinations, along with their attendant mystique, have long commanded the attentions of anthropologists who inadvertently bump up against the peculiar array of traditions and taboos surrounding twin births. Anthropologist J. Rendel Harris's formidable body of research in the area of twin cults lists in extensive and intriguing detail the host of rituals inspired by twin worship and defamation.[2] It is worth noting a few of those ceremonial rites here, as they lend insight into patterns that also emerge cross-culturally in myths of twin siblings.

The birth of biological Twins, past and present, is never a humdrum event. Twins are blessed, or cursed, with a special energetic charge. Harris rightly acknowledges that, even in those cultures wherein twins are revered, their elevation to divine status appears to be fueled more by fear than by admiration. The fear instilled by the uncanny birth of twins is often so well entrenched in a culture that any number of excuses for banishing or disposing of them are promulgated. Customary in many cultural histories is the practice of sacrificing one twin, typically the second born, and preserving, or even deifying, the other child. Favored rites of twin sacrifice involve abandoning the child to the elements or burying the infant alive in a special clay pot.

Murder of one or both siblings is common, is the regular sacrifice of the twins' mother or, should her husband retain a liking for her, of a slave woman in her place. The additional punishment extended to the twins' mother in many cultures appears to ensue from a common understanding that the habit of one birth at a time regularly distinguishes humankind from other animals. That the mother, through some unnatural offense, made herself akin or available to a lower order of animals is deemed deserving of severe and equally unnatural punishment, as by death or banishment to a "twin-town." A misunderstanding of biology also accounts for the common belief that the birth of twins could only result from a "dual paternity." This scenario has generated numerous legends of twins born of a divided immortality, one infant fathered by a mortal, the second by a good or evil divine spirit.

The wide distribution and central importance of Twin myths in native North and South American cultures encouraged anthropologist Paul Radin to consider the Twins "the basic myth of aboriginal America." Moreover, in researching Indo-European cultures, mythologist Jaan Puhvel has suggested that the Twins represent "the deepest layer" in our "mythological layer cake."[3]

When I began researching twin legends, my investigations were primarily limited to considering the centrality of Twinship in the formation of masculine gender identity. This research led me to catalog a wide variety of myths documenting the adventures and travails of Twin brothers. Indisputable parallelisms abound in apparently unrelated twin legends in widely separated cultures, supporting the great archetypal importance of the Twins in male mythology.

Twin male heroes appear in the mythologies of virtually every native culture: Mayan, Egyptian, Burman, African, Roman, Greek, Brazilian, Judeo-Christian. Male Twins often appear as the two creators of this world. As with historical records of twin births, the parentage of mythological Twins typically involves a common mother and a dual paternity which endows one Twin with divine immortality and the other with the earthbound aspects of mortal existence.

The dual creator motif has been explored in some depth by Marie-Louise Von Franz, who has suggested that the Twin Creators embody a "pre-conscious totality" which includes all the archetypes. Von Franz further suggests that the Twins contain the full range of multiplicities that characterize the single creator in our monotheistic culture.[4] The unmediated coexistence suggests that consciousness itself entails an awareness of the "twin" nature at its very core. Together, they embody that fundamental dichotomy, which Jung described as "the primary pair of opposites, consciousness and unconsciousness, whose symbols are Sol and Luna."[5]

Although Jung adhered to contrasexual terminology, he was well aware of the constrictions implicit in assigning gender labels to solar and lunar principles:

> Logos and Eros are the intellectually formulated intuitive equivalents of the archetypal images, Sol and Luna. In my view, the two luminaries are so descriptive that I would prefer them to the more pedestrian terms, Logos and Eros. . . . [Logos and Eros] offer us something more complete, whereas an archetypal image has nothing but

its naked fullness, which seems inapprehensible to the intellect. Concepts [Logos and Eros] are coined and negotiable values; images [Sol
and Luna] are life.[6]

The symbolic union of Sol and Luna in their primordial grace,
free of subsequently ascribed gender labels, emerges in the archetype of the Twin brothers. Myths of Twin males nearly always endow one Twin with the active "solar" attributes and the other with
more amorphous "lunar" characteristics. Joseph Campbell's first
published commentary on the legend of the Navaho Twins remains
perhaps the best, most succinct description of the solar/ lunar Twins'
relationship:

> The two, Sun-child and Moon-child, antagonistic yet cooperative,
> represent a single cosmic force, polarized, split and turned against
> itself in mutually supplementary portions. The life-supporting pow-
> er, mysterious in the lunar rhythm of its tides, growing and decaying
> at a time, counters and tempers the solar fire of the zenith, life desic-
> cating in its brilliance, yet by whose heat all lives.[7]

We find this solar/lunar dialectic duplicated over and over in
Twin myths. The patriarchal myths with which we are most familiar—
Romulus and Remus, Jacob and Esau—usually portray the Twins as
antagonistic. Typically, the Lunar Twin is slain in favor of the Solar
Twin. Up to now, our culture has hailed only the Solar Twin as its
prototype of masculinity, consigning the Lunar Twin to impotence
and oblivion. The character of this lunar companion spirit has become a mystery to us, having been eroticized (and devalued) as homosexual or feminine. The sacrifice or suppression of the Lunar
Twin runs so deep in our culture that most of us are unaware that
nearly every central male hero figure was originally a Twin. Even
Hercules, the quintesssential patriarchal Solar Hero, was born with
a Lunar Twin named Iphicles. An additional large body of Twin
myths also exists depicting Twins who work in accord, as is generally the case with Twin male creators. In fact, the phenomenon of
twinship is so pervasive in male creation mythology that Jungian
analyst Edward Edinger has stated conclusively: "the ego destined
for individuation is born as twins."[8]

It is important to consider how the Twin archetype differs from
the Shadow, which Jung posited as the predominant archetype

representing one's own gender and influencing relationships with one's own sex. The Shadow represents that which gets rejected by the conscious Ego. It contains those potential feelings and behaviors that we choose to disown because they do not fit our "ego-ideal." Jung suggested that rejected shadow-impulses emerge in one's "shadow projections."[9]

In our culture, the Lunar Twin is typically merged in the realm of the Shadow and can only be recognized in men's damaging projections. Men tend to project their Lunar Twin onto other men, seeing it as "effeminate" and "homosexual." In women, men often idealize lunar attributes, identifying them as the quintessence of "femininity." If the Lunar Twin remains undiffferentiated within a man's Shadow, he continues to prevent the possibility of a balanced relationship within himself and with other men or women.

While the Lunar Twin still resides in the Shadow, a man's Solar Twin exercises unmitigated power over all the dark contents of the Shadow. The solar Ego is, by definition, the power of light over darkness: it does not "see into" the darkness of the Shadow; it simply erases the darkness, replacing it with light.

If the Lunar Twin is identified in a man's shadow projections and reclaimed from the feminine, his relationship to his own Shadow is radically altered. The accepting Lunar Twin makes the solar/lunar twin-Ego more receptive to aspects of the Shadow that a solar Ego would obscure. As its name implies, the Lunar Twin illuminates the darker side of a man's nature, allowing him to experience the mysterious, numinous qualities of his being. Once his Lunar Twin has been differentiated from the Shadow, brought into consciousness, and incorporated into a man's Ego-ideal, a man can better relate to the Self. A solar/lunar Ego-structure also allows him greater Ego-strength, or libido, with which to contain the negative, destructive forces that threaten his well-being. Ultimately, the broader solar/lunar Ego-perspective may improve men's relationships as well. Much of men's isolation, homophobia, and misogyny can be attributed to our failure to recognize the Lunar Twin as the "missing piece" in the male psyche.

In the course of my preliminary research in masculinity, the regular appearance of male twins in creation myths prompted me to notice this "missing piece" in the masculine formula of alchemy. In the "monocolus" stage of the alchemical equation, solar and lunar aspects of the masculine principle are fused in a preliminary "union of the same." As a prerequisite step to the "union of opposites," the importance of this stage in male individuation cannot be exaggerated. It indicates that the bonding of solar/lunar aspects in a "union of the same" must take place before the male enters into a mature intrapsychic and external "union of opposites."

This type of solar/lunar balancing is not confined to alchemy. Most psychospiritual systems entail a transcendence of dualities as a prerequisite to spiritual awakening, and in nearly every case, the primary duality is portrayed in solar/lunar symbolism. The incorporation and ultimate transcendence of both solar and lunar aspects are earmarks of such epic figures as Osiris, Dionysus, and the Christ, each of whom is described as having attained "a superior stage of psychospiritual development since in their androgynous and sacrificial nature they incorporate both the solar and lunar modes and transcend them in death."[10] Osiris's solar/lunar cycle is completed with the birth of his son, the solar bird Horus, whose "sun eye" and "moon eye" are symbolic of the changed vision that accompanies spiritual transformation.

In mythology, the predominance of male solar/lunar Twins is certainly indicative of the patriarchal bent of our histories. It may also reflect a central difference in the male and female experiences of "otherness." Psychologically, the primary experience of separation from the mother seems to have a different impact on the male and female psyche. The female appears to retain a capacity for intimacy with the mother, without the fear of dissolving into her. The male, on the other hand, experiences a deep need for union with another, yet he ambivalently recoils from the mother, fearful of losing himself in her. Should the male fill that primary need with a female, he runs the risk of regressing again toward the mother. Yet his psychological balance requires an "other" to be able to "see" himself, or else he is likely to drown in narcissism. It appears that the "twinning" of the mythological male may express the male's deep need for a masculine "other" to generate the tension of contrast in his ego that he needs in order to have a frame of reference from which to view the Self. This critical difference of ego-perspective, combined with the male attitude that predominates in myth, may account for the surplus of male twins.

However, many parallel myths entailing sister–sister and sister–brother pairs, as well as brother–brother twins, show that the implications of the solar/lunar Twins archetype extend well beyond the realm of the masculine. Male-female Twin couples include Apollo (solar) and Artemis (lunar), and the Egyptian twins Shu (solar) and Tefnut (lunar). In Japanese creation mythology, the sun goddess Amaterasu is formed when her father bathes his left eye; and her moon-god brother, Susano, is born of the father washing his right eye.

Among the most familiar examples of Twin sisters are the Egyptian goddesses Isis (solar) and Nephthys (lunar), who are born with twin brothers/husbands Osiris (lunar) and Set (solar). Isis works with her lunar counterpart, Nephthys, to resurrect the male moon god, Osiris. This paradigm is reflected in many folk legends which portray Twin brothers rescuing their imprisoned solar sister. An earlier pair of Egyptian solar/lunar Twin sisters is Uatchit, the Vulture Goddess (solar), and her twin Nekhebet, the Cobra Goddess (lunar). Uatchit and Nekhebet shared sovereignty of all of Egypt, and, for centuries, the pharaohs made a habit of inscribing the Twin sisters' symbols over their tombs as insurance of power and protection for the passage into the netherworld. Another Twin sister pair includes the divine Helen of Troy and her mortal twin, Clytemnestra, sisters of the twin brothers, Castor and Pollux.[11]

The earmark patterns of mythological solar/lunar twinship are often duplicated in tales of non-twin siblings or heroic couples of both same and other sex. Because of the ambiguity that pervades mythic relationships, the solar/lunar energies may be inscripted in many mythic characters other than Twin. This is particularly true of female mythological figures who tend to display a dual nature, although they are rarely represented as Twins. For example, the Iroquois creation myth features male Twins and a congruent female bipolarity represented in the Twins' mother and grandmother. When the mother is slain by one of her sons, the bereft grandmother takes her daughter's corpse and creates from it the Sun and Moon and all the stars in the sky.

As the central paradigm of solar/lunar balancing, the Twins are likely to reappear with power now as we move into a century that will require universal, archetypal creation motifs to incorporate the various realities our new world encompasses. The ongoing breakdown of patriarchal mythology throws us into a whirlpool of global mythologies that we must learn to navigate. Just as we grew immeasurably from the ground-breaking work of Jung and his constituents, so too will the next generation benefit from new archetypal theories which, like Jung's, seek to amplify complementary, compatible aspects of a variety of viewpoints, rather than reducing them to their least common denominators. It is my hope that the solar/lunar perspective embodied in the archetype of the Twins will be one of many theories to contribute to ushering in our next stages of psychospiritual understanding.

Eileen Simpson

Orphans

It would have comforted me to know that I was not alone in hating Orphan Annie. Why my school friends were so crazy about her was a mystery to me. More mysterious, I see now, was why I disliked the comic so intensely. I thought it was because the garish color of Annie's hair caricatured mine, and because her smile was fake (the kind of smile you put on when you're afraid you'll cry). Also, there was something menacing about her guardian. He looked like a bully to me, and the massive diamond he wore in his tuxedo shirt front reminded me of the light doctors were always shining in my eyes when they told me to say, "Ahhh." I certainly wouldn't have wanted him to be *my* daddy.

It wasn't until I was in high school that I found the literary orphan I was willing to identify with, and the daddy I would have been happy to have, in Jean Webster's *Daddy-Long-Legs* (1912). Judy Abbott, after years of living in an orphanage, where she works as hard as Riley's Annie looking after the younger children in the asylum, is rescued by an anonymous benefactor who pays for her to go away to college. His one request is that she write to him. She fills her letters with accounts of her academic progress, and undergraduate activities (oh so innocent and girlish in the fictionalized Vassar of those days). She can't thank him enough for the allowance he sends, nor for the wardrobe which helps to erase the bitterness of having had for so many years to wear hand-me-downs.

What attracted me to the novel was that Judy's years in the asylum are passed over with merciful rapidity. (We are given only enough detail to highlight the contrast between the old life and the new.) She goes *away* to college (which I had little hope of doing). Daddy is as generous as I could have wished a daddy to be. And, best of all, there was the developing romance between guardian and ward.

My affection for the novel was shared by many other girls. It was immensely popular and was translated into sixteen languages. (What nonorphans found attractive about it, I think, was the facile resolution of the Oedipal conflict. There was no mother to be rivalrous with, and since Daddy-Long-Legs is not the heroine's real daddy, they can become lovers without guilt.)

Rereading "Little Orphan Annie" recently to discover why I found it so unappealing, I saw that it was not only the terrible separations that put me off (in one strip Warbucks even dies but, being Warbucks, he comes to life again). It was also that Annie's orphanhood is unending. There is no promise of a better future, no time when, being grown up, she will no longer be at the mercy of adults.

All true, perhaps, but the orphan's subliminal appeal from the time of Riley's poem to the movie was to the middle-class family. Annie's losses, her homelessness, were the family's gain. She reminded children that they were fortunate to have mothers and fathers, reminded mothers that but for them their offspring would be at the mercy of the Miss Asthmas, Mrs. Warbuckses, and Mrs. Bleating-Harts of this world; reminded fathers that but for them their daughters would be endlessly looking for a surrogate.

Children who wished they were orphans—and what child does not at one time or another?—were able to imagine themselves as Annie for the length of the strip, or the duration of the daydreams the strip engendered, and yet be free to return to the shelter, if not joy, of home and family when it was over. Those who suspected they were orphans (because of the way their parents treated them) could separate themselves from the adults they had to live with, and lead a happier or more adventurous life on their own.

Annie outside made those inside feel cozier than they would have without her to reflect their good fortune. As her readers sat at the kitchen table, or sprawled on the living room rug, Annie, out in the world, acted out their wishes and fears. Her pluck, energy, and resourcefulness gave her fans the comforting reassurance that though she was touching, she was also tough. They knew that no matter what peril she underwent, what pain she suffered, she would triumph. An indestructible little scapegoat, Annie was an orphan *for* them. Small wonder she was so well loved.

Olga Cabral

Occupation:
Spinster

Lawyer Dickinson's spinsterly daughter
was mad the neighbors said: she
hid inside a snowflake
there being nowhere else to go.
Fallen lightyears
from fields of star-hooved Taurus
into puritan body/Sapphic brain
she the lost Pleiad
mourned for the company of her blinding Sisters.

(They come before us, the Victorian women
prisoners of muslin caged in taffeta
with their dim hair and drowning eyes:
women of genius warm and womanly
who burned in that dry spare air to their
crystal bones.)

In Amherst Emily lived on
though the world forgot
moving with calm coiled hair through tidy days.
Her face shrank to a locket. She explored
miniaturized worlds known only to moths and angels
walked to the far side of a raindrop—
trespassed
on Infinity.

(How many Emilies
coughed and stitched
in silent bell jars
died too young in furnished attics
while the Universe boiled over in its
starry Pail?)

Robert H. Hopcke

Gay Relationship as a Vehicle for Individuation

Having spent by now quite a few years (and more than a few words) in attempting to bring Jungian psychology a view of homosexuality and male–male eros that reflects the reality of gay male lives, I am tempted by the topic of this volume to take refuge in theory and intellect. Arguments could be made using current research on gay relationships and the ongoing social-political critique of Jung's thought, which I think would probably persuade even the most conservative of readers that gay male relationships, too, can be a locus of wholeness and a vehicle for individuation—in short, a place where the Self is made manifest.

Those of us who have lived and worked in the gay community in the last two decades, however, were not persuaded of this truth through argumentation or research. We have come to know the power of men loving men through our experiences. Through our lives we have seen how gay men can create between them bonds of love and growth that are tested in ways many heterosexual relationships never imagine. We have lived and created family in the face of an entire society that denies not only our right to love each other but often our very existence. "Gay relationships don't last," "Gay relationships are self-destructive," "Men who love men are sick, perverse, immature"—these negative messages, on which we have all been raised, have been thrown over for us as gay men, not through clever reasoning or mountains of data, but through our continual experience of another reality. Thus, it is through my own experience, the way I have experienced the Self in my love for another man, that I hope to persuade in a way that theory and intellect could never do. In a public forum and an intellectual context, I suppose there is a certain risk attached to using one's private life as evidence, but my hope is that by taking a more personal approach, others may glimpse a bit of the experience I have had of the wholeness that love between men can bring. At the very least, this more personal view will counteract the invisibility and denial that reigns concerning gay relationships as a legitimate form of family structure in the United States today.

I met Paul ten years ago. I was a recently transplanted Easterner, twenty-two years old, a seminary student with energy to burn. He was thirty-one, settled into California after three years, managing a center for the study of new religious movements. I had heard of a gay seminarian's conference to be held in Berkeley that year and, after a number of phone calls to the schools of the Graduate Theological Union, was fortuitously shunted to Paul for more information. We met one afternoon to discuss the conference. Though he was not particularly polite (this, I learned later, was due to exasperation—the conference had been canceled), nevertheless, in the course of our conversation an attraction was born. We made a date for lunch a month later due to our crowded schedules, a lunch which Paul eventually had to cancel. So instead of lunch, we met at the White Horse for a drink. It was December 8, 1980, the day John Lennon was killed, the day of the feast of the Immaculate Conception, Paul's sister's birthday, the day after Pearl Harbor. We had a few drinks, spoke of Italy, especially Assisi, had a wonderful night of conversation and laughter, and went home together to his apartment. We didn't know it at the time, but I had just moved in.

We have both told this story many times to many people. It is our creation myth, and like all creation myths, it serves to remind us how and when something sacred came to be. Gay relationships all have a creation myth. Some perhaps tell of relationships born under an evil star, others arising in the sunlight of new hope, many, of course, shining forth out of a blaze of erotic excitement. But all lovers have a story to tell of how and when they met, what happened, how something new came to be from a union of two different people. The wonder of this meeting, the way its details are savored and recounted, the feeling of oneness and hope—these, I think, come from the Self, whose bounty is not available to heterosexuals alone. Ask any gay couple how they met, and I'll bet that they, too, will tell you their own creation myth.

Impulsively and without much thought, I transported my belongings down from my lonely room at the seminary dorm into Paul's poor little one-bedroom apartment in a very California pink stucco building with aqua-blue trim on Cedar Street. Blind with love, we expected, perhaps as all lovers do, that our togetherness would be perfect and complete, a continuation of the wonderful romantic days of our first month, a month spent apart during Christmas vacation, a month filled with passionate phone calls, torrid letters, and, finally, a post-holiday reunion. We found out soon that relationships are not that simple.

Our natural differences soon surfaced as we began our life together, and the next year or so was one of great tension. Of course, looking back with the wisdom of ten years later, I see that much of the conflict could have been avoided if we had gone more slowly and given ourselves more time. But that is not what we did. Instead, we battled it out.

We entered couples therapy to learn how to fight more productively and, in the course of our work together, continued to outline our many and varied differences in personality, style, and expectation of life together. Paul is in many ways a classic introvert—deliberate, at ease with solitude, overwhelmed in too public or too crowded a situation, with a very vivid interior life of the mind. When I characterize him to myself, I see him as a philosopher or as a monk. I, on the other hand, am undeniably extroverted—naturally seeking out activities and people, fond of huge gatherings, adrift if caught without anything to do and anyone to call, having a distinct taste for making things happen in the outer world. When Paul characterizes me in his kinder moments, he describes me as living my life as if it were an opera.

Further opposites characterize us as a couple, we came to find. Paul's thinking and sensation functions are quite strong—hence his taste for rational, ordered living spaces and his career in teaching philosophy and religion. For me, in contrast, with my long history of artistic and musical interests, my feeling and intuition tend to dominate; hence my longing for a piano and a pet, and my career as a psychotherapist. And more opposites still: I was twenty-two and at the beginning of my professional life, a child of the Me Decade of the 1970s when we met, whereas Paul was thirty-one and ready to settle down and build a life, his youthful years of schooling behind him, very much a child of the socially conscious 1960s. This youth–age dichotomy continues to dog us throughout our years together, ensuring always that he and I are just on the cusp of being in different stages of life and in different decades no matter how many years we spend together.

The list of opposites could go on and on, but the particulars are not what is most important. Rather, it is the existence of these opposites, or, to be precise, our framing of these differences as opposites which furnished us with the source of greatest tension in our relationship as well as the source of greatest growth. In the course of our couples work together and our own individual work, we were forced to hammer out a *union* of these opposites, though not in the usual sense this term is used in Jungian psychology; that is, to denote an inner process of balance between disparate parts of the personality. Rather, Paul and I were forced as a couple to *be* a union of opposites. In this way, our relationship served and continues to serve as a vehicle for our individuation, a place of growth and healing for us individually and for the community around us.

The youth–age polarity is the one set of opposites that perhaps best illustrates our success in creating a union, as well as being an archetypal set of opposites very often present in gay male relationships.[1] Early in our relationship, I drew upon Paul's age and experience to ground me, to give me direction, to settle me in, just as he counted upon my youth, enthusiasm, and physical activity to enliven our life together and protect him from a premature middle age. Likewise with the introversion-extroversion split: Paul's introversion taught me a way of being with myself that led to perhaps the most important transformation of my adult life—my discovery of Jungian psychology and my years of dreamwork—while my extroversion functioned as a kind of social reconnaissance, widening our circle of friends and activities to counterbalance the very inward style that we, like so many other academic couples, tend to have.

Why is this point about opposites so crucial to make? First, it is important to underscore, especially in reference to the way that the union of opposites is all too often characterized within Jungian psychology, that the opposites involved in gay male relationships are not the opposites of male-female relationships. Indeed, the very fact that there exist love relationships between two men should force one to rethink the validity or usefulness of our culture's conceptualization of gender as a matter of opposites, as well as the corollary to this gender ideology, namely, the primacy and universality of heterosexuality.

Both of these conceptions are confronted with a serious challenge in the face of gay relationships. The Self contains far more than our limited, contingent view of sexuality and gender. Even though they involve members of what our culture has identified as the "same sex," gay relationships incarnate a plurality of opposites that go far beyond the male-female duality that Western gender ideology would have us believe is so central. Gay relationships challenge this heterosexual ideology to its core and should lead thoughtful people to wonder just how many personality characteristics extrinsic to gender are projected onto "men" and "women." As two men in a relationship, Paul and I are free to simply see our extroversion or introversion, our youthfulness or older wisdom, as part of us as *individuals,* rather than something inherently linked to our "masculinity" or "femininity." Naturally, such freedom subverts the intention of our culture's heterosexual ideology, but I think any manifestation of the Self personally or socially tends to overthrow the egocentric illusion of control and structure we have built around ourselves as protection against the numinous and the extraordinary.

This leads me to the second important point about opposites, namely that gay relationships are in fact a locus of individuation, even though, or, in fact, precisely *because* the so-called opposites of "male" and "female" are not at issue. Having given the reader some sense of what opposites actually have come into play in my relationship with my lover, it should be fairly clear that our relationship contains all the tensions and all the potential of any love relationship between any two human beings. What was required of Paul and me is required of any heterosexual couple—consciousness, work, empathy, dedication, and commitment—the result of which was an enlargement of our personalities and an enrichment of our lives. As the incarnation of a union of opposites, all relationships, homosexual or heterosexual, serve to embody the Self not just for the inner satisfaction of the individuals involved but as a way, in my opinion, to effect a transformation of consciousness.

Here, however, we come upon the way in which the social realities of our culture's heterosexual ideology have an adverse impact on gay relationships and, to my mind, on society in general. Heterosexual marriage, both as a social institution and as a psychological relationship, is clearly understood and celebrated as a vehicle of personal and collective transformation. The wedding ceremony, at least in the Judeo-Christian tradition, is not intended solely as a legal formality or as social insurance for the protection of future children but is, from a religious point of view, a way of demonstrating to the individuals involved and to the community around them the nature of divinity itself, the way in which God is unity and wholeness made manifest in the world. This symbolism is essential to the ceremony; hence, marriage is a sacrament within Roman Catholic theology and practice, a means of God's grace in the world.

For gay relationships, the situation is considerably different. In the context of Western heterosexual ideology, anyone who deviates from the dominant pattern of male-female relationship is either denied social existence or punished. Gay men and lesbian women do not exist according to this line of thinking, or, if their existence becomes undeniable, they are branded as deviates, criminals, a danger to society, mentally ill. The effect of such attitudes is to deprive gay men and lesbians—as well as anyone else whose behavior or thinking varies from prescribed norms—of any sort of sanctioned community, any sort of visibility in the world at large. Gay people neither grow up with images of themselves in the culture that confirm their existence or goodness, nor do they have available to them images of same-sex relationship which stress the potentialities, sacredness, and fulfillment that come from knowing and loving another man or another woman. The isolation and invisibility imposed by heterosexual ideology on gay couples has an insidiously pernicious effect and is justified in a maddeningly circular way: gay relationships fail because they are not supported, and they are not supported because they are perceived as inherently unstable.

Well, all gay relationships do not fail. Paul and I were lucky to have resources and support to call on in the Bay Area. But such resources are not available to the vast majority of gay people across the United States. So, at the end of couples therapy, Paul and I decided to use our relationship to create and confirm the community that had lived around us and had known us both individually and as a couple. It felt right, after three years together, to declare our commitment to each other in some form, but I think it was of integral importance that this declaration occur in a public forum. In this way, our ceremony of union, which took place on May 7, 1983, made our relationship a vehicle not just for our own personal individuation process but for the growth and transformation of the community around us. Planned and written by ourselves, structured as a ritual journey that went from who we had been before we had known each other, to who we were then as a couple, to who we hoped to become in our lives together, this ceremony included personal testimonies from our friends, beautiful music, a Eucharistic celebration, and a ritual exchange of gifts. During the hard times that followed, the commitment I made to Paul in that ceremony and the support of our friends were often the sole factor in keeping me from ending the relationship out of frustration, anger, or despair. Our ceremony is one of the few actions I have taken in my life over which I can honestly say I have never had a single regret.

As I hope my own personal story has made clear, a relationship between two men that is based on love, respect, and a commitment to growth is a place where the symbolism and action of the Self can appear, regardless of gender or social oppression, regardless of hatred or intolerance. If the Self is the supraordinate personality toward which all individuation is directed, the source of union and connection with a reality greater than our own ego, then love, whatever its form, whatever its path, is always an instrument of divinity.

Caroline T. Stevens

Lesbian Family, Holy Family: Experience of an Archetype

Pondering the archetype of the family, I have recalled my secret joy as a child at Christmas time of arranging the painted plaster figures of the Holy Family under the tree. I took them from the straw-filled box in which they had waited all year and nestled them in cotton snow under the fragrant pine branches. They were attended by a circle of animals, a black-and-white cow (with one horn missing), a brown goat, and five white sheep. The figure of Joseph (who was and was not the Father) stood protectively behind Mary and the Child, and a blond shepherd leaned on his crook nearby. The three Wise Men, clad in purple, red, and blue, approached the central figures, reverent and bearing gifts. The Family and their attendants made up a tableau of love, joy, and awe, the final touch in the preparation of the tree, and their arrangement was my job alone, undertaken with a meditative care for just the right placement of each figure. My own family's gifts to one another were then laid 'round the tree, and the herald angels sang each year the carols that filled our house.

My annual ritual placed Mother and Child in the center of a protected circle, the focus of the welcoming faith of men, animals, and angels. Though hardships and dangers would shadow that Child, though His true worth was barely known on earth, a star shown on

His birthplace, and the ultimate power of the universe, so it was said, was His true progenitor. In my later years as a Jungian, I have felt what a central support that myth provided me in childhood and understood the urgency with which I tried to make it live in the arrangements of my life. And it seems to me now that the central message of the myth was this: the family exists to recognize, shelter, and enable creative possibility that awaits all of creation in every one of us.

In the manner of all human enactments of myth, the reality on earth is likely to fall painfully short of this ideal. Perhaps the very difficulties experienced in my own first family contributed to the stubborn way in which I tried and tried again, against the odds of "dysfunction," to create in that family and in the later ones I made with husband and children an expression of the archetypal possibility. Perhaps both the archetype and the human limitation contributed to my choice, at midlife, of a profession devoted to the recognition and furtherance of potentials awaiting birth in my own and other wounded lives—psychotherapy.

I have seen, in my later years, the power of the myth and my stubborn faith in it bear fruit at last, both in my work and in my life. The children of my early, most unconscious years survived my shortcomings to find productive paths of their own; I discovered, finally, that trying to heal a mate was not the way to create a healing family for them or for myself. And in my work I have found that faith in the soul's possibilities for recovery, renewal, and transformation can help enable their realization.

The story of the Holy Family, it seems to me, marks a significant moment in the inevitable conflict between the values supporting individuation and those requiring the individual's sacrifice to the group, a moment when the new life and vision brought by the Child is hunted as prey by a king who feels his hegemony to be threatened by an unknown potential. Old kings, old gods, it seems, must always respond in this way. The Babylonian Apsu sought the death of his offspring because they disturbed his sleep. Uranus buried his newborn children and Cronus swallowed his. These two Ancients were eventually defeated by the Mother Goddesses in league with their young. Jehovah found reassurance in the willingness of Abraham to sacrifice his son as an act of obedience to the All-High. And ultimately the Holy Child Himself became Christ on the Cross, feeling Himself, for a memorable moment, to be forsaken by the Father.

But Herod was a secular king, a prototype of many kings and emperors, dictators, presidents, and Fathers Who Know Best, an accumulating number of (male) human leaders attempting to embody the archetype of the One who represents the Many, whose prowess is supposed to guarantee the survival and well-being of the group, from family to nation. The human shadows of such leaders, however, have grown ever longer, until perhaps the threat they embody becomes more evident than the benefits they supply. Earth fathers such as Joseph, caretakers of the Child and responsive to a creative power higher than themselves, remain ideals, but the "manhood" of a Joseph comes into question as a one-sided vision of patriarchy grows stronger. Service to the family, most especially to the new life it nurtures, came to be seen as the purview of women, while success in a competitive world beyond the family came to be the measure of men.

Moreover, the most that a Herod can provide, be he the noblest expression of the archetype of the king, is to secure the well-being of a limited collective at the cost of service to the king and conformity to his goals, laws, and vision. The target of Herod's fear and rage was an unknown potential that threatened him but would grow to serve, so goes the myth, the spiritual well-being of all humankind. At the point of apparent conflict between the old and the new, between the established collective and the individual, there is always that uncertainty. We cannot know in advance where the new life, the new vision unsupported by custom, will lead. Often it seems, in a limited view, to be a threat. Each of us must decide, perhaps more than once in a lifetime, where our souls' loyalties rest. Most fundamentally, we discover the archetype that lives for us most deeply, and determine to rest our faith in it. For me it seems to have been the archetype of the Holy Family in a particular version encountered in my childhood: Mother and Child, in a circle of loving recognition and fealty to creative possibility.

For me, an image of family supports the ideal of individuation as the goal of personal development. In this archetype we discover the new One as a bringer of gifts to the Many—though not, of course, in human experience, of the literal magnitude of the Christ story. We find a welcome for the renewal of life, and a possible third way between the claims of the individual and the claims of the collective—the way of individuation. Individuation names a process by which we each move toward a full enactment of unique potential. When we find this process to be in opposition to the customs and understandings of the collective, we are encouraged to acquiesce in the guidance that comes from within, to choose personal authenticity over secure conformity. We are urged toward this choice with an awareness of its costs to ourselves and to others, and with an assumption of responsibility for its consequences. Obviously, it is not a choice to be lightly made, and no outer, human authority may rightly claim to judge it. In fact, the true authority is felt to be one that is more ancient and more universal than any collective, which speaks nevertheless to and through the personal life. The Jungian name for this authority is the Self.

At the heart of the idea of individuation lies the impulse to serve interests greater than that of the ego's or the collective's, to perceive as truly and to act with as much integrity and authenticity in that service as we can muster. We begin, perhaps, in the discovery and freeing of those parts of ourselves imprisoned by early hurts and the distorted perceptions that have grown from them. We learn to question our habitual projections of darker aspects of ourselves onto others, be they family members or members of other ethnic or racial groups. We begin to claim as our own the strengths and weaknesses we thought belonged only to the other sex. Enlarged and strengthened, we move by steps toward the real possibility of "selfless" service to others, no longer motivated primarily by personal needs for security, acceptability, or the appearance of virtue. Plainly, this is the work of a lifetime, and so we speak of the "path of individuation" and do not prophesy its ultimate goal. At any time, a new "Holy Child" may be discovered in the Bethlehems of our souls.

I now come to the lesbian family and the personal path that led to my experience of the archetype of family in an unexpected form. My choice of how to live has often proved difficult, both for me and for people I love. Again and again I have found myself divided between warring possibilities, sometimes felt as a conflict between the wishes and needs of others and the truth of my own life. More often, however, I have known these oppositions as competing needs of my own. Early in life I chose marriage to my high school sweetheart, newly home from the war, against my parents' wishes and ambitions for me. Later I struggled between a longing to be a singer and the love and security I gave and received with husband and child. And later still, I felt the conflict between a 1950s-style home and family and an overwhelming urge to return to school.

In a fundamental way these were struggles between competing primary identities: Shall I be daughter or wife, singer or wife and mother, wife and mother or student of human behavior and society? It might be more easily imagined today that none of these alternatives need exclude the other. But each choice seemed to me to be at the cost of the other, and in a sense this was true. Time, energy, and devotion were required by each, and each might have consumed all that I had to offer. But the question was this: What am I, who am I beneath the roles and commitments that have compelled me in the past? And for the first time no ready answer was at hand. Middle-aged students and female scholars were not common in that time and place, and women with passions that were not expressed in devotion to others were suspect. Nevertheless, the time was right, in my own life and in the culture of the dawning sixties, for a turn to guidance from within.

With this, the archetype of the family, so fundamental in my life, deepened to include a dimension never before so consciously considered. It had compelled me, as I have suggested, to try to create the circumstances in which the new lives of children and the unlived possibilities of a husband might appear and flourish. I felt a demand that my own unrealized potentials, both intellectual and spiritual, must be given new birth and respect. I struggled with this awareness over a period of five years, but at last I knew that I would have to give up the comfort of feeling virtuous, that in fact those I loved would be forced to pay for my sacrifice of the learning I craved—not a happy or a pretty truth, but one I needed to acknowledge. In 1962 I began full-time studies at the local university, the first overt step on my path of individuation.

That path has been filled with unexpected turns and separations as well as new meetings, arrivals, and departures into previously unimagined territories. Nothing has ever seemed or proved to be as predictable as life before that 1962 turning point, and difficult choices continue to present themselves. The family I serve has grown wider as well as deeper. I have asked myself again and again: What is now authentic in me, what new birth occurs, and how is it to be served in myself, in the others I meet along the way, in my culture, in the world we all must share? The answers are not easy and often seem to conflict, but the more consciously they are asked, and the more the conflicts they raise are suffered, the freer I grow.

Now I have entered into the creation of a new family, new to me

and new in its acknowledged appearance among us as a manifestation of the archetype. For those whose image of the family is ineluctably
and concretely centered in a heterosexual pair, the notion of a family
created by and centered in same-sex partnership may be, almost
literally, unimaginable. Yet I find in my own shared life with a woman all of the archetypal possibilities and many of the human difficulties
that are experienced in the traditional family unit. I come late in life
to this experience, and so I have escaped the full impact of societal
prejudice against a choice such as mine. That impact would have
had a cumulative effect on my self-experience had I suffered it young
and unseasoned by the other struggles and conflicts in my life. It
would have raised more questions if the rearing of my children had
occurred in this family: What would have been the effect on them of
social attitudes, and the effect on my son of family life without the
central authority of a father?

Yet I know from my own life and the lives I touch as an analyst
that the traditional family structure most certainly does not guarantee happy and productive adulthood to its children, that it typically
falls heartbreakingly short of the archetypal possibility. It is rather
the experience of a home made by two cooperative and loving individuals of whatever gender, bringing their varied gifts to the creation of a nurturing environment, that lays the foundation for well-
being of all its members, young and old. Had I come to this way of
living sooner, I might have lost less energy in the effort to overcome
social and cultural teaching about my potentials as a woman; I might
have lost less energy in the attempt to convince others that I was a
"real woman" and harmless, even desirable, despite my strong mind
and daring heart. And everyone who looked to me for nurture and
guidance might sooner have been blessed by that blessing.

My partner and I have joined our resources to create a home,
with room to share and rooms for the single enterprise of each. We
have combined our experiences of life to create both new understandings and new conflicts, the conditions for real growth in
awareness. I write, she creates visual art, and both of us work from
our respective perspectives and talents as therapists, attempting to
help others enhance the conditions for new birth in their lives. We
support and encourage each other in all our separate and mutual
endeavors. Our personal and professional associations with daughters and son, brother and sister, and other greatly valued men and
women constitute yet another circle of support, a set of interlocking
circles that constitute a wider context for the growth of all.

The recognition and support we supply to the growing possibilities and frail vulnerabilities in each of us express more fully than I have ever known the archetype I have honored, both consciously and unconsciously, for most of my life. The dark side of the archetype of family, most deeply of the mother, and the inevitable experiences of absence, rejection, or restriction, are part of our lives along with the light. It is there as a kind of undertow into the waters of old, familiar despair that can grow strong at times of loss or stress. Empathy can fail, old defenses can be marshaled, the bond between us can grow frayed and frail. But we find it is woven of something stronger than our failures: a colorful fabric embroidered with the ancient emblem of the Family.

III

Archetypal
Dimensions
of the
Life Cycle

We move from childhood to adolescence and then through maturity into old age, unless our lives are prematurely cut short. It sounds as though we neatly move through these stages in a progressive linear fashion. Actually, there is a sense in which all these stages are simultaneously present. The child lives on in the adult, and in us as children there lives a picture of the adult whom we imagine we will become. The figure of the inner child has become familiar to those involved in recovery and Jungian work; we talk less of the inner adult self, the inner wise old man or wise old woman, though I suspect they work on us just as powerfully. These, too, are archetypal images—numinous, ambivalent, potentially transformative.

Part III begins with Jung and his essay on the archetype of the child, which emphasizes the ambivalence inherent in the archetype: the vulnerability and invincibility of the child, its masculine and feminine aspects, the way it represents both our past and our potentiality, renewal, and hope. Freud, focusing on the lifelong impact of our actual individual childhoods, introduced us to the wounded child who still lives on in our adult psyches. Jung, whose emphasis falls more on the archetypal or divine child, sees the child as representing not primarily our woundedness but rather our recoverable capacity for playfulness, spontaneity, wonder, and creativity. This more positive view has had an enormous influence on contemporary popular psychology, for it promises that the resources we need for self-transformation lie within.

We then turn to the stages of *male* development viewed archetypally. As Jung notes, "The archetype does not proceed from physical facts, but describes how the psyche experiences the physical fact, and in so doing the psyche often behaves so autocratically that it denies tangible reality or makes statements that fly in the face of it."[1] Swiss analyst Marie-Louise Von Franz's classic description of the *puer aeternus,* the eternal youth, shows him as full of beautiful promise, yet sadly so wedded to endless possibility that to him decision, actualization, and commitment bespeak betrayal more than fulfillment. (Though the model is male, the pattern also often appears among women; the female equivalent to the puer is the puella.)

The puer is often linked with the senex, the old man, as likely to be the crabbed and rigid old man as the wise and wizened mentor. James Hillman writes insightfully about this pairing and how each of these figures defines and complements the other. He begins with mythological amplification, using the figure of the Greek god Cronus to bring into view the positive and negative aspects of the senex archetype. But what really interests Hillman is not mythology but psychology—our personal experience of the archetype's power to shape our lives not only in our later years but also whenever the longing for certainty, perfection, and order becomes dominant. He notes how likely it is for us to be in touch only with this archetype's negative aspect. To access its positive side requires that the split from the puer be healed.

The essay on male psychology, taken from Jungian analyst Robert M. Stein's book *Incest and Human Love,* shows how the male's typical focus on phallic potency ignores many of his soul's deepest needs. Stein helps us see the difference between the penis as a physiological organ and Phallos, the god who embodies a particular mode of impulsive and explosive energy to which men are particularly susceptible. But unless a man is also in right relationship with his receptive "feminine" qualities, with his "womb," his soul cannot be renewed or fertilized by Phallos.

I became aware as I was making these selections of how we don't really have a term for "male adulthood"—perhaps because this stage is almost invisible. It has so often not been looked *at* because it tends to be the typical standpoint *from* which to look. Yet I note that recently masculinity has become problematic, as femininity came to be some decades ago. Writers such as Robert Bly, with his image of the "wild man," and Robert Moore, with his exploration of four male archetypes (king, warrior, magician, and lover), are laying the groundwork for the emergence of what we might call "the conscious masculine."

When we examine the stages of the female life cycle, we do have familiar names for all three phases: maiden, mother, and crone. Yet, as many feminists have made clear, the identification of female adulthood with motherhood is profoundly problematic. There are so many other dimensions to an adult woman's life, but somehow the mother archetype (and culturally specific stereotypes about motherhood) tend to take over. For adult women, wrestling free of this archetype's hold, while also blessing how it enriches our lives, may be painfully difficult. Connie Zweig, editor of *To Be a Woman,* describes how contemporary women are engaged in midwifing a new archetype—the *conscious,* mature woman.

In *Woman's Mysteries,* pioneering Jungian analyst M. Esther Harding gave us a portrait of the maiden or virgin as one-in-herself, which has been an inspiration to generations of women and is included here. More recently, feminists such as Mary Daly and Barbara Walker have given us pictures of the crone as representing the strength and courage of self-sufficient, convention-defying older women. My own discussion both accepts and expands upon their visions. I agree that in a sense the maiden represents an irrecoverable (because never literally possible) innocence, inviolability, self-sufficiency, and the crone a longed-for but to some degree unrealizable attainment of a fulfilled wisdom and power. But such a view focuses only on the positive side of the archetypes. It ignores the confusion, loneliness, vulnerability, and emptiness of the maiden and the incompletion, impotence, and vulnerability of the crone. Such avoidance of the darker side seems to occur when we view archetypes independently of actual lives.

When the archetypal and the personal aspects of the life cycle are integrated, we discover the ever-recurring alternation between wounds and blessings in each phase, and how all the phases interpenetrate and enrich one another. We are never only puer or only senex, never only maiden or only crone. Indeed, as Jung's essay on the child suggests, we are never only male or only female. Thus what has been included here about puer, senex, and phallos may illuminate my self-understanding as a woman, as the essays on virgin, woman, and crone may prove insightful to men.

C. G. Jung

The Child
Archetype

THE ABANDONMENT OF THE CHILD

Abandonment, exposure, danger, etc. are all elaborations
of the "child's" insignificant beginnings and of its mysterious and
miraculous birth. This statement describes a certain psychic experience of a creative nature, whose object is the emergence of a new
and as yet unknown content. In the psychology of the individual
there is always, at such moments, an agonizing situation of conflict
from which there seems to be no way out—at least for the conscious
mind, since as far as this is concerned, *tertium non datur*.[1]

"Child" means something evolving toward independence. This
it cannot do without detaching itself from its origins: abandonment
is therefore a necessary condition, not just a concomitant symptom.
The conflict is not to be overcome by the conscious mind remaining
caught between the opposites, and for this very reason it needs a
symbol to point out the necessity of detaching itself from its origins. Because the symbol of the "child" fascinates and grips the
conscious mind, its redemptive effect passes over into consciousness and brings about that separation from the conflict-situation
which the conscious mind by itself was unable to achieve. The symbol anticipates a nascent state of consciousness. So long as this is not
actually in being, the "child" remains a mythological projection
which requires religious repetition and renewal by ritual.

THE INVINCIBILITY OF THE CHILD

It is a striking paradox in all child myths that the "child" is on the one hand delivered helpless into the power of terrible enemies and in continual danger of extinction, while on the other he possesses powers far exceeding those of ordinary humanity. This is closely related to the psychological fact that though the child may be "insignificant," unknown, "a mere child," he is also divine. From the conscious standpoint we seem to be dealing with an insignificant content that has no releasing, let alone redeeming, character. The conscious mind is caught in its conflict-situation, and the combatant forces seem so overwhelming that the "child" as an isolated content bears no relation to the conscious factors. It is therefore easily overlooked and falls back into the unconscious. At least, this is what we should have to fear if things turned out according to our conscious expectations. Myth, however, emphasizes that it is not so, but that the "child" is endowed with superior powers and, despite all dangers, will unexpectedly pull through. The "child" is born out of the womb of the unconscious, begotten out of the depths of human nature, or rather out of living Nature herself. It is a personification of vital forces quite outside the limited range of our conscious mind; of ways and possibilities of which our one-sided conscious mind knows nothing; a wholeness which embraces the very depths of Nature. It represents the strongest, the most ineluctable urge in every being, namely the urge to realize itself. It is, as it were, an incarnation of *the inability to do otherwise,* equipped with all the powers of nature and instinct, whereas the conscious mind is always getting caught up in its supposed ability to do otherwise. The urge and compulsion to self-realization is a law of nature and thus of invincible power, even though its effect, at the start, is insignificant and improbable. Its power is revealed in the miraculous deeds of the child hero.

The phenomenology of the "child's" birth always points back to an original psychological state of non-recognition, i.e., of darkness or twilight, of non-differentiation between subject and object, of unconscious identity of man and the universe. This phase of non-differentiation produces the *golden egg,* which is both man and universe and yet neither, but an irrational third.

The symbols of the self arise in the depths of the body and they express its materiality every bit as much as the structure of the perceiving consciousness. The symbol is thus a living body, *corpus et anima;* hence the "child" is such an apt formula for the symbol. The uniqueness of the psyche can never enter wholly into reality, it can only be realized approximately, though it still remains the absolute basis of all consciousness. The deeper "layers" of the psyche lose their individual uniqueness as they retreat farther and farther into darkness. "Lower down," that is to say as they approach the autonomous functional systems, they become increasingly collective until they are universalized and extinguished in the body's materiality, i.e., in chemical substances. The body's carbon is simply carbon. Hence "at bottom" the psyche is simply "world." In this sense I hold Kerényi to be absolutely right when he says that in the symbol the *world itself* is speaking. The more archaic and "deeper," that is the more *physiological,* the symbol is, the more collective and universal, the more "material" it is. The more abstract, differentiated, and specific it is, and the more its nature approximates to conscious uniqueness and individuality, the more it sloughs off its universal character. Having finally attained full consciousness, it runs the risk of becoming a mere allegory which nowhere oversteps the bounds of conscious comprehension, and is then exposed to all sorts of attempts at rationalistic and therefore inadequate explanation.

THE HERMAPHRODITISM OF THE CHILD

It is a remarkable fact that perhaps the majority of cosmogonic gods are of a bisexual nature. The hermaphrodite means nothing less than a union of the strongest and most striking opposites. In the first place this union refers back to a primitive state of mind, a twilight where differences and contrasts were either barely separated or completely merged. With increasing clarity of consciousness, however, the opposites draw more and more distinctly and irreconcilably apart. If, therefore, the hermaphrodite were only a product of primitive non-differentiation, we would have to expect that it would soon be eliminated with increasing civilization. This is by no means the case; on the contrary, man's imagination has been preoccupied with this idea over and over again on the high and even the highest levels of culture.

We can no longer be dealing, then, with the continued existence of a primitive phantasm, or with an original contamination of opposites. Rather, as we can see from medieval writings, the primordial idea has become a *symbol of the creative union of opposites,* a "uniting symbol" in the literal sense. In its functional significance the symbol no longer points back, but forward to a goal not yet reached. Notwithstanding its monstrosity, the hermaphrodite has gradually turned into a subduer of conflicts and a bringer of healing, and it acquired this meaning in relatively early phases of civilization. This vital meaning explains why the image of the hermaphrodite did not fade out in primeval times but, on the contrary, was able to assert itself with increasing profundity of symbolic content for thousands of years. The fact that an idea so utterly archaic could rise to such exalted heights of meaning not only points to the vitality of archetypal ideas, it also demonstrates the rightness of the principle that the archetype, because of its power to unite opposites, mediates between the unconscious substratum and the conscious mind. It throws a bridge between present-day consciousness, always in danger of losing its roots, and the natural, unconscious, instinctive wholeness of primeval times. Through this mediation the uniqueness, peculiarity, and one-sidedness of our present individual consciousness are linked up again with its natural, racial roots. Progress and development are ideals not lightly to be rejected, but they lose all meaning if man only arrives at his new state as a fragment of himself, having left his essential hinterland behind him in the shadow of the unconscious, in a state of primitivity or, indeed, barbarism. The conscious mind, split off from its origins, incapable of realizing the meaning of the new state, then relapses all too easily into a situation far worse than the one from which the innovation was intended to free it.

As civilization develops, the bisexual primordial being turns into a symbol of the unity of personality, a symbol of the self, where the war of opposites finds peace. In this way the primordial being becomes the distant goal of man's self-development, having been from the very beginning a projection of his unconscious wholeness.

THE CHILD AS BEGINNING AND END

The "child" is both beginning and end, an initial and a terminal creature. The initial creature existed before man was, and the terminal creature will be when man is not. Psychologically speaking, this means that the "child" symbolizes the pre-conscious and the post-conscious essence of man. His pre-conscious essence is the unconscious state of earliest childhood; his post-conscious essence is an anticipation by analogy of life after death. In this idea the all-embracing nature of psychic wholeness is expressed. Wholeness is never comprised within the compass of the conscious mind—it includes the indefinite and indefinable extent of the unconscious as well. Wholeness, empirically speaking, is therefore of immeasurable extent, older and younger than consciousness and enfolding it in time and space. This is no speculation, but an immediate psychic experience. Not only is the conscious process continually accompanied, it is often guided, helped, or interrupted, by unconscious happenings. The child had a psychic life before it had consciousness. Even the adult still says and does things whose significance he realizes only later, if ever. And yet he said them and did them as if he knew what they meant. Our dreams are continually saying things beyond our conscious comprehension (which is why they are so useful in the therapy of neuroses). We have intimations and intuitions from unknown sources. Fears, moods, plans, and hopes come to us with no invisible causation. These concrete experiences are at the bottom of our feeling that we know ourselves very little; at the bottom, too, of the painful conjecture that we might have surprises in store for ourselves.

Primitive man is no puzzle to himself. The question "What is man?" is the question that man has always kept until last. Primitive man has so much psyche outside his conscious mind that the experience of something psychic outside him is far more familiar to him than to us. Consciousness hedged about by psychic powers, sustained or threatened or deluded by them, is the age-old experience of mankind. This experience has projected itself into the archetype of the child, which expresses man's wholeness. The "child" is all that is abandoned and exposed and at the same time divinely powerful; the insignificant, dubious beginning, and the triumphal end. The "eternal child" in man is an indescribable experience, an incongruity, a handicap, and a divine prerogative; an imponderable that determines the ultimate worth or worthlessness of a personality.

Marie-Louise Von Franz

The Puer

P*uer aeternus* is the name of a god of antiquity. The words themselves come from Ovid's *Metamorphoses*[1] and are there applied to the child-god in the Eleusinian mysteries. Ovid speaks of the child-god Iacchus, addressing him as *puer aeternus* and praising him in his role in these mysteries. In later times, the child-god was identified with Dionysus and the god Eros. He is the divine youth who is born in the night in this typical mother-cult mystery of Eleusis, and who is a redeemer. He is a god of life, death and resurrection—the god of divine youth, corresponding to such oriental gods as Tammuz, Attis, and Adonis. The title *puer aeternus* therefore means "eternal youth," but we also use it to indicate a certain type of young man who has an outstanding mother complex and who therefore behaves in certain typical ways, which I would like to characterize as follows.

In general, the man who is identified with the archetype of the *puer aeternus* remains too long in adolescent psychology; that is, all those characteristics that are normal in a youth of seventeen or eighteen are continued into later life, coupled in most cases with too great a dependence on the mother. The two typical disturbances of a man who has an outstanding mother complex are, as Jung points out,[2] homosexuality and Don Juanism. In the latter case, the image of a mother—the image of the perfect woman who will give everything to a man and who is without any shortcomings—is sought in every woman. He is looking for a mother goddess, so that each time he is fascinated by a woman he has later to discover that she is an ordinary human being. Having lived with her sexually, the whole fascination vanishes and he turns away disappointed, only to project the image anew onto one woman after another. He eternally longs for the maternal woman who will enfold him in her arms and satisfy his every need. This is often accompanied by the romantic attitude of the adolescent.

Generally, great difficulty is experienced in adaptation to the social situation. In some cases, there is a kind of asocial individualism: being something special, one has no need to adapt, for that would be impossible for such a hidden genius, and so on. In addition, an arrogant attitude arises toward other people, due to both an inferiority complex and false feelings of superiority. Such people usually have great difficulty in finding the right kind of job, for whatever they find is never quite right or quite what they wanted. There is always "a hair in the soup." The woman is never quite the right woman; she is nice as a girl friend, but . . . There is always a "but" which prevents marriage or any kind of commitment.

This all leads to a form of neurosis which H. G. Baynes has described as the "provisional life"; that is, the strange attitude and feeling that the woman is *not yet* what is really wanted, and there is always the fantasy that sometime in the future the real thing will come about. If this attitude is prolonged, it means a constant inner refusal to commit oneself to the moment. Accompanying this neurosis is often, to a smaller or greater extent, a savior or Messiah complex, with the secret thought that one day one will be able to save the world; that the last word in philosophy, or religion, or politics, or art, or something else, will be found. This can progress to a typical pathological megalomania, or there may be minor traces of it in the idea that one's time "has not yet come." The one situation dreaded throughout by such a type of man is to be bound to anything whatsoever. There is a terrific fear of being pinned down, of entering space and time completely, and of being the specific human being that one is. There is always the fear of being caught in a situation from which it may be impossible to slip out again. Every just-so situation is hell. At the same time, there is something highly symbolic—namely, a fascination for dangerous sports, particularly flying and mountaineering—so as to get as high as possible, the symbolism of which is to get away from the mother; i.e., from the earth, from ordinary life. If this type of complex is very pronounced, many such men die at a young age in airplane crashes and mountaineering accidents. It is an exteriorized spiritual longing which expresses itself in this form.

A dramatic representation of what flying really means to the *puer* is given in John Magee's poem. Soon after the poem was written, Magee died in an airplane accident.

High Flight

Oh! I have slipped the surly bonds of Earth
    And danced the skies on laughter-silvered wings;
Sunward I've climbed, and joined the tumbling mirth
    Of sun-split clouds,—and done a hundred things
You have not dreamed of—wheeled and soared and swung
    High in the sunlit silence. Hov'ring there,
I've chased the shouting wind along, and flung
    My eager craft through footless halls of air...

Up, up the long, delirious, burning blue
    I've topped the wind-swept heights with easy grace,
Where never lark, or even eagle flew—
    And, while with silent, lifting mind I've trod
    The high untrespassed sanctity of space,
Put out my hand and touched the face of God.[3]

Pueri generally do not like sports which require patience and long training, for the *puer aeternus*—in the negative sense of the word—is usually very impatient by disposition. I know a young man, a classical example of the *puer aeternus*, who did a tremendous amount of mountaineering but so much hated carrying a rucksack that he preferred to train himself even to sleep in the rain or snow outdoors. He would make himself a hole in the snow and wrap himself up in a silk raincoat and, with a kind of yoga breathing, was able to sleep out-of-doors. He also trained himself to go practically without food, simply to avoid carrying any weight. He roamed about for years all over mountains in Europe and other continents, sleeping under trees or in the snow. In a way, he led a very heroic existence, just in order not to be bound to go to a hut or carry a rucksack. You might say that this was symbolic, for such a young man in real life does not want to be burdened with any kind of weight; the one thing he absolutely refuses is responsibility for anything, or to carry the weight of a situation.

In general, the positive quality of such youths is a certain kind of spirituality which comes from a relatively close contact with the collective unconscious. Many have the charm of youth and the stirring quality of a drink of champagne. *Pueri aeterni* are generally very agreeable to talk with; they usually have interesting subjects to talk about and have an invigorating effect upon the listener; they do not like conventional situations; they ask deep questions and go straight for the truth; usually they are searching for genuine religion, a search that is typical for people in their late teens. Usually the youthful charm of the *puer aeternus* is prolonged through later stages of life.

However, there is another type of *puer* that does not display the charm of eternal youth, nor does the archetype of the divine youth shine through him. On the contrary, he lives in a continual sleepy daze, and that, too, is a typical adolescent characteristic: the sleepy, undisciplined, long-legged youth who merely hangs around, his mind wandering indiscriminately, so that sometimes one feels inclined to pour a bucket of cold water over his head. The sleepy daze is only an outer aspect, however, and if you can penetrate it, you will find that a lively fantasy life is being cherished within.

The above is a short summary of the main characteristics of certain young men who are caught up in the mother complex and, with it, are identified with the archetype of the *puer*. I have given a mainly negative picture of these people because that is what they look like if viewed superficially, but, as you will see, we have not explained what is really the matter. The question is why the problem of this type, of the mother-bound young man, has become so pronounced in our time. As you know, homosexuality—I do not think Don Juanism is so widely spread—is increasing more and more; even teenagers are involved, and it seems to me that the problem of the *puer aeternus* is becoming increasingly actual. Undoubtedly, mothers have always tried to keep their sons in the nest, and some sons have always had difficulty in getting free and have rather preferred to continue to enjoy the pleasures of the nest; still one does not quite see why this in itself, a natural problem, should now become such a serious time-problem. I think that is the important and deeper question we have to put to ourselves because the rest is more or less self-evident. A man who has a mother complex will always have to contend with his tendencies toward becoming a *puer aeternus*. What cure is there? you might ask. If a man discovers that he has a mother complex, which is something that happened to him—something that he did not cause himself—what can he do about it? In *Symbols of Transformation,* Dr. Jung spoke of one cure— work—and having said that, he hesitated for a minute and thought, "Is it really as simple as all that? Is that the only cure? Can I put it that way?" But work is the one disagreeable word which no *puer aeternus* likes to hear, and Dr. Jung came to the conclusion that it was the right answer. My experience also has been that it is through work that a man can pull out of this kind of youthful neurosis.

There are, however, some misunderstandings in this connection, for the *puer aeternus* can work, as can all primitives or people with weak ego complexes, when fascinated or in a state of great enthusiasm. Then he can work twenty-four hours at a stretch or even longer, until he breaks down. But what he cannot do is to work on a dreary, rainy morning when work is boring and one has to kick oneself into it; that is the one thing the *puer aeternus* usually cannot manage and will use any kind of excuse to avoid. Analysis of a *puer aeternus* sooner or later always comes up against this problem. It is only when the ego has become sufficiently strengthened that the problem can be overcome, and the possibility of sticking to the work is given. Naturally, though one knows the goal, every individual case is different. Personally, I have not found that it is much good just preaching to people that they should work, for they simply get angry and walk off.

As far as I have seen, the unconscious generally tries to produce a compromise—namely, to indicate the direction in which there might be some enthusiasm or where the psychological energy would flow naturally, for it is, of course, easier to train oneself to work in a direction supported by one's instinct. That is not quite so hard as working completely uphill in opposition to your own flow of energy. Therefore, it is usually advisable to wait a while, find out where the natural flow of interest and energy lies and then try to get the man to work *there.* But in every field of work there always comes the time when routine must be faced. All work, even creative work, contains a certain amount of boring routine, which is where the *puer aeternus* escapes and comes to the conclusion again that "this is not it!" In such moments, if one is supported by the unconscious, dreams generally occur which show that one should push on through the obstacle. If that succeeds, then the battle is won.

In a letter[4] Jung says about the *puer:* "I consider the *puer aeternus* attitude an unavoidable evil. Identity with the *puer* signifies a psychological puerility that could do nothing better than outgrow itself. It always leads to external blows of fate which show the need for another attitude. But reason accomplishes nothing, because the *puer aeternus* is always an agent of destiny."

James Hillman

The Senex

According to the Warburg Institute's authoritative study of Saturn, in no Greek god-figure is the dual aspect so real, so fundamental, as in the figure of Kronos, so that even with the later additions of the Roman Saturn who "was originally not ambivalent but definitely good," the compounded image remains at core bipolar. Saturn is at once archetypal image for wise old man, solitary sage, the *lapis* as rock of ages with all its positive moral and intellectual virtues, *and* for the Old King, that castrating castrated ogre. He is the world as builder of cities *and* the not-world of exile. At the same time that he is father of all he consumes all; by living on and from his fatherhood he feeds himself insatiably from the bounty of his own paternalism. *Saturn is image for both positive and negative senex.*

In astrology this duality was handled by the examination of Saturn's place in the birth-chart. In this way, the good and bad poles inherent to his nature could be kept distinct. His temperament is *cold*. Coldness can be expressed also as *distance*; the lonely wanderer set apart, out-cast. Coldness is also cold reality, things just as they are; and yet Saturn is at the far-out edge of reality. As lord of the nethermost, he views the world from the outside, from such depths of distance that he sees it, so to speak, all upside down, yet structurally and abstractly. The concern with structure and abstraction makes him the principle of *order*, whether through time, or hierarchy, or exact science and system, or limits and borders, or power, or inwardness and reflection, or earth and the forms it gives. The cold is also *slow*, heavy, leaden, and dry or moist, but always the *coagulator* through denseness, slowness, and weight expressed by the mood of sadness, depression, or melancholia. Thus he is *black*, winter, and the night, yet heralds through his day, Saturday, the return of the holy Sunday light. His relation to *sexuality* is again dual: on the one hand he is patron of eunuchs and celibates, being dry and impotent; on the other hand he is represented by the dog and the lecherous goat, and is a fertility god as inventor of agriculture, a god of earth and peasant, the harvest and Saturnalia, a ruler of fruit and seed. But the harvest is a *hoard*; the ripened end-product and in-gathering again can be dual. Under the aegis of Saturn it can show qualities of greed and tyranny, where in-gathering means holding and the purse of miserliness, making things last through all time. (Saturn governs coins, minting, and wealth.) Here we find the characteristics of avarice, gluttony, and such rapaciousness that Saturn is *bhoga*, "eating the world," and identified with Moloch—which again on its positive side demands the extreme *sacrifice*, and can be understood as Abraham and Moses, the Patriarchal mentor who demands the extreme.

His relationship to the *feminine* has been put in a few words: those born under Saturn "do not like to walk with women and pass the time." "They are never in favor with woman or wife." So Saturn is in association with widowhood, childlessness, orphanhood, child-exposure, and he attends childbirth so as to be able to eat the newborn, as everything new coming to life can become food to the senex. Old attitudes and habits assimilate each new content; everlastingly changeless, it eats its own possibilities of change.

His *moral aspects* are two-sided. He presides over honesty in speech—and deceit; over secrets, silence—and loquaciousness and slander; over loyalty and friendship—and selfishness, cruelty, cunning, thievery and murder. He makes both honest reckoning and fraud. He is god of manure, privies, dirty linen, bad wind, and is also cleanser of souls. His *intellectual qualities* include the inspired genius of the brooding melancholic, creativity through contemplation, deliberation in the exact sciences and mathematics, as well as the highest occult secrets such as angelology, theology, and prophetic furor. He is the aged Indian on the elephant, the wise old man and "creator of wise men," as Augustine called him in the first systematic polemic against this senex archetype.

This amplification may give a phenomenological description of an archetype, but it is not psychology. Psychology may be based on archetypal themata, but psychology proper begins only when these dominants, experienced as emotional realities through and within our complexes, are felt to pull and shape our lives. Amplification can give us mythography, or anthropology, or *Kunstgeschichte*; yet it remains outside us, interesting but hardly involving. But let it touch us through the archetypal core of the complex in our individual lives—then the descriptions of myths and rites, art and symbols, suddenly are living psychology! Then it hits us as "inner" and "important," belonging to us or possessing us. Then it matters, becoming a necessity, and we are driven to amplify our psychological problems through archetypal understanding. Then it is urgent. Because of the complex we search the books.

Psychologically the senex is at the core of *any complex* or governs *any attitude* when these psychological processes pass to end-phase. We expect it to correspond to biological senescence, just as many of its images: dryness, night, coldness, winter, harvest, are taken from the processes of time and of nature. But to speak accurately the senex archetype transcends mere biological senescence and is given from the beginning as a potential of order, meaning, and teleological fulfillment—and death—within all the psyche and all its parts. So the death which the senex brings is not only biophysical. It is the death that comes through perfection and order. It is the death of accomplishment and fulfillment, a death which grows in power within any complex or attitude as that psychological process matures through consciousness into order, becoming habitual and dominant—and therefore unconscious again. Paradoxically, we are least conscious where we are most conscious.

The negative senex is the senex split from its own puer aspect. He has lost his "child." The archetypal core of the complex, now split, loses its inherent tension, its ambivalence, and is just dead in the midst of its brightness which is its own eclipse, as a negative *Sol Niger*. Without the enthusiasm and eros of the son, authority loses its idealism. It aspires to nothing but its own perpetuation, leading but to tyranny and cynicism; for *meaning cannot be sustained by structure and order alone.* Such spirit is one-sided, and one-sidedness is crippling. Being is static, a pleroma that cannot become. Time—called euphemistically "experience," but more often just the crusted accretions of profane history—becomes a moral virtue and even witness of truth, *"veritas filia temporis."* The old is always preferred to the new. Sexuality without young eros becomes goaty; weakness becomes complaints; creative isolation only paranoid loneliness. Because the complex is unable to catch on and sow seed, it feeds on the growth of other complexes or of other people, as for instance the growth of one's own children, or the developmental process going on in one's analysands. Cut off from its own child and fool the complex no longer has anything to tell us. Folly and immaturity are projected onto others. Without folly it has no wisdom, only knowledge—serious, depressing, hoarded in an academic vault or used as power. The feminine may be kept imprisoned in secret, or may be Dame Melancholy, a moody consort, as an atmosphere emanating from the moribund complex, giving it the stench of Saturn. The integration of personality becomes the subjugation of personality, a unification through dominance, and integrity only a self-same repetition of firm principle. Or, to reawaken the puer side again there may be a complex-compelled falling-in-love. (Venus is born from the imaginal froth in the unconscious out of the dissociated sexuality cut off through Saturn.)

To sum up then with the senex: It is there from the beginning as are all archetypal dominants and is found in the small child who knows and says "I know" and "mine" with the full intensity of its being, the small child who is the last to pity and first to tyrannize, destroys what it has built, and in its weakness lives in oral omnipotence fantasies, defending its borders and testing the limits set by others. But although the senex is there in the child, the senex spirit nevertheless appears most evidently when any function we use, attitude we have, or complex of the psyche begins to coagulate past its prime. It is the Saturn within the complex that makes it hard to shed, dense and slow and maddeningly depressing—the madness of lead-poison—that feeling of the everlasting indestructibility of the complex. It cuts off the complex from life and the feminine, inhibiting it and introverting it into an isolation. Thus it stands behind the fastness of our habits and the ability we have of making a virtue of any vice by merely keeping it in order or attributing it to fate. The senex as complex appears in dreams long before a person has himself put on his *toga senilis* (*aet.* 60 in Rome). It manifests as the dream father, mentor, old wise man, to which the dreamer's consciousness is pupil. When accentuated it seems to have drawn all power to itself, paralysing elsewhere, and a person is unable to make a decision without first taking counsel with the unconscious to await an advising voice from an oracle or vision. Though this counsel may come from the unconscious, it may be as collective as that which comes from the standard canons of the culture. For statements of sagacity and meaning, even spiritual truths, can be bad advice. These representations—father, elders, mentors, and old wise men—provide an authority and wisdom that is beyond the experience of the dreamer. Therefore it tends to have him rather than he it, so that he is driven by an unconscious certainty, making him "wise beyond his years," ambitious for recognition by his seniors and intolerant of his own youthfulness. The senex spirit also affects any attitude or complex when the creative contemplation of its ultimate meaning, its relation to fate, its deepest "why," become constellated. Then the husk of any habitual attitude deprived of all outward power shrinks to a grain, but imprisoned in the little limits of this seed is all the *vis* of the original complex. Turned thus in on itself almost to the point of disappearing altogether, leaving only a melancholy mood of *mortificatio* or *putrefactio*, in the black cold night of deprivation it holds a sort of lonely communion in itself with the future; and then with the prophetic genius of the senex spirit reveals that which is beyond the edge of its own destructive harvesting scythe, that which will sprout green from the grain it has itself slain.

This duality within the senex itself that is imaged for us by the positive-negative Kronos-Saturn figure gives each of us those intensely difficult problems in our process of individuation. How does the Old King in my attitudes change? How can my knowledge become wisdom? How do I admit uncertainty, disorder, and nonsense within my borders? How we work out these issues affects the historical transition since we are each a makeweight in the scales.

The duality of the senex rests upon an even more basic archetypal polarity, that of the senex-puer archetype. Thus the crucial psychological problem expressed by the terms "negative senex" and "positive senex," ogre and Old Wise Man, which concerns our individual lives and "how to be," which is reflected in the symptoms of the aging millennium, and which influences the nature of our effects upon today's historical transition—this crucial psychological problem arises from a fundamental split between senex and puer within the same archetype. Negative senex attitudes and behavior result from this split archetype, while positive senex attitudes and behavior reflect its unity; so that the term "positive senex" or old wise man refers merely to a transformed continuation of the puer. Here [we] reach the issue: *the difference between the negative and positive senex qualities reflects the split or connection within the senex-puer archetype.*

Robert M. Stein

Phallos
and Male
Psychology

Masculine and Feminine are qualities of the human personality common to both sexes. But a man's nature tends to be more rooted in a Phallic spirit, while a woman's tends to emerge out of a Womb spirit.

The Phallic spirit, like the penis, functions autonomously, independent of control by the rational mind. One might argue that the reactions of the penis are subject to rational control, but this is dubious. Although the penis can apparently be manipulated to perform, without doubt it has a will of its own which resists all the trickery of the rational mind (ego) if it so desires. Furthermore, men who habitually employ the ego to control the reactions of the penis accomplish this by varying degrees of numbing detachment. Ultimately, the phallic spirit in the penis responds to such treatment by causing some form of psychological or physiological impotency. Obviously, the control of the ego over the penis is minimal and of limited duration. However, the attitude and relationship of ego to penis can effect profound changes in the reactions of this primary organ of masculine sexuality.

The sudden uncontrollable surge of blood into the penis, causing it to stand erect, is a great mystery. The desire behind it may be love for another, or it may also be pure lust or desire for power over another, or it may be a mixture of all these elements. Often the penis becomes aroused by sexual fantasies having no relationship to an actual person. And at times, a sudden erection totally unrelated to sexual desire will occur, which suggests that the phallic rush of energy into the penis is a spirit which transcends the sexual drive.

If we accept the idea of the penis as an organ particularly under the influence of the phallic spirit, we can deduce something about the nature of this God, Phallos. We recognize, above all, its essentially unpredictable quality. Experientially, it seems to manifest itself as a sudden powerful surge or thrust from within, flowing rapidly with the desire to make contact with another object—be it idea, image, another person or an inanimate object. While it is the desire of the feminine Womb spirit to be entered, to receive and embrace, the desire of Phallos is always to move toward penetration of an unknown realm. Phallos therefore is fundamental to all human initiative. Without it we can be moved, but we can not move. Anyone who fears being moved out of old stabile structures into areas that are new, unknown and unformed, will fear the sudden, irrational influx of Phallos. Consequently, the right relationship to this spirit is essential for change and psychological development. At the same time, it is a spirit constantly on the move: curious, impulsive, explosive, daring but incapable of commitment; filled with the joy of its own power and ready to use it against anything that gets in its way, unconcerned with tending and nourishing human relationships unless tempered and contained in Eros. When women complain about men only wanting to get into their pants and not caring about the relationship, they are really speaking of Phallos. When a mother is unable to cope with the constant activity, playful curiosity and demands of her child, she is often suffering from a bad relationship to Phallos.

I recall a young mother who was having great difficulty with her unmanageable male child; she dreamt that her son was zig-zagging and bouncing off the walls of his room with such velocity that she constantly had to duck in order to keep from getting hit. Suddenly he became a huge Phallos and she awakened terrified. Obviously this woman was in a bad relationship to Phallos. A boy's relationship to the phallic root of his masculine nature will be profoundly influenced by a mother so threatened and judgmental in her attitude toward his essential maleness.

Love and Phallos are often difficult to differentiate because both are fundamentally active, initiating life forces. Both are experienced as a force moving one away from where one is toward another object or person. Furthermore, the Goddess of Love herself is believed to have been born out of the severed genitals of the Sky God, Ouranos. No doubt there is a close relationship between Phallos and Love. Perhaps Phallos is the primal source of the energy contained in every emotion that motivates man to move, to act, to initiate. Since Love is primarily a great movement toward union with another, it too must be rooted in Phallos.

Still, Love and Phallos are not identical. How do they differ? Perhaps the main difference is that Love is always a desire to merge, to unite, while Phallos is primarily a desire to penetrate and explore. In addition, Love always evokes great concern for preserving the beauty and integrity of the other, while Phallos lacks such concern; in its pure form it tends to rape and ultimately destroy the object of its fascination.

Clearly, Phallos is the source of all of man's creative energies. It is a force which always moves away from the old, from what is, toward the new and unknown. Phallic curiosity is the activating principle behind man's creative imagination, but the penetrating, dissecting quality of curiosity becomes destructive and anti-human without Eros to preserve the integrity and mystery of the unknown object.

Phallos, the generative source of life, is pure emotion, pure desire. Any thought, impulse, image or idea is brought to life by Phallos. It is pure spirit, pure energy using anything and everything as its material for giving shape to the creative urge. In its insatiable hunger to fertilize and create new forms, it has neither awareness nor concern for human limitations. Without Phallos nothing moves, nothing changes. Fear of Phallos results in fragmentation and stasis. I must be open and desirous to receive Phallos or it can not enter me. Consequently, if I do not have the right relationship to the receptive feminine qualities of my soul, my womb is closed and I begin to dry up because I can not be fertilized and renewed by Phallos. The womb, receptive earth, is, therefore, primary. Without it the Life Force has no vessel to receive it, and the blood of my own life will soon cease to flow. Death.

Let us return now to the woman who was so threatened by her son's phallic qualities. The inner image of the archetypal feminine is largely shaped by a man's experience of his mother. Typically, most Western men experience the receptive maternal aspects of their own psyche as rejecting of Phallos. How could it be otherwise? Everything we know about the ancient feminine mysteries indicates that they were centered around the worship of Phallos. Modern woman is as cut off from these mysteries as was Oedipus. Instead of her Eros embracing and humanizing her son's potent phallic energies, she attempts to subdue and control this irrational spirit with her ego. So long as a man's internal image of the feminine is rejecting of Phallos, he can never come to a right relationship with his own creative spirit, and the same situation applies to women, as we shall see presently. Consequently, the inner feminine (the anima) must change before a man can truly open up to Phallos.

How does this negative experience of the feminine manifest itself internally and in life? In men's dreams, a frequent motif is the sudden appearance of mother or a mother figure just as the dreamer is about to surrender to his sexual desires. *Mother inhibits Phallos.* Since mother is also associated with soft, tender, loving feelings, and Phallos is the source of all passion, a man has great difficulty getting his passion together with his love when his experience of the mother archetype is so castrating. More often than not, this same archetypal pattern will be constellated in relationship to his wife. I have often heard a woman express her pain about not being able to be physically close and tender with her husband because when she does he immediately wants to fuck. And I have often heard a man complain about how his wife says no to sex after having aroused him with physical intimacy. This common dilemma is a clear indication that both partners are suffering from the same negative relationship to Phallos. Should the woman yield to her husband's sexual passion, she knows the close tender feelings will be obliterated, for she, too, is plagued from within by this rejecting maternal archetype.

Impotency—mental, spiritual, and physical—is the consequence of a man's inability to embrace Phallos. Nothing will alter his basic feeling of inadequacy until he overcomes his fear of Phallos as it begins to stir, to rise up numinously at the root of his being. It is different for a woman. As long as she feels connected to the softness and receptivity of her womb, she will feel womanly—unless her soul is dissatisfied with living only the archetypal feminine. However, any woman who has a need to think creatively, to become spiritually free of her dependency on a man, to individuate, will feel inadequate and unfulfilled until she, too, can allow the full potency of Phallos to enter consciousness. Still, a woman can lead a relatively full, if unconscious, life for many years before she is forced to come to grips with her fear of Phallos. A man can not. It is essential for his initiation into manhood.

When the generative life force (Phallos) is full and flowing, one might be fearful, but it is always awesome and fascinating. Phallos erect is to be respected. But Phallos is not always erect, the Life Force is not always flowing outward. Often it retreats, or lies peacefully dormant. To love Phallos means not only to embrace one's potency, but one's impotency. Unless one can accept being weak, foolish, helpless, one will always fear the potent surge of Phallos. The other side of tumescence is detumescence. Phallos, like life, rushes in as a great flowing force, but life ebbs just as suddenly and rapidly as it flows.

Now that we have made the connection between the fear of phallic potency and the fear of impotency, we can discuss some important differences between masculine and feminine psychology. The inability to initiate effective action toward the realization of a desire tends to make a man feel impotent. He need not necessarily act so long as he feels the power to act. A woman tends to feel impotent mainly when she is *without* desire; at least this seems to be the case when she is connected to the ground of her womb-like nature. As long as a woman feels open to respond to the quick of life, she can, without feeling inadequate, accept her passivity as well as her incapacity to act effectively upon her desire. She may, of course, experience pain and frustration about her unfulfilled needs; however, her sense of potency is not as dependent on her power to act, but rather on the connection to her desire and the belief in her capacity to respond to its fulfillment. For example, a young, extremely passive woman lived for years in a state of isolation devoid of any relationship to a man. After months of analysis, in which she refused to examine her relationship to men and sexuality, she finally revealed that she had felt nothing wrong with herself in these areas. Her sense of adequacy came from her fantasy that as soon as the right man came along she would be ready to receive him. This exposure of her identification with the princess of the Sleeping Beauty myth came as a consequence of her sudden realization that she would be incapable of responding to her Prince Charming even if he should appear. A man, too, can live for years in a fantastic delusion about his potency. But his myth is that he has the power actively to effect the realization of his desire, and that he is only holding back until the time is right.

So, a man would seem to gather his sense of strength and potency from his capacity to act, while a woman's strength would seem to be more rooted in her desire to respond. The demand that Phallos be always erect and capable of asserting itself is naturally more prevalent among men than among women, although many women are plagued from within by a similar demand. A man will be continually undermined and spiritually crippled as long as he is caught in the equations: Erect Phallos Potency; Limp Phallos Impotency.

Furthermore, he is forced to escape into his fantastic delusions of phallic potency in order to maintain any sense of adequacy and self-respect. Life for him becomes a series of evasions. He finds the realities of his existential condition and the non-phallic dimensions of his personality intolerably painful, so that the soul's authentic needs are forever slipping away from his grasp and left unfulfilled.

Our Western culture identifies progress and productivity with masculine vitality and strength. Productive potent and creative; counterproductive impotent and destructive. Clearly, such attitudes reflect a misunderstanding and distortion of masculinity. A man can free himself of this phallic fixation only if he experiences and joyfully accepts those states of passive, unknowing, helplessness as expressions of his receptive feminine nature. Rather than shrivelling up with feelings of impotency, a man must be able to sink deeply into the *strength* of his own desire to be fertilized.

M. Esther Harding

The Virgin

The Great Mother is always represented as *Virgin*, in spite of the fact that she has many lovers and is the mother of many sons, or of one son, who dies only to be born again and again, year after year. This term "virgin" needs some investigation, for obviously, with its modern connotation of chaste, innocent, it cannot be used of the Magna Mater, unless we assume that she remains miraculously virgin in spite of experiences which would seem to make the term inapplicable. Frazer, however, has an illuminating statement on this point. "The [Greek] word *parthenos*," he says, "applied to Artemis, which we commonly translate Virgin, means no more than an unmarried woman, and in early days the two things were by no means the same... there was no public worship of Artemis the Chaste; so far as her sacred titles bear on the relation of the sexes, they show that, on the contrary, she was, like Diana in Italy, especially concerned with the loss of virginity and with child-bearing... Nothing, however, sets the true character of Artemis as a goddess of fecundity though not of wedlock in a clearer light than her constant identification with the unmarried, but not chaste, Asiatic goddesses of love and fertility, who were worshipped with rites of notorious profligacy at their popular sanctuaries."[1] In a footnote Frazer comments on the line in Isaiah, "and a virgin shall be with child," and says that the Hebrew word here rendered as "virgin" means no more than "young woman," and that "a correct translation would have obviated the necessity for the miracle." This comment does not quite cover the point of difficulty, however, for whatever the Prophet Isaiah may have meant by his saying, there is no doubt that the Virgin Mary was venerated by the medieval church and is still venerated by Catholics today, as virgin in our modern sense of the word, even though it is recognized by tradition that she bore carnal children to Joseph after the virgin birth of her Eldest Son, and is also hailed in Latin hymns as spouse as well as mother of her Son. These things would form a flagrant contradiction or require an impossible miracle, if they were to be taken as true on the objective plane. If, however, we recognize religious concepts as symbolic and interpret these contradictions psychologically we realize that the term "virginity" must refer to a *quality*, to a subjective state, a psychological attitude, not to a physiological or external fact. When used of either the Virgin Mary or of the virgin goddesses of other religions, it cannot be used as denoting a factual situation, for the quality of virginity persists in some unexplained fashion in spite of sexual experience, childbearing, and increasing age.

Briffault gives a clue to this enigma. "The word virgin," he says,

> is, of course, used in those titles in its primitive sense as denoting "unwed," and connoting the very reverse of what the term has come to imply. The virgin Ishtar is also frequently addressed as "The Prostitute"; and she herself says, "A prostitute compassionate am I." She wears the "posin," or veil, which, as among the Jews, was the mark of both "virgins" and prostitutes. The hierodules, or sacred prostitutes of her temples, were also called "the holy virgins." . . . Children born out of wedlock were called "parthenioi," "virgin-born." The word "virgin" itself has not, strictly speaking, the meaning which we attach to it; the correct Latin expression for the untouched virgin is not "virgo," but "virgo intacta." Aphrodite herself was a Virgin.[2]

The Eskimo mother goddess has the same characteristic of virginity in the old sense of the term. The Eskimos call her "She who will not have a husband." Demeter also is said to have "execrated marriage." She presided not over marriage but over divorce. The Chinese holy virgin, Shing-Moo, the Great Mother, conceived and bore her son while yet a virgin. She is venerated as a pattern of purity; her conception of the Holy Child is deemed to have been immaculate, but her ancient character is revealed in the fact that she is the patroness of prostitutes.

The term virgin, then, when used of the ancient goddesses, clearly has a meaning not of today. It may be used of a woman who has had much sexual experience; it may be even applied to a prostitute. Its real significance is to be found in its use as contrasted with "married."

In primitive times a married woman was the property of her husband, often bought for a considerable price from her father. The basic idea which underlies this custom still holds sway to some extent among us. In the period of "arranged marriages" and of "marriage settlements" the assumption that the woman was a purchased possession might be glimpsed beneath the decorous negotiations, and the custom of "giving away" the bride recalls the same underlying psychological concept, namely, that a woman is not her own mistress but the property of her father who transfers her *as property* to her husband.

Under our Western patriarchal system the unmarried girl belongs to her father, but in earlier days, as still in some primitive communities, she was her own mistress until she married. The right to dispose of her own person until she marries is part of the primitive concept of liberty. There are many evidences of a general careful guardianship of the young girls in primitive societies, both within and without the tribe; they are guarded, for instance, against violence and especially from "incest" with their "clan brothers," but with men of a clan into which they may marry they can follow their own wishes. This liberty of action involves the right to refuse intimacies as well as to accept them. A girl belongs to *herself* while she is virgin—unwed—and may not be compelled either to maintain chastity or to yield to an unwanted embrace.

As virgin she belongs to herself alone, she is "one-in-herself." Gauguin remarks on this characteristic of the Tahiti women in his book *Noa Noa*. To him it seemed strange. He tells how any woman would readily give herself to a stranger if he attracted her, but that she gave herself not to the man with whom she had intercourse, but to her own instinct, so that even after the relation had been completed she remained one-in-herself. She was not dependent on the man, she did not cling to him or demand that the relationship should be permanent. She was still her own mistress, a virgin in the ancient, original meaning of the word.

It is in this sense that the moon goddesses can rightly be called virgin. The quality of virginity is, indeed, characteristic of them. Other goddesses of ancient and primitive religions do not partake of it; they are not one-in-themselves. They have apparently no separate existence of their own, but are conceived of only as the wives or counterparts of the gods from whom they derive both their power and their prestige. Thus the goddess has the same name as the god, the same attributes and powers, or perhaps she has the feminine version of his more masculine qualities. They form a pair, undifferentiated except in sex. The goddess is merely mate to the god as the woman was to the man. Her name even was a matter of no concern. She was designated merely by the feminine form of the male deity's name. For example the wife of Faunus was Fauna; Dio was the feminine of Zeus, and Agnazi of Agni; Nut corresponded to Nu, and Hehut to Hehu. Even the primitive earth and sky gods formed a pair united in marriages, Mr. Heaven and Mrs. Earth.

Goddesses existing in this way as the counterparts of the gods are of distinct type. They represent the ideal of the married woman and personify that aspect of feminine nature which is clinging and dependent. They deify the domestic virtues of the wife, who is concerned only with the interests of husband and children.

This is the ideal expressed in such terms as "the two shall become one flesh." It is also the archetype underlying the story of the creation of Eve from Adam's rib. In such a situation the "entity" or unit is the pair, the married couple, the family. The members who make up this unit do not have a separate or complete existence, nor do they have a separate or complete character or personality of their own. For in such a marriage the man represents the male part of the entity and the woman the female part. The psyche itself, however, is both male and female. Each human being contains within himself potentialities in both directions. If he does not take up both of these aspects and develop and discipline them within himself, he is only half a person, he cannot be a complete personality. When two people form a complementary marriage, where all the male is in the man and all the female is in the woman, it follows that each of them remains one-sided, for the unlived side of the psyche, being unconscious, is projected to the partner. This condition may work fairly well so long as both are living and remain on good terms. But when one partner dies the other will find himself seriously at a loss and, perhaps not until then, when it may be too late, is it borne in upon him how limited and one-sided his life has been.

In Western patriarchal society, during many centuries, man was concerned to be dominant and superior, while woman was relegated to a position of dependence and inferiority. Consequently the feminine principle has not been adequately recognized or valued in our culture. And even today, when the outer manifestations of this one-sidedness have undergone considerable change, the psychological effects persist and both men and women suffer from a maiming of the psyche, which should be whole. This condition is represented by the goddess who is counterpart of the male god and nothing else.

The relation of the Moon Mother to the god associated with her is entirely different. She is goddess of sexual love but not of marriage. There is no male god who as husband rules her conduct or determines her qualities. Instead she is the mother of a son, whom she controls. When he grows up he becomes her lover and then dies, only to be born again as son. The Moon Goddess belongs to a matriarchal, not to a patriarchal, system. She is not related to any god as wife or "counterpart." She is her own mistress, virgin, one-in-herself. The characteristics of these great and powerful goddesses do not mirror those of any of the male gods, nor do they represent the feminine counterpart of characteristics originally male. Their histories are independent and their functions, their insignia, and their rites belong to themselves alone, for they represent the essence of the feminine in its sharpest contrast to the essence of masculinity.

Connie Zweig

The Conscious
Feminine:
Birth of a
New Archetype

*Someday there will be girls and women whose names will
no longer signify merely an opposite of the masculine, but
something in itself, something that makes one think not of
any complement and limit, but only of life and existence:
the feminine human being.*

RAINER MARIA RILKE

Women are made, not born. Without enduring the fires
of individuation, some remain girls. Carefree and perhaps careless,
they remain wed to the ideals of childhood, the promise of perfection, the dream of human potential without limits. They remain
afloat without contact with the depths, full of optimistic smiles but
unable to bear the burdens of responsibility, the tensions of compromise, the sobering reality of adulthood.

Others become ladies. Outfitted with the symbols and matching
behaviors of traditional femininity, they shape themselves to cater
to the needs of others. Known in Jungian circles as anima women,
they willingly (though perhaps unknowingly) carry the projections
of men, taking on society's stereotypical images of beauty in order
to please men and stay connected with them.

Still others become pseudo-men. Known as animus women, they shape themselves to become independent, strong-willed, and productive. Popularly called "father's daughters," they discard their mothers' ways and identify more with the masculine world. One friend told me that, in order to deflect the constant seductive pressures of men in her early teens, she intentionally neutered her appearance and learned to act gruffly, like "one of the guys." Today she sports highly tailored clothes and has an air of uncompromising rigidity.

Animus women tend to be adept in society, competent and confident—except, perhaps, about their own femininity, which is not expressed in stereotypically attractive ways. Men want to befriend them and talk with them but go elsewhere when choosing romantic partners, which can leave these women feeling abandoned and perplexed. For many women, this experience may lead to a painful internal conflict between feeling powerful in the world and feeling attractive as a woman. But it also can wake up a woman to her deeper longing to be authentically feminine, to experience herself fully as a female human being and, at the same time, to be a strong, independent individual whose power and authority are rooted within her.

Today our society is so structured that it leaves this longing unmet. As Polly Young-Eisendrath and Florence Wiedemann point out in their book *Female Authority*, a woman cannot be both a healthy adult and an ideal woman. If she adopts a vocal, capable attitude, she is deemed too "masculine" and therefore becomes unattractive to men. Or she attracts soft, boyish men who seek her strength and clarity.

On the other hand, if she chooses a traditional style of femininity that is defined by men and a male-dominated culture, she is left dependent, powerless, and without choices. Either way, many women report feeling deeply dissatisfied *as women*.

Unfortunately, the archetypal images of depth psychology as described above don't meet women's deeper needs. To develop only the puella (eternal girl), the anima woman (Aphrodite/lover), or the animus woman (Athena/Amazon) is to leave our feminine souls deprived and without an answer to our pressing question:

What does it mean to be a woman in a man's world for those of us who don't wish to stay home and "become like our mothers" or to strive aggressively and "become like men"? What rites of passage will enable us to imagine and embody a kind of femininity that is consciously chosen—and that contains the benefits of our hard-won independence?

During several years of research for my book *To Be a Woman*, I uncovered clues that point to some answers. I believe that, in response to our unprecedented economic, educational, and psychological opportunities, we are witnessing the emergence of a new archetype of women's development. While Marion Woodman speaks of conscious femininity, I have chosen to call it the "conscious feminine," referring to the feminine's status as an archetypal principle rather than its modifying power as an adjective.

There are many gateways to the conscious feminine. They open continuously and simultaneously for a woman who is doing inner work. For example, we need to explore the roots of our mother-daughter wounds. Every girl's essential feelings about herself, her body, and her relations with others are rooted in her bond with her mother. She is our source, and she is our model of how to be a woman.

Because most mother–daughter relationships are sorely lacking in intimacy and/or independence, we find ourselves longing for the mother who never was—and who never could be. For this reason, as adults, we may want to learn to re-mother ourselves by finding, through a range of options, a means to awaken within ourselves those mothering qualities that we seek from outside. These options may include reconnecting with the young girl within, nurturing and mentoring by a surrogate mother such as a therapist or friend, revitalizing the relationship with our own mothers, undergoing motherhood as consciously as we can, or receiving the gifts of a wise grandmother.

As Kathie Carlson writes in *In Her Image*,

> we must be willing to *suffer* our mothers within us, to see to the roots of their behavior within us, and to forgive and transform it in ourselves. We also may be able to see through to our common lot as women, finding in our inner mothers responses to powerlessness, perversions of the spirit, or distorted potentials.

Becoming conscious of the negative effects of our mothers on our lives is not enough. Carlson adds, "It is as if we must take our mothers *in* and carry them psychologically as they once carried us physically."

In addition, we need to explore the roots of our father–daughter wounds. These roots run deep and include our intertwined connections with our personal fathers, significant other men, the patriarchal culture in which we live, and the internal masculine principle (or animus) within us. All these influences work together to form our images and expectations of men and the masculine domain. When we start to clarify and make conscious their hidden dynamics, we begin to re-father ourselves.

Like our mothers, our fathers could not meet the more-than-human needs we projected onto them as children. Sometimes, sadly, they could not even meet the all-too-human needs as well, perhaps because of their own insufficient parenting. So most women have greatly wounded feelings in relation to our fathers, ranging from intense hatred to idealized adoration.

To develop psychologically, we need to carefully examine these feelings and their ripple effects in our lives. We need to look closely at how we have owned and disowned our fathers' qualities, how we have identified with our fathers and become like them, how we have feared them, and how we have rebelled. For example, one woman told me she knowingly adopted some of her father's traits and even tried to fulfill his career dreams. Her sister, on the other hand, veered off in the opposite direction to thwart her father's wishes. In the first case, the woman tried to live his unlived life; in the second, she tried to escape his influence. However, from the point of view of individuation, each is trapped in a dynamic that is determined by intense feelings about him and not by her own adult choices.

Our fathers also have great impact on how we experience our feelings of power and attractiveness. A father's anima (his internal feminine image) can be carried unknowingly by a daughter, giving her a sense of sway over him, yet trapping her in his personal pictures of beauty and femininity. Alternatively, a father may devalue a daughter's style of femininity, criticizing her growing shapeliness or her tomboyish ways and destroying her budding feelings of self-confidence at a young age. At that time, she begins to yearn to be a woman other than the one she is.

Later in life, as we are attracted to lovers and mates, our fathers (now fully internalized within us) continue to affect our choices and behaviors. Women with absent fathers may project their imagined, perfect ideals onto men, forever searching for "the one that got away" who has the power to make things all right. Others seek their fa-

thers' opposites, their shadow qualities, determined, even unknowingly, not to re-create the original father-daughter relationship. For instance, I interviewed one woman whose father remains a
very loving and involved presence in her life. He is a great conversa-
tionalist who achieved success in business and highly values a knowledge of politics and history. For years, this woman has become
intimately involved with men who, unlike her father, remain un-
worldly and unaccomplished financially, and whose priority has been
to develop their emotional and psychic abilities. In effect, she has
sought out her father's opposite, almost as if one man of his kind is
enough in her life.

For these reasons and more, it is essential to begin to sort out
the complexities of this primary relationship. Whether we overly
identify with our fathers or overly reject them, we are not free to
create a femininity of our own until we detect his invisible hand on
our destiny.

A father and other father figures in a woman's life are also the
source of her animus—the masculine element within. So re-fathering
involves awakening and separating out this element in the unconscious. The archetypes of animus and anima are universal patterns
in the human psyche. Jung used the terms *animus* and *anima* as
they derive from the Latin *animare*, which means to enliven, because he believed they act like enlivening souls or spirits to men
and women.

Jungian analyst John A. Sanford, in his book *The Invisible Partners*, explains that a woman's animus is usually difficult for her to
detect. Like men who, identified primarily with the masculine, project their femininity onto women, so women, identified solely with
the feminine, project their unconscious masculine side onto men.
For this reason our animus appears to belong to someone else, perhaps to a lover who appears to be the living image of the "perfect
mate." Sanford calls these projected elements "the invisible partners" in our male-female relationships.

Sanford adds that if a woman projects onto a man her positive
animus image—the savior, hero, or spiritual guide—she overvalues
him. If he does the same and sees her as his ideal woman, their
projections match—and they call it love. In their fascination and
attraction, they may come to feel completed only through each other, remaining blind to the mechanism of projection that colors their
reality. If, however, she projects her negative animus image, he be-

comes a source of disappointment and betrayal, a "bastard"; if he does the same, she becomes a "bitch."

To begin to understand the role of animus projection in our relationships with men is to begin to discriminate between what is "in here" and what is "out there." When we learn to own the masculine side of ourselves, developing an inner source of autonomy and spirituality, we will rely less on men for these qualities. Then, the longing for the ideal mate, which causes so much suffering and which no living man can fully satisfy, can be met to some extent by these living parts of ourselves, which can become a rich source of creativity.

There is a flip side to a woman's projection of the masculine onto men: a woman's overidentification with the animus within. This psychological stage is widespread among women today. In our efforts to be free of stereotyped patterns of femininity, we have adopted instead a "masculinized" way of coping, thereby becoming "father's daughters."

Unfortunately, the language commonly used to explain this dynamic is overly simplistic and lacking the depth and complexity that our experience as women today deserves. It is said that a woman with a highly developed animus becomes overly aggressive, intellectual, and power-hungry in an effort to end patterns of passivity, dependency, and moodiness.

In the early days of feminism, for instance, many women wished to dispel the myth of biology as destiny and to prove women's capacities to think clearly, handle authority, and achieve what some men can achieve. As a result, some women grew addicted to the heady rush of productivity, becoming workaholics and taking it upon themselves to be "superwomen." Just as their mothers may have sacrificed work for love, they in turn may have sacrificed loving relationships in order to develop their careers. These women may find that their relationships with men suffer from a loss of clear gender identities. Some observers, such as poet Robert Bly, have remarked that during the heyday of feminism many men became more soft, receptive, and nurturing in response to women developing what men perceived as "masculine" traits.

The gift of this shift, of course, is that for the first time, large numbers of women have had and will continue to have a tremendous impact on a patriarchal culture. Through a greater use of our wide-ranging capacities, we have begun to leave our mark on every field of endeavor. In addition, and again for the first time, male-female relationships can become a vehicle for the growth of consciousness through an increasing understanding of projection and the withdrawal of those projections from our loved ones. The suffering that results from unclear gender roles brings with it the exploration of deeper forms of love, and more meaningful connections that can emerge only after the anima-animus projections have been brought to consciousness.

When women no longer place the masculine outside of themselves onto men, the animus is no longer unconscious. When men no longer place the feminine outside of themselves onto women, they are no longer in the clutches of the unconscious anima, forever searching for the ideal woman. This, then, portends a huge shift in our intimate relationships, as well as in our creative inner lives. And it calls on us to develop a new language that goes beyond Jung's classification, which was more appropriate for his time—"when men were men and women were women."

We are in the midst of these psychological transitions today. Many women have emerged from an unconscious identification with the traditional feminine mode into a more focused, active "masculine" style. At the same time, the next step also has begun: women now report feeling dissatisfied with the limits of these newfound ways, mourning our lost femininity.

Jungian analyst June Singer calls this syndrome "the sadness of the successful woman." It stems, she says, from losing touch with our feminine instincts by giving priority to developing individual identity at the cost of relationship values. Singer is not proposing that women undergo a regressive return to being full-time caretakers; rather, she is suggesting that deep feelings of conflict will erupt when life is one-sided, such as when the goals of career do not validate the feminine self.

This trend toward dissatisfaction with career-driven lives signifies a new stage in women's development. We can predict the beginning of the breakdown of animus identification, and with it the beginning of the emergence of the conscious feminine.

Aside from working to heal her personal history, a woman may want to explore the mythological realm as well. Today many women are redefining spiritual life by reawakening the divine feminine. Growing up as young girls, we are told by adults that we were made in the image of God. Yet, in our newly forming imaginations, the face of God looks more like a smiling, kind, white-haired grandpa or a stern, finger-wagging old patriarch than the face we see in the mirror. As a result, God is something Other, outside of ourselves—and boys and men have a closer link to him than we do.

However, we *are* made in the image of God—our God. We are what we imagine. The form we give to our divine ancestors in our collective and personal imaginations is the form we aspire to become. If we imagine a male figure who is perfect and all-powerful, we hold these qualities as ideal. If we imagine a female who is bountiful, compassionate, and generative, we exalt these qualities. If we imagine a fluid partnership, a male/female divinity in which we embrace each other while embracing all of life and death, then the power of the masculine and the power of the feminine will both be honored.

Tragically, for us, the many faces of the divine have been reduced to a one-dimensional snapshot. For women, this singular God with male gender has been a terrible loss; our imaginations have been impoverished, our abilities to identify with the divine diminished. Ultimately, life under the rule of God the father came to mean that much of what had been valued in the female experience during earlier times—such as sexuality, menstruation, birth, mothering, menopause, aging, ritual, and female generative power—lost its meaning and its sacred authority. Ultimately, "female power" became an oxymoron; a woman can identify with God only by denying her own identity. That means that to be a woman is not to participate in the divine.

As a result of the movement toward a feminine spirituality, the Goddess has emerged, whether we conceive of her as a single transcendent figure or as plural goddesses representing the many energies of life. She brings us a vision of Woman that stands outside the walls of patriarchy. She affirms our bodies, minds, hearts, powers, and sisterhood.

To imagine the divine feminine is to meet a deeply felt need and to turn our priorities topsy-turvy. In her book *The Goddess*, Christine Downing explains it this way:

> To be fed only male images of the divine is to be badly nourished. We are starved for images which recognize the sacredness of the Feminine and the complexity, richness, and nurturing power of female energy.... We seek images that affirm that the love women receive

from women, from mother, sister, daughter, lover, friend, reaches as deep and is as trustworthy, necessary, and sustaining as is the love symbolized by father, brother, son, or husband. We long for images which name as authentically feminine courage, creativity, loyalty, self-confidence, resilience, steadfastness, capacity for clear insight, inclination for solitude, and the intensity for passion.

Perhaps the emerging archetype of the conscious feminine can add to the rich legacy of archetypal images we have uncovered from ancient cultures. The feminine is, in Edward C. Whitmont's words, the "priestess of the fullness of life." She changes life's meaning and direction. She initiates a new relationship to Self, to Other, and to the Divine.

With this comes a shift in our relationship to matter, to our bodies, and to the earth. Jungian analyst Marion Woodman points out that the world has never known the archetype of conscious mother; I would add it has not known the archetype of conscious mature woman. We need to contact her, as Woodman says, "because the power that drives the patriarchy, the power that is raping the earth, the power drive behind addictions has to be transformed. There has to be a counterbalance to all that frenzy, annihilation, ambition, competition, and materialism."

The paradox of the patriarchy has peaked: an underdeveloped sense of self coupled with an overdeveloped technology has created the crisis we face. In response, the feminine has appeared in many forms: a renewed respect for the earth, for relationship, for children; a surge of interest in healing, compassion, and altruism. Ecology itself implies action in the context of relationship, a quintessentially feminine kind of action.

As the archetype of the conscious feminine becomes more conscious, its allied archetype changes as well. We have never known the conscious masculine either. We have confused the patriarchal power principle, which controls and shapes nature at any cost, with the masculine. The masculine, too, suffers from imbalance due to the loss of the feminine, and it, too, may become renewed, clarified, and reborn in us. With its emergence, we have a very real opportunity to do spiritual alchemy, to meet the mystery of the Other in the sacred marriage.

Christine Downing

The Crone

"Crone"—the very word stirs up profound ambivalence in me. On the one hand, I feel myself unworthy of this designation— not wise enough, not completed enough, not old enough, not transcendent enough. On the other hand, I feel myself still too powerful, too active, too happy and healthy to be her.

I know that the Crone is often identified with a longed-for but to some degree unrealizable attainment of a fulfilled wisdom and power. But I'm not happy with a view that focuses only on the positive side of the archetype and ignores her incompletion, impotence, and vulnerability. Such avoidance of the dark side seems to occur when we allow archetypes to exist independently of actual lives or actual myths.

I suspect that my disavowal of the Crone is somehow integral to what this archetype implies, requires, gives, and withholds. I believe that my disavowal is not mine alone. I see my mother, almost ninety, still warding her off. As I read the accounts of women much older than I am, attempting to articulate their experience of being seventy, eighty, ninety, I discover that for them, too, there is acknowledgment of the Crone and denial. Perhaps this is because the Crone is inherently a transcendent figure. (The Greeks, I recall, recognized old age as specifically liminal, embodying the threshold between life and death, not so much as a final stage of life but as the passage away from life.[1])

She stirs ambivalence in us. Women of my age inevitably remember the negative connotations that "crone" and its analogues, "hag," "witch," "harpy," "shrew," "vixen," and "virago" used to evoke. These words referred to ugly, repulsive, and terrifying women who were in compact with evil spirits. We have celebrated the reclaiming of these words by such feminists as Mary Daly and Barbara Walker who encourage us to think of crones as long-lasting survivors, as wise and powerful, self-affirming women, as wanton, willful, intractable women, as women who refuse to yield to patriarchal power and thus represent all that men find terrifying in independent women.[2]

Yet there is something too simple in this positive feminist view of the Crone. It equates the Crone with the power of women-identified women which men find frightening and ugly and consequently vilify. But it doesn't seem to fully recognize the Crone as the *old* woman. The sense we get is that the Crone is woman as resolutely *not*-mother, perhaps *never*-mother, at the least *after*-mother. These women, more or less my contemporaries, are proud to call themselves crones, but in a way that seems to ignore the realities of true old age and the dark side of the Crone archetype. I'm less sure that only men are frightened of the Crone, for she may represent something in ourselves that frightens us, and that we avoid by claiming that we are already crones.

Thus it seems important to be honest about where I am now, just on the edge of my sixtieth birthday. There are valid reasons for my resisting the relevance of the Crone archetype to *me*. I certainly have little experience yet of the most important losses that older women emphasize: the loss of a familiar body, the loss of friends, losses which in sum comprise the loss of one's world. Indeed, I am struck by the resentment some "real" Crones feel at the readiness of the midlife woman to speak authoritatively about old women and thus "unconsciously silence the inherent radicalism of the only one who can tell her how it really is."[3]

Although I recognize the inappropriateness of a premature identification with the Crone, I also see the dangers in denying that identification. It feels important to look honestly at what is being avoided in such denial. The same women who write so passionately against younger women's usurping their right to define old age also protest vigorously against the self-deceptions involved in "passing" for younger than one is. So I realize I need to ask, What fear, what rage, what misogyny am I hiding from in regarding the Crone as Other?

Last summer I went to a gathering of women who, for at least that afternoon, were self-identifying as "crones." It struck me to find that almost all were about my age but that what most of us wanted to talk about was our mothers! I have found this true of so many of my contemporaries. We are engaged in our relation to our mothers as we have not been since we became mothers ourselves. And what so many of us voice is, first, concern with the unhappiness, the rage, the helplessness, and the resented dependence on us evidenced by so many of our mothers; and, second, but somehow even more forcibly, our fear of becoming them. Whereas once we may have said, "I don't want to grow up to be like her," now we find ourselves saying, "I don't want to grow old like her." We know that is not rational; *I* know it's not rational. I have made very different decisions in my life from those my mother made in hers. There is little likelihood that I would feel the same anger at gifts not actualized, at recognition not received, at status not acquired, at a lifepartner for whom I'd "sacrificed" my life, all of which fuels my mother's obsessive litany. I feel deep empathy for her; I understand that her rage is one that feminist analysis justifies—yet it terrifies me, partly because I can do nothing to assuage it. To confirm her view of the real tragedy in her life seems only to keep her more mired in her sorrow and anger. To remind her of how creative her life *has* been doesn't seem to honor the not-enoughness of how this feels to her now. To suggest that the regretted shape of her life is in part the consequence of choices *she* made, not entirely due to what others imposed on her, makes no sense to her and is not something she is willing to explore. I feel for and with her, and I am angry at her not only for being unhappy but because I am afraid I will become her. I am so aware of how even now she is *in* me—in my body, my gait, my smile, my frown, my gestures. Perhaps someday she will take me over.

I know many other old women, some of whom seem much happier than my mother. I am moved and impressed by the continuing creativity into advanced old age of women such as Meridel LeSueur, Georgia O'Keeffe, Louise Nevelson, and Martha Graham. Nevertheless, *the* exemplar of the Crone for me remains my mother. It seems that somehow, as one approaches old age, disentangling the personal mother from the archetype, from the Crone, becomes difficult again. I thought I had done *that* long ago. But it is still there to be done again.

The Crone's body, her relation to death, her power, her rage, her wisdom, and her memories—these are the themes that engagement with the archetype brings to the fore. In her simple and wise book *Old Age*, Helen M. Luke writes of the three gifts reserved for the old: the changes taking place in the body, helpless rage, and memory. She acknowledges that it may sometimes be difficult to remember that these things are "gifts."[4] Perhaps it is precisely the way in which each is blessing and curse that makes them so profoundly relevant to an understanding of what constitutes the full meaning of the Crone archetype.

In looking at the significance of the bodily changes associated with this archetype, it might be relevant to go back to the etymology that links "crone" to the Latin, *carn* ("flesh"), and thus see it as cognate with "carnal," "carnival," and "incarnate." I like this recognition that crones are *embodied*, that we cannot do justice to the Crone unless we associate her with her aging body and expect that her soul-state will be related to her body-state.

This, like so much else, is two-edged. We women have been socialized to attach much significance to our body's appearance, and thus may find accepting our body's aging difficult. Obviously I am best off in those moments when I can become genuinely interested in the physical changes occurring in my body: the brown spots that cover my arms and chest, the prominent veins on my hands, the flabby belly, the facial lines that record my anxieties and my delights, the skin hanging loose on my upper arm, the flat and flaccid buttocks, the thinning pubic hair. Barbara Macdonald moves me deeply with how naturally she seems able to do this:

> I say to myself frequently in wonder, "This is my body doing this thing." I cannot stop it. I don't even know what it is doing. I wouldn't know how to direct it. My own body is going through a process that only my body knows about. I never grew old before, never died. I don't really know how it's done.[5]

This reminds me of how I felt when I was pregnant: in awe at my body's knowledge of how to do this. I have also felt in awe about menstruating, orgasm, and nursing but had not thought to feel likewise about aging until I read these words! My body knows how to do this: it will teach me. But such acceptance is not easily won. The acceptance we do achieve may cohabit with regret, based on something much deeper than identification with youthful attractiveness and sexual allure—the regret at being mortal. The body that knows how to age is a body preparing to die.

The old woman not only has to come to terms with her own oncoming death but also with the way she is viewed as a representative of death, as death-bringer, not only by men but also by women. Indeed, I believe we need images of death which honor our fear of death as well as our acceptance. The notion of women as unambiguously reconciled with death is too simple. It may be true that we women have an easier time accepting our human participation in the natural cycles of life, death, and renewal than do men, but I'm not persuaded it is easy even for us.

I suspect that the longing for the Crone to mean a fully worked-through acceptance of death is connected to the persistent fantasy of the possibility of a truly *completed* life. Carolyn Heilbrun believes this fantasy has particular power over women: "We women have lived too much with closure...There always seems to loom the possibility of something being over, settled, sweeping clear the way for contentment. This is the delusion of the passive life."[6]

Embracing the Crone, making her our ally, seems in so many ways to be more difficult than we might wish. We want so much affirmation from her that in the end it will be easy. We want her to stand before us not only as a woman fearless before death but as a woman powerful in life. Yet as I have already suggested I have deep reservations about an emphasis on the Crone's *power*, especially when we forget how much of the Crone's peculiar power lies in her acknowledgment of weakness, her need for others, and her hatred of that fragility and dependence.

Helen Luke speaks of the task of learning to live *without* the powers we have spent a lifetime building up, "powers which will be taken from us anyway in the fulfilling of the pattern of life and death." She sees the power of the old to depend on their willingness to accept their dependence on others and to renounce the will to power, the "will to dominate people or things or our own souls." For if we continue to depend on the ego or the creative spirit to provide us with a sense of meaning and achievement, old age will become nightmare and despair.[7]

Luke mentions "helpless rage" as one of the gifts of old age, but without the unquestioning approbation of women's anger and rage that sometimes accompanies reflections on the Crone. She notes how often "the ego will endure the worst agonies of neurotic misery rather than consent to the death of even a small part of its demand or its sense of importance." For her the rage becomes "a training ground" for learning the difference between what she calls "depression" and "suffering." It is an occasion for learning to see differently, for coming to see that the darkness we project onto others or onto circumstances is our own, yet also for winning freedom from an arrogant guilt about our failures that supposes we *should* have been able to live free of culpability. Ideally, Luke suggests, the old would arrive at a transformed rage that would accept the givenness of their suffering—and yet would still welcome release from it.[8]

Just as the power of the Crone is a strange kind of power, so her wisdom seems to be a strange kind of wisdom, permeated with a recognition of how little one knows, of how, apart from that acknowledgment, one is really no wiser than one ever was.

The Crone is busily engaged with her memories, with telling her story to herself and to all who will listen. The Greeks believed that what occupied the psyches, the souls of the dead, in Hades was remembering—not new experience, new thoughts, but simply going over and over the already lived. Remembering becomes re-membering, putting the pieces back together to make a new whole. I have listened, as perhaps most of us have, to my mother going over and over the same vividly recalled events from her years as a child, as a young woman, as middle-aged woman. Often, from outside, it seems as though no progress is being made, no new insights gained; often, from inside, it feels as though this remembering is almost a passive experience. Yet, as I listen to my mother, I know what she is doing is clearly *work*, not just passive recall. Many of the memories are painful, often more painful than the actual event. She is learning to see them differently, to see herself differently. But the new perspective must be rediscovered over and over again before it is fully absorbed. Luke sees such re-evaluating of our past as the point of such remembering. We may discover to our horror that much of what we've done was really done for recognition, comfort, or spiritual merit; that much we thought virtuous or kind really brought harm to others; and that in most of our actions there was as much evil as good.[9]

As I have tried to listen attentively to what old women have said or written of their aging experience, I have come to believe that no one is a crone, in the sense of knowing what it is to be one. Seventy-year-old women and even those in their eighties and nineties are still *discovering* what it's all about. In the words of Meridel LeSueur, we are all but initiates in the "rites of ancient ripening."[10]

IV

Archetypal Roles

Perhaps the most familiar of all archetypal images is the figure of the hero. Joseph Campbell's *The Hero with a Thousand Faces* introduced us to the ever-recurring pattern of the hero's journey and to the almost infinite variety of ways in which this pattern is lived out. Campbell's exploration also made evident how the archetype shapes the lives of mythological figures like Odysseus or the Buddha, as well as our own.

More recently this focus on the hero as the archetype of archetypes has been put into question. In his essay, Professor of Liberal Studies Daniel C. Noel shows how constrictive this archetype can be and how it seems to impose (or reimpose) precisely the egocentric model of the Self from which an archetypal psychology would free us. He writes as a man who acknowledges the power of the archetype, struggles with its limitations, and discovers that the hero has his place after all, even if it is not the only place.

Annis Pratt, author of the book *Archetypal Patterns in Women's Fictions*, notes the degree to which the heroic quest as described by Campbell and others is a *male* quest. She seeks to delineate the archetypal pattern characteristic of *female* quests. She finds that there seem to be two quite different patterns, one characteristic of younger women, which focuses on the social world, and the other having a more spiritual focus, whose participants are usually in the second half of life.

We have noted earlier how archetypes often appear in pairs: puer and senex usually appear together, as do persona and shadow. Similarly, the hero typically appears engaged in battle, complemented by the monster. In her study of children's dreams, Denyse Beaudet, author of the book *Encountering the Monster: Pathways in Children's Dreams*, shows that even in young children this monster appears as a figure in the inner landscape. It is through engagement with the monster that a more resilient Self begins to emerge.

Jungian analyst Lyn Cowan suggests that another counterpart to the hero is the victim. Her essay helps us to see this archetypal role in a fresh way. We immediately recognize the victim's negative aspect, but Cowan reveals a deeper and more creative side. Attending to the victim may teach us to acknowledge and honor the inescapability of human woundedness and limitations.

Of course, not all archetypal roles are versions of the hero or other figures constellated by the hero archetype. Professor of Religious Studies William G. Doty gives careful consideration to the trickster's appearance in the mythic traditions of cultures all over the world. In his piece he explores how this archetype acts in our own lives to upset our comfortable assumptions about ourselves, to trick us into growing and changing even when we have no longing to do so or believe we aren't ready. The trickster is the psychopomp who appears, as Jung said the gods do, bidden or not.

Following Doty is Jungian analyst Jan Clanton Collins's look at the shaman, the healer figure of traditional cultures, as a prototype of the modern psychotherapist. She suggests how important it is not to see this archetype as existing only "out there" in past or alien cultures, or only in the professional clinician. Like James Hillman, she wishes to free the psyche from its imprisonment in the consulting room by helping us to discover what she calls "the inner shaman."

My essay on the healer and Jungian analyst Adolf Guggenbühl-Craig's piece on the invalid share this concern and emphasize the importance of seeing healer and invalid as coexisting in each of us. Without this recognition, there is little hope of responding to archetypal experience in a way that might truly reshape our lives.

Mary E. Hunt describes how attending to the archetype of friendship moves us beyond a narcissistic concern with *my* soul, *my* psyche, *my* transformation to a recognition of our interdependence with one another, a recognition of how much we need from others and how much we have to give. This archetype reminds us that we are connected to others not only in the depths of our souls but also *here*, in the social world where we encounter actual living others.

Hunt doesn't say this, but she might have: we need to learn to befriend the archetypal images, too—not only those we've focused on in this book, but the many others that live in us and through us. As we noted earlier, there is no definitive list of archetypes, and each of us would probably make our own list of the most important ones. But all archetypes need befriending. For, as Hillman says, "we cannot get to the soul of the image without love for the image."[1]

Daniel C. Noel

Re-Visioning
The Hero

More than anyone else in recent years, the late mythologist Joseph Campbell has instructed us on the Hero's role. The mythologies of all cultures, Campbell said, highlight figures, often seen as semi-divine, who participate in a three-part journey. In the guise of local images, these figures pursue a quest that is essentially identical and therefore reflective of a deep structure in human culture, a single archetypal motif, or "monomyth."

At the beginning of the quest, a typical Hero-figure, troubled by the status quo at home, is lured or shocked by circumstance to leave the family and the familiar, to initiate an adventure into parts unknown. Confronting threshold guardians as he departs, his journey may entail that he "die" to achieve separation, so the adventure takes place in an underworld or supernatural domain of terrors and wonders, gods and demons. His initiation requires him to deal with these as tests or trials, aided in his struggle by a wise mentor or helping animal spirits. At the lowest point of his underworld ordeal, the Hero must face his supreme challenge: slaying the dragon or stealing the boon, rescuing the princess or finding the treasure. His rewards for succeeding are great—consummation in a sacred marriage, reconciliation with the father, even becoming a god himself.

But there is a third and crucial stage of the quest beyond departure and initiation. The Hero must sacrifice the supernatural benefits of his personal triumph and return with his elixir to the world of ordinary mortals. This return is the true justification and goal for the entire journey: society as well as the Hero needs spiritual restoration, and he must bring back the boon for his fellows, who can be the family, the village, the nation, or, in the case of Jesus, Mohammed, or the Gautama Buddha, the world.

Campbell's picture of this archetypal protagonist, so central to his entire notion of the power of myth, can be persuasive. From the fairy tales, mythic legends, and religious texts of traditional cultures, to the arts, sciences, and popular media of our own time, warriors, sages, and saints inspire us, evoking our admiration and emulation. The life stories of such men as Martin Luther King, Jr., or Luke Skywalker—real or fictional—still feel today "larger than life." This is because, Campbell would argue, such a figure

> has been able to battle past his personal and local historical limitations to the generally valid, normally human forms. Such a one's visions, ideas, and inspirations come pristine from the primary springs of human life and thought. Hence they are eloquent, not of the present, disintegrating society and psyche, but of the unquenched source through which society is reborn.[1]

In addition, Campbell has reminded us that these cosmically creative powers may personify themselves in modern life in seemingly humble forms as people like ourselves: "The latest incarnation of Oedipus, the continued romance of Beauty and the Beast, stand this afternoon on the corner of Forty-second Street and Fifth Avenue, waiting for the traffic light to change."[2]

Moreover, the separation, initiation, and return of the ancient or modern Hero can be our personal inner adventure, too. In the sentences preceding this much quoted passage Campbell had already pointed to the strong psychological reverberations of the Hero pattern, its reflection in the development of our individual personality. "Freud, Jung, and their followers have demonstrated irrefutably that the logic, the heroes, and the deeds of myth survive into modern times. In the absence of an effective general mythology, each of us has his private, unrecognized, rudimentary, yet secretly potent pantheon of dream."[3]

Erich Neumann, a distinguished follower of C. G. Jung, spelled out in the greatest detail the relation between the cultural Hero-quest and the personal psychological process. Neumann's *The Origins and History of Consciousness* is a sprawling two-volume work that sets forth the stages in the evolution of consciousness both for Western culture and the individuals within it. Extrapolating from Jung's concept of "individuation," the development of each person's unique selfhood, Neumann reads the Hero's mythic journey psychologically as "the history of [the] self-emancipation of the ego, struggling to free itself from the power of the unconscious to hold its own against overwhelming odds."[4] Since the unconscious is seen in classical Jungian terms as "maternal," the struggle of the Hero is to be born from, and then to overcome and leave, the Great Mother of myth (or her symbolic analogues, such as the all-encircling "uroboros" dragon with its tail in its mouth).

Once it has moved out from the maternal unconscious and established itself in the world of opposites, the heroic ego faces the final stage of what Neumann calls "centroversion": the transformative return to a new relationship of equality with the unconscious, a relationship that promotes the balanced unity of mature selfhood. For Neumann, Western culture is both *filled with* Hero myths and *constitutes* a vast Hero myth itself in the evolution of its consciousness from primitive animism through skeptical rationalism to the prospect of a harmoniously centered interaction between science and spirituality. The three stages of movement toward the centroversion of culture, on the one hand, and toward the centroversion of personality, on the other hand, are models for each other.

Such a summary of Neumann's psychohistorical rendition of the Hero's adventure hardly does justice to his two-volume account. Like Joseph Campbell's work, Neumann's is characterized by multiple examples of heroic symbolism supposed by the author to exemplify the one master pattern, and there is much to applaud in both men's theories. Certainly they make the aggressive actions of the Hero seem called for in the name of onward development in the first half of life for the individual and the culture, while the final stage in each case is presented as an admirable reconciliation of opposites, a fruitful marriage for all. Indeed, it is difficult to fault Joseph Campbell's vision of forty years ago that "the hero is the man of self-achieved submission."[5]

However, I have developed an aversion to this archetypal figure that has at least two major sources. First, I found feminist criticisms of the often subtle machinations—and not-so-subtle machismo—of patriarchal culture impossible to isolate from my understanding of Jungian psychology in terms of traditional religious symbolism. As a scholar of religion and culture employing Jungian perspectives, I was forced by these criticisms to "re-vision" what Jung and successors like Campbell and Neumann had to say about the spiritual heroism of personality development. In doing so, I came to see the Hero as a deeply problematic model of the self.

For one thing, the Hero is inevitably male and unfortunately macho. Despite Campbell's reference to his self-willed submission and the ways in which one might speak of a final balance in the Hero's dealings with the mothering depths, despite the examples of gentle Asian mystics as heroes or women in childbirth, and despite the fuzzy boundaries between the Hero and such other more pleasing archetypal roles as the Explorer or the Magician—I believe that placing the Hero at the center of selfhood is like installing a dull-witted but dominating warrior male to control the psyches of each of us, women as well as men, people of color as well as whites, old as well as young.

Psychologist Carol Gilligan and education theorist Mary Belenky and her colleagues have published works that convinced me that women have other ways of growing and knowing than that accounted for in the Hero model.[6] Feminist psychologists of religion Naomi Goldenberg and Demaris Wehr focused directly on Jungian theory, questioning the viability of psychomythic categories like "the feminine" as applied to the real lives of individual women.[7]

Philosopher Michael Zimmerman sums up this first source of my distaste for the Hero archetype in his work on ecofeminism:

> The "history of consciousness," then, has turned out to be the story of *man's* development. The heroic male struggles violently to free himself from the clutches of the subconscious and collective powers of the Great Mother. Only by the matricidal act of slaying the beast (representing the Great Mother) does the hero achieve individuation. The fierceness of the ego's repression of the female, the bodily, and the natural is directly proportional to the ego's recognition of its ultimate *dependent* status. But the anxious ego finally claims to be independent of everything, including the Divine.

Zimmerman then adds that "most feminists... have concluded that Jung and Neumann's history of individuation, despite its critique of the lopsidedness of patriarchal consciousness, is itself so colored by masculinist categories that it cannot be of help in developing an alternative conception of individuation."[8]

A second source of my negative view of the archetypal Hero was at least as influential. Another of Jung's followers—albeit one who had strikingly deconstructed his thought along with psychology in general—offered a critique of all ego-centered ideals of selfhood. James Hillman's writings underscored how insidiously such a sense of selfhood can permeate even the benign goals of harmony between ego and unconscious.

This happens, says Hillman, for many reasons. Especially important among these are our tendencies to envision only one sort of ego, to see the ego as heroic in only one way, and to view the relation to the rest of the self as too centrally controlling. In holding to this ego-dominated, monocentric sense of self, we forget that the ego is itself a heroic *fantasy* of modern psychology, not a solid empirical fact. And when we equate the ego with the mythic Hero in a partial acknowledgment of this fantasy factor, we forget that heroes in Greek myth (the "home base" of Western heroism) had gods and goddesses as the controlling forces they were serving.

In *Re-Visioning Psychology*, Hillman seeks to honor the imaginal priority of these other forces by depicting selfhood as "soul-making" in a nonheroic psychology (soulGreek *psyche*Latin *anima*) which allows for the reality of our wounded, ambivalent, and scarcely controllable lives, grounded in the ongoing flow of multiple fantasy images. Here ego-consciousness is not the domineering force, pretending to a secular divinity; room and reverence are given as well to "anima-consciousness," an awareness in touch with the confusing moods of imagining and the assurance of mortality.

This nonheroic consciousness is triggered, according to Hillman, by something we experience in our actual lives almost every day (and find reflected in our nightmares, if not regularly masked in less frightening dreams): anxieties and perplexities, aches and pains—in short, "the symptom," which he refers to as "that thing so foreign to the ego, that thing which ends the rule of the hero." The process of *heeding* the symptom as a step toward anima-consciousness or soul-making he then calls "pathologizing": "Pathologizing forces the soul to a consciousness of itself as different from the ego and its life—a consciousness that obeys its own laws of metaphorical enactment in intimate relation with death."[9]

Hillman has said that "the Hero archetype is active, struggling, victorious. But the soul makes that Hero vulnerable because it is the place where he is susceptible to disease or death, to falling or weakening. . . . Usually whenever the word 'soul' is used, it evokes another set of things. It evokes love, emotions, dying, value, beauty."[10] Such evocations, it seems to me, contribute to a more authentically holistic ideal of self than does the rulership of the heroic ego.

Although such feminists as Naomi Goldenberg and Demaris Wehr have found things to praise in Hillman's writing, he seldom makes overtly feminist statements. However, his critique of ego-heroics can be combined with the insights of women scholars who point to the male bias in the narrative of the Hero. Hillman says:

> Through this narrative we've set up the Mother to be grasping and clutching, because we say we must leave her. But she may be saying, "You don't have to leave me. I'm nature and rocks. I'm the Earth. I'm eternal love. I'm constantly sending up new things. You don't have to leave me. . . . The most important thing is that the Mother is whatever the Mother is. She may want to hold you forever, but you have to learn what that holding is. Why must the Hero pull away, cut away from her?[11]

With these powerful arguments arrayed against the Hero model of selfhood in my mind, I was stymied when Christine Downing asked me to write this essay. In fact, I was fully prepared to turn down the request.

But that night I had a dream. At first, after I awakened the next day, I could remember no details except the knowledge that George Foreman is in my dream. Soon, however, I recalled a dream episode in which I am tempted to buy some fattening food item, and a woman friend with me in the store says "Look at you." I wondered whether she meant my face looked fat or she was referring judgmentally to my being about to go off my diet.

But I knew that "looking at" myself could involve a more important self-exploration: a call to inspect my identity was being issued by this dream. And George Foreman, a former heavyweight boxing champion in the day-world whom I had not thought of for months, had arrived to play some part in that identity.

Throughout the day I tried to think of what I had heard about Foreman's life from the media in the last year or two. He was, by 1990, an aging and overweight giant attempting to make a comeback sixteen years after losing his championship to Muhammed Ali. During the three years of his comeback—having been out of the ring for a full decade—he easily defeated a succession of opponents but was not taken very seriously as a contender. His victims had been carefully chosen for their ineptitude, it seemed, and he was now in his forties, head shaven, and forty pounds heavier than he had been as a lean young champion.

Yet everyone agreed he was still a puncher of formidable power. Perhaps more significantly, his attitude was reported as being very different from the uncommunicative, sullen stance with which he faced the earlier world he had conquered in the seventies. In the interim he had become a lay preacher in a conservative Christian denomination and appeared to be enjoying every bit of new notoriety he was earning.

Here, I mused uncomfortably, reviewing this information, might be an archetype image of *my hero*—a term that had occurred to me as I woke up from the dream—or of my inner heroism. Beyond my academic reservations about the Hero archetype as a *concept*, perhaps the dreaming soul was sending a message that a style of heroism personified by this massive brown Buddha-like man was helping to sustain my selfhood. If so, George Foreman seemed no ordinary warrior, earnest and armored like Rocky Balboa or Rambo. Involved though he was in a violently male world which, morally and intellectually, I found quite reprehensible, my "fore-man" also appeared to be offering a different definition of how one might be out front, in charge, heroic.

Two weeks after the dream I received a kind of confirmation of these possibilities. The real-life George Foreman, who provided the distant day residue in my dreaming and the raw material to imagine it onward into the future, was fighting on television. I was ready and wielding the remote control for my vcr, taping a boxing match in the service of soul-making. What I learned initially was that "the laughter has stopped": George's opponents were becoming more credible, and with twenty-two knockouts in his twenty-three–fight comeback he was now considered a viable contender for the world title. His bout was in London against Terry Anderson, a respected heavyweight twelve years his junior.

The British media and George Foreman, meanwhile, had been having a love affair. Headlines about the "punching preacher" included his own facetious quip, "I used to eat twelve eggs for breakfast. Now I'm on a diet. I only eat eleven." Videotaped at various London venues signing autographs and eating ice cream cones, pointing to the Houses of Parliament and then to himself ("Big Ben—Big

George," he proclaimed), he was relaxed and joking in a pre-fight interview. He remarked that for the people who come out to see him at age forty-two, "It's not about boxing." When the other top heavyweights fight, "It doesn't mean anything . . . it's just another sports card. But if George Foreman becomes the heavyweight champion of the world," he continued with a raised fist and a sweet smile, "everyone can have a grand toast with Geritol." He also poked fun at another contender for "lifting weights and trying to look like a he-man." And then he took his 259 pounds into the ring and knocked out 230-pound Terry Anderson in the first round.

Afterward the TV announcer emphasized George's power, his experience, and what was called "this carefree attitude—every fight is not a do-or-die situation, having to prove himself as he did years ago." For his part, George was barely sweating but gracious in victory, complimenting the force of Anderson's punches and adding that "all these youngsters think they're going to wear the old man out, but that's not necessarily so." Besides, there were other things than boxing on his mind even at this moment of macho triumph: "They have grand food over here and I didn't come over to Europe to sacrifice. I'm going to eat."

By the time I had heard that the Foreman–Anderson fight was going to be on TV, I had already reversed my decision about writing this essay. Just reflecting on my dream had convinced me that the psyche held a different opinion on the matter than my intellectual reluctance. The Hero was alive and well somewhere inside me. I had maintained the notion that the Hero was the representative of a warrior ideal, which was unacceptably unidimensional and politically incorrect. But perhaps I, in my conscious ego-attitude, was being heroic in this rigid, controlling fashion, embodying the very sort of heroism I had damned as definitive. I was as humorlessly inflexible and sacrificially moralistic about the Hero as I had been about dieting.

My political rectitude could also stand some re-visioning; its tendency to self-righteous dogmatism was ripe for seeing through. Here was a non-young, non-white Hero, and while he was certainly a strongly male figure—George referred to having fathered nine children—he did not appear to be imposing his pattern on women's psychological development. (It was the woman in my dream who advised me to look at myself, which could mean focusing on my own men's issues just now aside from the legitimate grievances of feminism.)

To be sure, it is possible that the Hero is not the right category for the image of "George Foreman" that undid my clenched resistance. Perhaps this was the "positive Shadow," a Jungian concept I had always found somewhat baffling. A powerful dark man had arrived to oppose a conscious attitude, not as a menace but with a soft elbow to my psychic ribs and a comic summons to "come off it." Alternatively, despite the fact that I am older than George and possess more formal education, his stress on aging and his implied lessons on how to go about it might place him in the role of Wise Old Man.

Or maybe the *process* of archetypal manifestation just allows for far greater variation than we often suppose: the Hero does truly come in a thousand guises, including many that are mixed with other archetypal imagery. It is these specific faces, in fact, that I suspect most need our attention. Concerning the real experience of selfhood (in this case mine), the particular manifestations of archetypal heroism decisively inform the meaning of its supposed essence. We need to ponder the idea that the Hero is a George Foreman–figure, and vice-versa.

That kind of specificity, after all, is the hallmark of the fantasy image, which in turn is, as Jung insisted, soul herself.[12] As an old man, Jung wrote that serving soul and her images in self-development does not require us to abandon the Hero but to relativize his hold on the ego when he, and it, become dictatorial.[13] In his splendid study *The Quest of Self in the Collected Poems of Wallace Stevens*, Michael Sexson points out that

> ego psychology and the hero myth, with their literalistic pretensions, are also movements in imagination, in soul, in anima. When this is forgotten, there is a temptation to fall into the same kind of literalism by accusing them of "killing" the imagination and then attempting to "overthrow," "go beyond," or otherwise "defeat" them.[14]

Those words from a decade ago—which I only recalled and reread after my dream—anticipate my own initial forgetfulness and temptation. Today, however, my conclusion accords with his, and I would simply add that the imagination can even see the Hero as shading off from single-mindedness, as being capable of relinquishing control to the many other archetypes of a multicentered self.

Annis Pratt

The Female
Hero

Female heroes are engaged in two kinds of quests: the younger hero's quest for development, which Carol Christ calls the "social quest," and the rebirth journey, more commonly undertaken in midlife or later. Christ defines the first as "a search for self in which the protagonist begins in alienation and seeks integration into a human community where he or she can develop more fully." The second involves "a relation to cosmic power or powers."[1]

In studying fiction written by British and American women, I have found that women authors often subordinate female heroes to gender constraints at an even more crippling level than the authors experience in their own lives. I discovered, however, that women's fictions are not entirely determined by the enclosing patriarchal culture. Even the most conservative authors weave into their texts strands of a more holistic feminine possibility that subverts men's ideas of what women should be and do. In their accounts of young women engaged in the social quest, even the most feminist authors depict their protagonists as weighed down by patriarchal prescriptions that limit their development of authentic adult selfhood, so that the female hero is forced to grow down rather than up. But in novels of transformation and rebirth, women authors often posit a more complete psychological maturation of women heroes than patriarchy approves. Women's fiction, like our dreams, strengthens us to resist what we most dread and to creatively imagine alternate worlds.

Literature by women suggests that the social quest of the female hero typically involves a series of stages markedly different from those that Joseph Campbell and others have seen as characterizing the male hero's journey:

The Green World. As the young woman hero approaches puberty, she is often moved to a longing for nature. Expected to conform to adult femininity, which in patriarchy entails enclosure under male control, she feels that in the green world she has possessed herself and is reluctant to relinquish nature's empowering ties. This is a time when she experiences in nature a completion of selfhood that she fears she will lose as she grows up.

Crossing the Threshold. At this stage, the young woman must leave the parental household for differentiation to take place. While young men revolt against their fathers and wish to avoid a fatal complicity with the mother as "other," they nonetheless seek to outdo father's sexual and social life in a male social world. Young women tend to look back over their shoulders at a powerfully victimized maternal archetype with whom they fear a fatal fusion. The mother being left behind serves less as a role model than as an example to be contradicted. This makes the female quest for Eros, whether heterosexual or lesbian, fraught with the danger of reenacting infantile attachments or adolescent antagonisms.

The Green World Lover. The female hero typically turns to a fantasy lover who is wholly nonpatriarchal, who desires participation in mutually pleasureful lovemaking rather than power over her. However, this figure of desire can be projected upon inappropriate and patriarchally infected lovers, leading to...

The Rape Trauma. Although in its most dramatic and damaging form this experience constitutes violent penetration against a woman's erotic will, it also includes any lovemaking that the young woman hero does not desire. Penelope Washbourn writes, "To 'make love' to a man she does not love, to pretend erotic attraction or arousal, to carry a child she does not want, to have sex with a man against her will are forms of spiritual female death."[2] Vestiges of the theory that a woman who enjoys sex is unwomanly are often internalized and block access to authentically desired Eros and psychological maturation.

Enclosure in Patriarchy. Conformity to marital and other gender norms threatens to shut the doors of the quest for self. As one young female hero describes her feelings on her wedding day, acquiescing to marriage against her deepest instincts feels like being stuffed inside a marshmallow.

Completion of the Quest: Achievement of Erotic and Vocational Wholeness. A successful completion of the female hero's quest for authentic selfhood rarely happens in the novels I studied, except in fantasy fiction where she earns a world in which she can lead a full adult life as a contributing member of a fantasized nonpatriarchal collective. What is normal in the male hero's quest is deviant for the female hero. Although the male hero may also rebel against his social identity, the woman hero has no choice in the matter. If she is to be complete, if she is to experience the totality of sexuality, competence, intellectual growth, and vocational mastery that constitutes human selfhood, she is likely to be punished and marginalized. In the realm of sexual self-determination, the male is rewarded, while I found only two or three fictional female heroes who were allowed to survive an enjoyable and self-chosen sexual pleasure. The young woman who completes the quest is by definition an outcast from society, her social quest by definition asocial.

The stages of the female hero's rebirth quest also differ significantly from the stages typical of the male hero's journey:

Persona Rejection. At the beginning stages, the female hero experiences first vague and then more conscious dissatisfaction with the social roles she has assumed. She may have masculinized herself in a kind of psychological cross-dressing, developing competitive, blunt, aggressive, and overly rational characteristics she considers necessary to get ahead in the world of work. Alternatively, she may have conformed to gender norms for feminine submission in a series of roles in which she gives of herself to the detriment of her own selfhood. Often the rebirth journey begins with a splitting off from husbands or love partners, or a decision, at long last, to stop identifying with one's father.

Encountering the Shadow. The shadow plays a markedly different role in the female hero's rebirth quest than that of the male. Jung's male shadow, or antiself, is antisocial, having to do with impulses spring-ing from rebellion against cultural norms and mores and arising from impulses repressed in the unconscious. I have found that the women's shadows depicted in fiction are socially conformist, incor-porating women's self-loathing for their deviations from gender norms, including norms that forbid feminine sexuality. The wom-an hero is more apt to encounter in her shadow her own socially internalized rejection of deeper feminine archetypes. In women's fiction or poetry, the female hero's shadow takes the form of an especially horrific male partner, the gynophobic shadow and ani-mus fused into a "horrible husband" or lover who reinforces her self-blame and tries to drag her back into compliance with social standards. If the woman hero remains stuck in this phase, unable to transcend messages communicated through everyday social experi-ence in patriarchy, her rebirth journey fails.

Encounter with Parental Figures. On her journey, the female hero reencounters the figures of her parents, either in reality or in memo-ry. This is the time to complete a psychological differentiation achieved through physical distancing earlier in life. Only at midlife or later does the female hero successfully come to terms with the father and mother of personal memory. Once the positive and negative ele-ments of the biographical father and mother are absorbed and transcended, and any over identification or antagonistic fusion with the actual living parents ruptured, can the encounter with the deeper maternal archetype take place.

The Green World Guide or Token. While engaged in the rebirth quest, the female hero spirals back to earlier issues that were passed over in favor of conformity to society. Green world guides and tokens that seem to push one toward further development arise as a desire to revisit a special spot in nature, or as a dream of an animal. As in the social quest of the young Native American hero who "cries for a vision" and often finds an animal or natural familiar, fictional fe-male heroes at this stage encounter dream seals, imaginary turtles, phrases of music suddenly portentous, and, even in the case of an older single woman who kicks over the patriarchal traces to become a witch, an apparently innocent jar of fruit sent in from the country. Black women heroes may feel drawn to study their West African heritage or to return to their family's land of origin.

The Green World Lover. In women's fiction, the encounter with an erotic goddess or god figure is apt to be natural, antisocial, and profoundly nonmarital, free of patriarchalized shadow content. Female fictional heroes end up mad, dead, or at least socially outcast when they indulge in love affairs with the green world lover. Whether it is an actual figure or an imaginary one, this ideal lover appears as an initiatory guide and often aids women at difficult points in their quest. He (or sometimes she) does not constitute the turning point or goal of the rebirth journey. The encounter with the green world lover enables the female hero to accept her potent, feminine sexuality and continue on her rebirth journey.

The Maternal Archetype. In the male version of the rebirth quest, the ultimate encounter is with an "other," different in gender, and takes the form of a struggle with the feminine within the male psyche. The danger in this process is fatal complicity with an alien contrasexual being: the goal is subordination of her as an element of the reborn masculine self. Jung's polarization of gender and valorization of power-over behavior subverts his goal of a balanced or androgynous psychology.

The female hero's encounter with a feminine and maternal figure at the depths of her psyche involves a clarity about what is to be abjured and what is to be absorbed from her original mother figure and from her personal feminine experience. Once gendered submission is overcome and the personal mother dealt with at the subconscious level, the female hero moves on to a transformation of personality in an enhancing fusion or to a complementary symbiosis with the maternal archetype. Whereas earlier in the social quest she might have experienced loss of selfhood or fusion in this process, her personal boundaries are now sufficiently differentiated from those of the biological mother for her to attempt reempowerment through the maternal archetype.

The Return to Society. When the terror of the maternal archetype is overcome, natural imagery, sharply particular and embodying sensual participation in the ongoing stream of early life often bursts forth. Returning to society from a journey on which she has been transformed into an agent of her own destiny in turn with nature and filled with sexual pleasure, competence, self-love, and courage, the female hero is now a Crone, or Wise Woman. In Eurocentric societies, there is a lack of respect for elders, especially middle-aged and older women, a disrespect that is often reinforced by men and women who have not completed their own rebirth journeys and who retain fear and antagonism against anyone on whom they can project their unassimilated maternal archetype. Because of this, the newly birthed Crone often gets little reverence from the community for her spiritual wisdom and is likely to elicit fear or even loathing.

The outlines that I have provided of the social and rebirth quests are based on literary observation. Although the fictional data are often more discouraging than women's lived experience, the poetry that I have examined is often more hopeful. Also, many of the most exuberant rebirth journeys in recent fiction are written by black women empowered by black feminists' rejection of white European standards—works such as Gloria Naylor's *Mama Day*, for example, and Paula Marshall's *Praise for the Widow*. Native American novelists and poets, though even more marginalized and often devastated by white American values, have recently written books (such as Leslie Marmon Silko's *Ceremony* and Louise Erdrich's trilogy, *Love Medicine, The Beet Queen,* and *Tracks*) that work back through social and rebirth quests to archetypally empowering traditional materials. While white female heroes cannot simply usurp spiritual archetypes from black or Native American women's religious systems, they may seek correspondingly powerful archetypes in European pagan pasts.

I am convinced that for all of us literature can serve as a catalyst for life choices. Women novelists and poets have both warned us with tales of patriarchal horrors and encouraged us with stories of female heroes whose quests we may want to emulate. They have provided us with moments of epiphany, of vision, when we can feel rising from our depths a female quality that altogether transcends the gender polarities destructive to human life.

Denyse Beaudet

The Monster

The monster mediates the archetypal realm, bringing the underside of life to expression. The monster renews itself perennially and gives rise to an infinite variety of images. Beneath this variety, more universal patterns can be discerned, such as the monster as engulfer, which transcends not only differences among cultures and historical periods but also differences in age.

When we approach the dream life of children attentive to images of the monster, we recognize that children contending with the monster go through the stages of the heroic quest identified by Joseph Campbell in his book *The Hero with a Thousand Faces*. In a dream, the child often journeys to a forest, a mountain, or an ocean, and there encounters a monster. Or, the monster summons the child on an adventure by breaking into the family home. The child's first impulse is usually to retreat, but then he or she takes up the challenge and moves forward into the adventure, alone or with an ally. As I have observed, the child encounters the monster by one of three pathways: combat, taming, or engulfment.

Of the three pathways, engulfment appears the most paradoxical. In my study, the dreams of one five-year-old girl, Marjorie, illustrate engulfment. The eleven dreams she described to me during a ten-week period depict a passage through the belly of the whale and its aftermath. This series reveals her progress through descent and resurgence.

In her first dream, Marjorie is a young child being pushed in a baby carriage by her friend Caroline. She and Caroline see a monster. The monster's appearance marks the beginning of Marjorie's adventure, even though the stroll in the baby carriage seemed like a harmless enterprise at first. Marjorie's identification with the young child suggests going back in time.

She reaches into an even more remote past in another dream. She goes by car to the ocean and drowns, then she sees a whale and a shark. The whale eats her. In her drawing of the dream, Marjorie pictures herself in the belly of the whale. Her head is down, and she is surrounded by green matter that represents the entrails of the whale.

Marjorie's passage through water before entering the belly of the whale suggests a dissolving and a return to the uroboric, or undifferentiated, consciousness which characterizes the beginnings of life.[1] Marjorie returns to water as the first element of her fetal existence. The belly of the whale is her place of origin.

Engulfment by the monster partakes of the mysteries of death and rebirth. Some puberty rites of initiation include the ritual introduction of a child into the belly of a sea monster such as a crocodile, a whale, or a big fish. The child is later born from the monster as an initiate. In many cultures in Africa, Oceania, Lapland, and Finland, and among the Eskimos, myths of engulfment tell of heroes who are men, women, and also children.[2]

The swallowing by the monster "signifies the re-entry into a pre-formed embryonic state of being," the "return to the germinal mode of being," which implies death as well, since one must die in one's existence to return to "the beginning."[3] Marjorie's return to the belly of the sea monster may bear the meaning of a symbolic death. Frances G. Wickes notes that death and rebirth govern the evolution of human life from early childhood on: "Progress and regression, rebirth and death are present from the earliest days, and are shown in the little acts of the little child as well as in the larger acts of the larger adult."[4]

The green that Marjorie uses to depict the entrails of the whale suggests that she is surrounded by a fertile terrain. While the whale has eaten her, suggesting death, this verdant fertility may also contain the potential for renewal and rebirth. Jung writes how those engulfed by the monster undergo regression both to intrauterine life and to the deepest layers of existence, and from there stay caught or free themselves from the maternal hold with new life.[5]

In contrast with the dream in which she is accompanied by Caroline, Marjorie's engulfment dream does not contain another human. She is alone, for the encounter with the monster is a direct and intimate meeting. Marjorie and the mammal are almost one. Marjorie's body, as she draws it, follows the contours of the whale's entrails closely, as if she were enveloped and held closely on all sides.

To encounter the monster by engaging it in combat or by taming it implies action originating from the dreamer, but engulfment implies participating by being acted upon. The pathway of engulfment involves letting oneself become the object of absorption and transformation. But this transformation, insofar as it passes through symbolic death, also means a new beginning.

Marjorie's dream series unfolds between the deep archetypal realm where the sea monster has taken her and day-to-day reality. As she journeys into the depths of the sea monster, her sixth birthday approaches, and she then dreams of being able to ride a two-wheeled bicycle that her parents have given her as a birthday gift. The dream shows her in complete mastery of her vehicle, reflecting a newfound competence.

The dream that follows shows her climbing onto a cross and returns her to the archetypal realm of the whale dream. In this dream she climbs to the top of a mountain and sees a small baby. She takes it and later drops it. Then she sees a cross and climbs onto it. "I was doing like Jesus," she confides after drawing the dream. Her drawing shows Marjorie (in black) climbing the mountain (yellow). On top of the mountain, we see Marjorie holding the baby (both are orange), the dropped child (in black), and the cross with Marjorie upon it (both are orange).

After the return to early childhood and the descent into the belly of the whale, Marjorie engages in a contrasting movement of ascending to the summit of a mountain. She finds a baby and holds it in her arms. Whereas she occupied the role of a young child in the first dream, she now assumes the role of a mother. Once picked up, the baby is dropped, marking the end of the return to early childhood observed in the dream of the baby carriage and the dream of being engulfed by the whale. After dropping the baby, Marjorie climbs onto the cross, thereby identifying herself with an adult spiritual hero. The symbol of the sacrificed god can be found at the heart of several religions. Jung conceives the sacrifice of the hero as a renunciation of the return to the maternal womb for the sake of immortality. In this sense, the sacrifice is the opposite of regression: "The sacrifice is the very reverse of regression—it is a successful canalization of libido onto the symbolic equivalent of the mother, and a spiritualization of it."[6] Marjorie's climb onto the cross, "like Jesus," an adult spiritual hero, counterpoises her return to the belly of the whale.

Marie-Louise Von Franz observes that when the conflict between the unconscious process of psychic growth and the will of the conscious personality is represented in the form of crucifixion, it can mean that the conflict has reached its acute phase.[7] In this light, Marjorie's climbing onto the cross points to an inner conflict and to the pain that such a conflict entails. The cross bears a creative potential as a place of sacrifice, just as the belly of the whale contains the potential for a new beginning in life. In discussing creation myths that include a sacrificed divinity, Mircea Eliade writes that life can be born only through the sacrifice of another life: "The fundamental idea is that life can only take birth from another life which is sacrificed. The violent death is creative—in this sense, that the life which is sacrificed manifests itself in a more brilliant form upon another plane of existence."[8]

Although amplifying of the cross as a symbol illumines some of its meaning in the context of Marjorie's dream, Marjorie's climb onto the cross remains, in Joseph Campbell's phrase, "to the eye and heart a sign of silence," a gesture that preserves its full mystery.[9]

The next four dreams again concern Marjorie's day-to-day reality. Marjorie reckons with three forms of violence: natural violence from a storm, animal violence from her dog, and human violence from a male neighbor aimed at her family. Up to this point she has progressed forward from her earlier dreams, but now her dreams take her back home.

Marjorie's path of return again passes through water, and for the second time she drowns, but this time she emerges. Marjorie finds herself on the seashore, and she wants to try to swim. She goes into the deep water and drowns, then she comes up again. Someone comes and picks her up. After drawing her dream, she says that this person "saves" her. Marjorie expresses the magnificence of the moment when she puts the sun in her drawing "because it is beautiful."

While the return to water in the engulfment dream pointed to ego-dissolution, Marjorie's move into water in this emergence dream reveals her intention to remain in contact with her own power through swimming. She wants to try to direct herself in the fluid element, but for the second time she sinks to the bottom. This time, however, her descent stops and she begins to ascend again. The drawing shows her above the surface of the water, and on the shore is the benevolent character who saves her, portrayed in many colors (yellow for the head and arms, red for the trunk, and blue for the legs). Her emergence from water signifies rebirth. Eliade says, "Breaking with all forms, doing away with all the past, water possesses this power of purifying, of regenerating, of giving birth; for what is immersed in it 'dies', and, rising again from the water, is like a child without any sin or any past, able to receive a new revelation and begin a new and *real* life."[10]

The mystery of the return to origins suggested by being engulfed by the monster repeats itself from childhood to adulthood. Marjorie's voyage into the belly of the sea monster, followed by her emergence, finds its echo in the odyssey described in Julie Stanton's poem *La nomade*. When the poem begins, the Nomad, an everywoman, is pulled by the Beast with the golden nostrils. The Nomad is blind. She and the Beast travel forward on the red earth. On the Nomad's back, where "stillborn children sleep," "women of water and wind cry," and "presumptuous men lay," her past weighs upon her. As she journeys with the Beast, she simultaneously returns in her memory to other eras of her life. Her journey takes her into water, through a storm, to a mountain, and to a volcano. The Nomad gradually surrenders her hair, her beauty, her breasts, and her genitals, and eventually enters the chest cavity of the Beast.

The Beast has chosen the place. Suddenly a tongue darts forth and a voice bellows like a storm:

> *The bray of the Beast opens its chest up*
> *passageway greatly allowing*
> *exiting already*
> *she has recognized the surroundings*
> *"the deep enchantment" where one becomes prisoner*
>   *without dying*
> *and supreme under the day's wound*
> *the throatcanyon of time*
> *sun deep in the cloister...*
>
> *And so She is in the Beast*
> *her life suspended and yet she has life*
> *passenger on a boat henceforth dockable*

henceforth this place the acquiescing
silky slide of mucous membranes.

The Nomad is left inside the Beast, "where she waits for the date of light." Through the darkness, though, a new dawn is presaged, for "mornings of origin walk at the heart of the Beast."[11]

Marjorie's engulfment and emergence is also in resonance with a contemporary woman's experience of being swallowed by Kali, the Hindu goddess of death and rebirth. While immersed in a period of intense emotional pain, Marianne Paulus had a vision of Kali and surrendered to being swallowed by her:

> One day Kali's fierce face appeared beneath me, mouth opened wide, teeth dripping with blood, eyes flaming with fire. Her aspect was one that would ordinarily have inspired fear or horror, but instead I felt deep comfort when I saw her there and a rush of love went out from my heart to her. At once she began to swallow me whole.

Paulus gave herself to the experience, feeling warmth and great comfort as she was being swallowed up in Kali's total darkness:

> When I was completely inside her, my breathing ceased and I was in utter stillness—totally enveloped in darkness, warm, secure, safe. . . . The whole of me had been taken in. I felt healed in the all-encompassing taking of myself into herself. There was no horror to Kali. Only the most incredible tenderness. She was indeed big enough to envelop whatever is, into herself. . . . From inside Kali where all was bloody, I could only sense the wonder, the awesomeness, of such a life-giving force. . . . I remained inside the belly of Kali—in the heart of the earth, so it would seem, where fire burns and consumes all that cannot endure it—for weeks, in total darkness. But in the darkness began to come understanding and knowing. Understanding of my process. Knowing about the inner nature of life.[12]

Marjorie enters the belly of the whale; the Nomad returns to the chest cavity of the Beast with the golden nostrils; Marianne descends into the darkness of Kali's belly. Marjorie drops the baby; the Nomad loses her eyes, her hair, her beauty; Marianne undergoes the fire that burns and consumes all that cannot endure it. Marjorie emerges from the water; the Nomad waits for the date of light; understanding and knowing come to Marianne.

Marjorie's journey, the Nomad's voyage, and Marianne's descent all constitute symbolic forms in resonance with one another. The level of consciousness engaged by the experience of engulfment at age five and at age forty could not be the same, but the similarity in symbolic pattern attests that both child and adult participate in the mystery of death and rebirth that shapes the evolution of human life.

Lyn Cowan

The Victim

Cordelia: We are not the first who, with best mean-
            ing, have incurred the worst. For thee,
            oppressed king, I am cast down . . .
Lear: Upon such sacrifices, my Cordelia, the
            gods themselves throw incense.
                        SHAKESPEARE, KING LEAR

The archetypal figure of "the victim" is fraught with social connotations, religious associations, and psychological paradoxes,
but I will limit my scope here to two aspects: the secular and the
sacred. I will speak less of the psychosocial experience of literal victims than of the victim figure in the psyche, an archetypal image
appearing in as many forms as there are woundings, injustices, and
sacrifices.

We are all victims, though some of us, in whom the inner victim figure is denied or projected, may not be aware of a deeper psychic resonance in those critically important moments when suffering is inflicted. We all suffer, either randomly or by some seemingly
inscrutable design. We all have far less power to control our sense of
well-being in an increasingly chaotic world than we would like.
And sooner or later, Death chooses each of us as its victim.

The archetypal victim image is a personification of how an individual or group imagines itself in its suffering. This is the "sacred
victim," with its attendant associations of eternity and transcendence.
The sacredness of the victim image refers primarily to its "set-apart-
ness," its interiority as a psychic figure and its inner meaning.

By distinction, a criminal act is a literal event that forces a condition of victimhood on an individual or group, usually through violent means. The locus and temporality of this victimization make it secular: it happens in the world, in the dimension of time. The distinction between the secular and the sacred, the "out there" and the "in here," does *not* make them mutually exclusive; to do so would split the archetype.

In our culture and time, the word *victim* evokes the negativity attached to the darkest and most painful experiences: suffering, injustice, powerlessness, and death. We almost always think of "victim" in its secular sense, perhaps because we have lost much of the sense of the sacred *in* the mundane, and feel only with difficulty (if at all) the deeper resonance of ancient claims of near-forgotten gods and goddesses being made upon us. Our world is largely and one-sidedly secular, and we are confined in it. Having no other "world" to appeal to for help or justice, the victim in contemporary America is indeed a victim of the world of crime, homelessness, contagious disease, and drug madness.

The word *victim* evokes as well the terrible fear and insecurity of arbitrary randomness, or the equally terrible fear of having been singled out, "chosen," for unbearable pain. We use the word in connection only with those experiences we dread: cancer victim, rape victim, crash victim, victim of mental illness, victim of starvation. Whoever or whatever does the victimizing is important to the constellation of the victim experience, for it is these agents—cancer, rapist, car, or plane—that create the context in which a person becomes a victim. Part of the horror of victimization is the realization that victim and victimizer share a terrible affinity: something in one may be found in the other. This does not mean they are simply two sides of the same coin; rather, both may be constellated in one person at one time, and that one may victimize oneself. To the victim, the agent of victimization has the power to inflict suffering and pain, to deny justice, to cause death. And since the victim is, by definition, powerless, the primal emotion that always accompanies victimization is fear.

Yet, just because it arouses such fear and complete negativity, it is possible that no other archetypal image so constellates the human psyche's need to make suffering meaningful as the figure of the victim. The first desperate cry of the victim is, "Why me?" The horror of that violent act which creates the victim cries out for some meaning in pain, some purpose in anguish; there can be no acceptance of, or coming to terms with, one's victimization without the psyche's constellation of the sacred victim. We may be able to endure much pain, far more than we ever deserve or think ourselves capable of enduring; but Jung was right when he said that human beings cannot tolerate a meaningless life.

Keeping these two aspects of the victim image together provides a way of imagining the victim which incorporates a multiplicity of meanings and emotions without denying the raw terror and despair that accompany the psyche's constellation of the victim image. It may also be that the only way out of the senseless hell of secular victimization is through the purposeful hell of sacred victimization—a shift in perception that moves the victim from the despair of random happening to a sense of conscious purposefulness.

The Secular Victim

The New Age in America is not a favorable climate for victims; the New Age is for winners, not losers. The relatively unconscious "victimizer" in the American collective psyche seems to be increasingly hostile to victims; indeed, such hostility is probably producing more victims. One need only look at the rising number of victims of violent crime, child abuse, drugs, AIDS, environmental toxins, scams, and -isms of all kinds.

The apparent antidote to victimhood is paranoia: trust no one, use deadbolt locks in your home, practice safe sex in your own bed, buckle up in your car, wear a hard hat and keep a cool head at work, know your rights when dealing with smooth-talking salespeople, police, and therapists. The assumption is that the more you protect yourself, the less likely you will become a victim. The image of the victim has been devalued by the long-cherished American conviction that victims are merely losers who didn't try hard enough to win.

The image of the secular victim and the situations that create it turn negative attention toward the victim, usually in the form of blame. Since the meaning of victimhood cannot be divorced from the cultural value context in which it is experienced, the victim will always appear blameworthy and at fault in a culture that most highly values dominance, conquest, power, competition—just the things needed to victimize.

The victim embodies those qualities that conflict with, threaten, or challenge that value system. The most obvious example is of the Nazi (mis)perception of the Jews as an "infectious" and powerful people who would poison the purity of Aryan society and take over the world. Projection happens everywhere, in everyone, collectively and individually. Secular victims are thus made by projection: those who support and maintain the culture's dominant values project their own fear of powerlessness, helplessness, weakness, and vulnerability onto whomever can be victimized. And since our culture does not have an equitable distribution of power, there are more victims than perpetrators: victims are likely to be individually victimized as women, people of color, children, animals; or collectively, as blacks, Jews, Native Americans, lesbians and gays, old people, handicapped people, and so forth.

It is of course the victims who are blamed for whatever trouble befalls them. Since the victim sustains the effect, she or he must in some way be the cause. Perhaps the root of this odd situation lies in the old Christian idea that sin invites retribution, while goodness deserves blessing. In this view, the victim's suffering is understood as retribution by divine justice through human agency; where there is retribution, there must be sin. The idea is still alive and well, though cast now in secular terms: whatever the victim "gets" the victim "deserves." In New Age terms, the victim "created" his or her reality.

But we do not, in fact, always create our own suffering; to think otherwise is to fall into the negative inflation of assuming a grandiose, godlike capability to make awful things happen. For the sake of psychological maturity, we must be able to separate the dictum that we are each responsible for our actions from the assumption that victims are responsible for their own victimization. If we cannot make this differentiation, the victim then becomes a pathologized figure, neurotically and one-sidedly regarding the world as victimizer. We are then unconsciously identified with the victim, either introjecting the guilt or projecting the blame. The psychological task, however, is not necessarily to eliminate blame but to learn to place it where it properly belongs.

The victim's horror, shame, and powerlessness at the hands of a perpetrator, and the collective blame that reinforces these feelings make the victim a figure of no value in a culture that despises weakness. But at the same time, it is precisely the horror, shame, and powerlessness that evokes our sense of tragedy, empathy, outrage against injustice, and sometimes even love. We perceive the victim as that figure in each of us who is weak, who suffers, feels wrongly accused, and is powerless to command justice. It is perhaps because the victim figure embodies the paradox of bearing unbearable suffering that it is able to move us so deeply to compassion, empathy, grief, and love. Only a psychopath is impervious to the suffering and power of the victim, because the psychopath is untouched by the power of Eros to be in some relationship to pain.

It is the experience of the victim figure in our own psyche that makes us conscious of our human capacity for sacrifice.

THE SACRED VICTIM

While most dictionaries define *victim* primarily as a person who suffers from an injurious or destructive action or agency, personal or impersonal, the older meaning of the word retains the sense of the original root: "victim" as "sacrifice." The original meaning of the word *victim,* from the Latin word *victima,* means "sacrificial beast," and refers to any living creature that is killed and offered to a god or godlike power. The word *sacrifice* comes from the Latin word *sacer,* from which we derive the English word *sacred,* meaning that which is holy, set apart, "devoted for sacrifice," dedicated to a god or some religious purpose.

It is significant that *sacer* also means "forfeit," "accursed," and "criminal." The victim, then, may be both innocent and accursed at the same time. While this "accursedness" may not accurately describe the nature of a victimization, it often corresponds to the victim's feeling of being cursed, singled out for punishment. The victim image often appears in psychic life as "the accursed one," as in the scapegoat figure, the one singled out for the sins of the many— precisely because it is innocent and undeserving of its fate.

In his wonderful essay "Cancer in Myth and Dream," Russell Lockhart notes the paradox in the word *victim,* having in its older Latin roots the meaning of "increase" and "growth."[1] (In Greek, the root of *victim* is *auxo,* meaning "increase" or "growth," and is the name of one of the Charities, *Auxo,* the "waxing.") The victim image thus unfolds as a complex weave of apparently contradictory meanings. It is an image simultaneously evoking collective emotions and ideas of fear, negativity, divine power, holiness, persecution, doubt, innocence, anguish, growth, sacrifice, condemnation. Thus the victim image may present itself in its secularity as ugly, fearful, and secretly despised, or the victim image may appear as sacred, beautiful, and desirable.

How the victim consciously perceives her or his suffering can give meaning to personal victimization: one is not only sacrificed but becomes capable of making, or enacting, a sacrifice. Victimization, then, is as much a condition of some meaningful relationship with a god as it is a condition of meaningless suffering.

The realms of the sacred and the secular are not mutually exclusive; the terms are merely devices to help us differentiate aspects of experience. The psychological task of the victim is to perceive them as joined, to make the secular sacred, to make a worthy sacrifice of one's suffering: to honor the wound, value the vulnerable, cultivate compassion for one's injured soul.

The person who perceives or feels oneself as suffering *for* (not only *from*) a deity, cause, principle, or beloved, experiences a different aspect of victimhood: the value of sacrifice. What redeems the suffering and anguish of the victim is not necessarily the cessation of suffering, but the experience of meaning in it. Simone Weil reminded us, "At every blow of fate, every pain, whether small or great, say to oneself, 'I am being worked on.' "[2] The *willingness* to sacrifice has long been regarded by some religious systems as a moral virtue, antithetical to the sin of selfishness. But my focus here is not on morality or virtue or selfishness, but rather on the *capacity* for sacrifice when the experience of victimization makes sacrifice psychologically necessary.

It goes against the grain of all our ideas of justice to place the burden of sacrifice on the victim; it smacks of victim-blaming. But it is precisely within one's capacity to offer sacrifice that one finds meaning: the victim who is able to make a sacrifice becomes psychologically active in her or his affliction, a participant in the holy work of making meaning out of incomprehensible chaos. Whether the sacrifice consists of one's naivete, innocence, cherished ideal, or self-image, the capacity to yield to a deeper necessity is tested in victimization.

The value and importance of the figure to whom the sacrifice is made, or on whose behalf it is offered, is paramount in the making of meaning, for a unworthy object demeans the one who sacrifices. The perpetrator of a violent crime is never worthy of the victim's sacrifice; he is merely a mindless agent of archetypal forces, enacting their impersonal cruelty. Neither he nor those godlike powers he serves are concerned with the individual fate of the victim. The victim must find a worthy altar in her or his own psyche on which to lay that which has been taken. Thus the victim "redeems" what has been lost not by revenge, but by a sense that some deeper purpose in life has been served. Choosing what has already happened and giving conscious assent, not consent, to the reality of one's victimization is the beginning of conscious sacrifice.

On a collective level, the demand for sacrifice historically has been disproportionately placed on women in ways that most men (and many women) do not regard as truly or worthily sacrificial. Perhaps because of this legacy and the ongoing reality of woman-as-victim, it is difficult for many women, as well as many men, to imagine that anything is to be gained by making or being a sacrifice for any reason. Self-sacrifice goes against both self-absorbed New Ageism (where it is now called "codependency") and some of the deepest and strongest currents of feminist thinking.

Yet, surely, there must be a place for sacrifice. Is there a place in life for the value of suffering or enduring pain for the sake of someone dearly loved, or for a cherished cause? What else can it mean to be "holy" or "set apart" or "dedicated" unless there is some person or idea worthy of such devotion? Of what value is all our strength and power if we cannot yield them up and submit them to a greater value? Are we so consciously determined not to be victims that we have become incapable of sacrifice? If we cannot or will not give up or yield anything, have no sense of deeper ethical claims upon us than our own small selves, we have lost not only a vital capacity to relate to one another but a fundamental experience of being human. Because it entails irreparable loss, it seems a tragedy to become a victim under any circumstances. But it is an equally terrible tragedy to be unwilling to sacrifice, because this signifies an inability to love.

The need of the victim to find meaning in her or his victimization is not the same as finding a "reason" for it. There may be no "reason" why one particular person becomes the victim of a drunk driver at a particular time and place. The "reason" *why* one becomes a victim may be profoundly different from the meaning the victim takes from the experience. And because each victim comprehends her or his victimization differently, the discovery of meaning is always an individual experience.

The first cry of the victim is, "Why me?" Since there is rarely an answer, it may be that "Why *not* me?" is a more productive question. Victimization tends to make one visible: one has been "chosen" by a victimizer. But the experience of victimization makes aspects of the victim visible to herself or himself as well, and with the shocking emotional immediacy characteristic of genuine trauma. From whatever circumstance or agent, victimization reveals the victim's courage or lack of it, the victim's limited control over circumstance, the victim's depth of fear and shame, the victim's capacity for self-compassion, or the depth of the victim's self-recrimination.

Contained within the figure of the victim is a lesson concerning the nature of the god to whom sacrifice is being offered, for the victim bears the likeness of the god. The ancients believed there was a profound, though sometimes hidden, affinity between the sacrificial victim and the god to whom such offering was made. In Jewish tradition, the justice of God required a sacrificial animal to be innocent and well-formed; hence the lamb without blemish. The Christian myth requires that the sacrificed Son be like the sinless Father. In that region of the soul where we are victimized, we must look for the likeness of a god, and there build an interior altar to ensure that our sacrifice is made holy. The wisdom to be discovered is not that "you brought it on yourself," but that it brought you to your Self.

How we treat the inner "sacred victim" is the measure of how we treat the "secular victim" in the world. If our response to an injured animal or abused child in a night dream is to banish it (by forgetting the dream or denying the disturbance) or blame it ("bad dream," "didn't make sense," "made me afraid so I hit it with a shovel"), our ruthlessness will enable us to banish out-there victims from sight, memory, and responsibility, or else we will treat such victims with the unconscious contempt that appears as pity. Anything but real concern, real compassion, real love.

The psychological necessity is not that we save the inner victim from all hurt and pain, but that we learn to accept and care about it in its woundedness. This means a sacrifice of the "savior" role, a conscious and voluntary giving up of our fantasies of total independence and self-sufficiency. We cannot save ourselves, and we are not sufficient unto ourselves. Only someone with a pathological compulsion for autonomy and do-it-yourselfism would argue this. But the temptation to save and heal the victim is very great, and perhaps nowhere is it felt more deeply than among psychologists and psychotherapists who work with victims and are expected to do just that.

For this is where we take our inner victim: to the doctor. We take our victim-feelings to a healer-god regularly (as to church), bringing sacrifices (as in fees), making confessions, feeling vulnerable and defenseless behind our mechanisms, feeling betrayed and enraged when our expectations (as in prayers) are not answered. We want rewards for humility, solutions to problems, recognition for hard efforts, safety always, and, most of all, we want the doctor to love us while it hurts, and then stop the pain. For some, being a victim becomes confused with a misunderstood need to stay in pain to ensure that the love will not stop. The doctor may become a victim, too, especially when she or he has an unconscious affinity with the patient. In those areas, the healer falls victim to the wounded, the persona of professional capability collapsing under the weight of impossible demands and expectations. The torment of the patient becomes the doctor's own.

Some victim images have exceptional power to move us emotionally because they incorporate nearly all the essential characteristics of the archetypal victim. The image of Jesus, broken and bloody on the cross, is a complete and singular example of the sacred victim figure, embodying holiness, innocence, unjust persecution and suffering, and voluntary sacrifice. As a collective example, the Jews historically have been forced to enact the victim role with such repetition that the very name of the people has become practically synonymous with "victim." Photographic images of skeletal death-camp inmates have given us an austere visual definition of archetypal victimization, which is why Jews began referring to the Nazi genocide as a holocaust, literally a "burnt offering." Most recently we have seen pictures of blind rabbits, gassed cats, and tuskless dead elephants—victimized animals who, though sentient beings, cannot willingly sacrifice themselves for humankind's benefit (and no doubt would not, if asked). These are images whose strength is derived from the innocence of the victim (Jesus), the magnitude of suffering (the Holocaust), and the utter helplessness of the victim's condition (animals). Then, if Psyche's lamp wakens and illuminates Eros, these powerful images may call us into relationship with them and evoke our compassion and love.

As noted earlier, the root of the word *victim* carries an ancient meaning of "increase" or "growth." However, I am not suggesting that victimization ought to be considered an occasion of "positive growth." To do so minimizes the horror and fear and shame or represses them completely. The injunction to the victim to "grow" through adversity is a subtle appeal to the victim's ego to leave the victimization experience behind (a form of denial). "Growth" in this usage is defensive, the demand of an anxious parent who does not know what to do for a child in pain (as in "Grow up, stop crying, stop feeling sorry for yourself").

A deeper objection to the demand on the victim to "grow" is that it keeps the experience of the victim within a fantasy of the child. Whatever complex meanings victimhood may have for the soul is obscured and reduced to false simplicity by forcing it into the single perspective of the child archetype. Thus the victim appears passively childlike or irresponsibly childish. This may be one reason why our culture takes a profoundly ambivalent attitude toward victims that is either total neglect and abuse or idealization and galvanic convulsions to rescue. (Remember little Jessica McClure, who fell down a well in Texas in 1989? The whole country vicariously participated in the rescue operation.) When perceived through the child archetype, the victim is infantilized: whatever injury has been done can now only be understood as a sign or consequence of psychological immaturity— the naïveté of a child, the innocence of a child, the carelessness of a child, the abuse of a child, the child who cries for grownups to play fair. Instead of an adult drama deep in the soul's sacred interior, victimization is seen as one of many misfortunes that befalls a child. We demand either excessive responsibility of the victim ("She should have known better") or expect him or her to be as helpless in trauma as a child.

The victim figure needs rescue not from victimization but from the child fantasy. The idea of "increase" in the root of the word refers to something other than developmental "growth." What happens to us happens, avoidably or not; what we do psychologically with those happenings is what makes for "increase" or decrease. Russell Lockhart writes:

> The psychology of . . . unwilling sacrifice is quite different from that of the willing sacrifice. There are moments and seasons in one's life when genuine sacrifice of the most valued thing is essential for further

growth. If this sacrifice is not made willingly, that is, consciously and with full conscious suffering of the loss, the sacrifice will occur unconsciously. One then will not sacrifice to growth but be sacrificed to growth gone wrong.[3]

When the inner victim figure is thrown to the lion of the great goddess Necessity (Ananke), it is in that arena—wherever we are torn to pieces by pain or injustice—where blind Necessity must be turned into purposeful Fate. The events and experiences that bring us pain, loss, grief, injury, and abandonment are the rites of passage and sacrificial offerings that "increase" us, that force maturation upon us.

The victim figure within us, wounded and helpless, is some-times rescued by interior reflection, when the interior victimizer is also acknowledged. We may be victimized by any of our own thought less follies, character flaws, failures of foresight, errors of judgment, or self-betrayals. We may fall victim to any deity or archetypal pow er whose service we have neglected: Eros taunts us with insatiable desire, Saturn holds our joy and freedom hostage in his prison of depression, Hera drives us mad for monogamy, Aphrodite tortures us with jealousy and the insecurity of love.

But the interior victim is not always to be rescued: indeed, once rescued, it is no longer truly a "victim." That suffering, powerless figure within derives its meaning precisely from its suffering and powerlessness: it is this acceptance of human limitation and wounded-ness that is offered up as sacrifice to the powers, deities, gods, or archetypes that rule psychic life. It may be that the archetype of the victim, with its infinite loneliness in pain, is that image which holds the deepest knowing ("gnosis") of what it is to be "human." To know the "sacred victim" in oneself is that experience of the fatefulness and finitude of life that makes submission to one's humanity possi-ble, sacrificing the very human desire to be god in all things.

William G. Doty

The Trickster

Who and what is the trickster within? How can we contact the useful fool or trickster image within each of us? Most of us marshal our energies toward repressing it, ignoring or refusing to admit that *we* could be so ill-bred, so crude, so rough-and-ready as most trickster/fool figures seem to be. One of my dreams illustrates it. Stalking down the ramp at the beauty pageant, suddenly, as the spotlights play upon me, I strip blazer and shirt from my hairy chest: "See how my Maidenform bra . . ." The rest is lost, as the judges yell for the houselights, and my female companion blanches and runs for the exit.

So odd, this dream-scene of being in the wrong script at the right time? I doubt it, and I suspect that everyone has such a dream at some point. Wrong place, wrong context, wrong everything, and yet we wake up with the smiling knowledge that what our dream-person did was after all quite appropriate, just what that stuffy, sexist beauty contest needed.

Tricksters seem to find exits where there are no exits. They laugh at established customs and give us a second slantwise view of life that depicts customary everyday reality as too often cheap, banal, tawdry, underdeveloped. Such views upset the going consensus definitions, trailing snickers and laughter in their wake. They cause us to experience an almost overpowering challenge to the going order, in a blitz of insight about what *else* might be possible. Seeding metaphors of growth, they demolish the aridity of the system that would squeeze out new life.

Let's stay with the incongruous elements, the sense that another realm intrudes into this one. *What if?* What if men did wear bras, or women jockstraps? What if night were day, or day night? *What if . . . ?* Right there we get close to what trickster/fool is all about: the image is one of turning upside-down all the usual, customary, called-for responses. Tricksters substitute a divine chaos for the daily ordinariness. This chaos is strangely full of promise, since "Once upon a time, long, long ago" Coyote/Raven/Hare worked the will of the Great Changer, bumbling along through life, to be sure, but in the process learning to differentiate the extremities of his body, and organizing the alteration of night and day, creating the mountain ranges and the fresh water streams. He doesn't stay in one place but is a traveler like Hermes. We learn to recognize the areas he travels around in as the mythical geography of Our Town, our often-disguised but actual reality. And we are placed again within the tension between the originative and the merely repetitive, the archetypal and the purely local.

Some trickster stories are creation myths. After deceiving the primal monster into letting him enter his belly, the Nez Percé trickster Coyote discovers all the animals that the beast has swallowed. Then he cuts up and kills the monster and lets out all the animals before creating the various tribes of human beings by flinging about the pieces.

The Winnebago trickster causes a waterfall to move to another location so that people could live there; "I am telling you," this trickster says, "that the earth was made for man to live on, and you will annoy him if you stay here. I came to this earth to rearrange it."[1]

Such trickster works are accomplished by what often seem unnecessarily antisocial or obscene acts: tricksters are likely to steal holy power-objects or to create by means of piles of their own shit, or by farting loudly to split obstructing rocks! No more gentrified high-culture politeness, but the culture-shifting upset. Not the benign white-gloves-for-tea etiquette we heard about in grammar school, but the superordinary reshuffling, the refractive clarity of the moments when one sees between the seams and behind the scenes into the ob-scene. Clearly in trickster myths such boundary crossings are regarded as *creative*, as creational and catalytic.

Sometimes I wonder why the societies that produce trickster cycles find it necessary to image creativity as a continual stepping beyond the expected and sanctioned mores and social limits. Are they somehow aware of the human deadness that polite society fosters? Do they sense the need for the outrageous pun or joke to help us imagine how we *ought* to be connecting? Coyote, especially, is fond of having intercourse in some of the strangest places, or with as many women as he can at once, or by using his extraordinarily long penis. The trickster extends his penis across rivers, around corners, and even across distances underground: "Oh!" says one female victim, "this ISN'T a mushroom I've sat upon!"

But these mythical creatures, precisely in their awkwardness, precisely in their uncouth gaucheries, point to satisfying relationships as they bring into existence those items without which we are helpless. They bring food, a world on which to dwell, sexuality, and a constantly reiterated moral order, even if it is emphasized indirectly by their diametrical oppositions to normal ways of doing things. Trickster stories are paradoxically moralistic; they preach about the norms by dramatizing the abnormal.

Many trickster stories map the human enculturation of the natural: Coyote learns not to use his enormously long penis to chase squirrels out of hollow logs, but only after the squirrels bite off the penis bit by bit! He learns how to differentiate his right hand from his left, but only after both hands fight for dominance, almost maiming the rest of his body in the process. From such exploits come cultural benefits, the reconstructions of primal chaos that have made the earth an inhabitable arena: food crops result from the discarded pieces of penis, or parts of the monsters that the tricksters overcame become this ridge and that valley.

Change comes as growth and transformation: Raven on Puget Sound manages to hang up the sun, moon, and stars, even though he smokes his gorgeous white feathers totally black in the process. Or Raven tries to steal blueback salmon from his father-in-law, but because he is so noisy, he is discovered and manages to escape with only a mouthful of scales. Nonetheless, when he spits them out in disgust, the fish scales fall into rivers and magically reproduce, becoming the first schools of salmon.

In many of these tales a rudimentary social ordering is being explored and founded, as when trickster's right and left hand finally cease struggling, each demanding to be primary, and humankind has begun to understand something about dualistic oppositions and how to deal with them. When Raven steals both fire and water at the same time, bringing to earth both daylight and fresh water, we cannot help but question whether our usual contrasts and exclusions and oppositions always hold. Fire versus water; intellect versus intuition; feminine versus masculine traits. We begin to comprehend that life is never one versus another, either/or, but BOTH/AND. Tricksters don't simplify but make more complex the inflections of being human. Signifying pluralisms of meanings, they refuse condensation in favor of multidimensional breakthrough into realms we otherwise think of as accessible only to wonderworkers beyond the realm of our own experience.

Like all true psychological images, trickster images hint that beyond the quotidian dictionary world of definitions there is always a cross-meaning or meanings. Wherever we are most complacent, wherever we feel that we have "made it," there tricksters appear and call into question the sacred ego-stability and economic success of it all. Remember the dream in which your clothes were torn and filthy, just as you stepped forth to get your diploma, the dream that made you wonder just what you were really aspiring toward with all your technological, metaphysical, or pedagogical expertise?

In life, we are led into no fewer potentially rich situations than are Raven and Coyote. Whether or not we heed the trickster's call to set our horizons of expectations slightly to the side of the well-beaten path, to see that the extraordinary always lies immediately beyond the comforts of the daily and ordinary, we do begin to comprehend that even our own small world and vocation can become world-founding, if we heed what this clownish, antiestablishment fool offers. "Dare to be different!" the trickster calls. "Hear and speak that which shatters tradition!"

A long trail of tricksters throughout world literature suggests that this figure has indeed an archetypal quality. Confidence men (Melville, Mann), jokester-reformers (Kesey), or contemporary figures in Native American fiction (Momaday, Welch)—we find tricksters across a very wide range of literary imaginings.

The trickster is a figure involved with transitions, especially death (Hermes as psychopomp led souls from this to the next world); with marginality and transcending boundary-restrictions; with the poetic creativity of the liminal and temporary; with the fertilizing opposition of the outsider who grants us the mirroring that brings recognition of who we truly are; with the humor and self-mockery that is aesthetic in the deepest sense of artistically re-visioning ourselves and our culture. He represents the unbridled generativity of both culture and nature that refuses the three-piece business suit, the stockings and high heels, because, just around the corner, there's the possibility of change and growth.

Jan Clanton Collins

The Shaman

The roots of all healing professions reach down to the archetype of the shaman. I became aware of this about twenty years ago when I was studying psychology in New York. In that most urban of all environments, I began to dream of Native American women and men who healed me, taught me, and called me to be a vessel for the healing of others.

Because of my dreams I began to explore my biological ancestry and found that my great-grandmother had a Native American heritage. About that time, I met Michael Harner at the New School for Social Research. He taught me about shamanism and introduced me to Essie Parrish, shaman of the Kashia Pomo.

I soon found myself driving up the California coast, toward Essie's house, turning east at Stewart's Point, and continuing through forests thick with blossoming rhododendrons and sunlit ferns. For what was I searching? A grandmother? A spiritual heritage? Confirmation of a sacred calling? I found all of these in my conversations with Essie, a powerful, natural, and unassuming teacher. Above all, I found the strength to trust my dreams, to "brave up" as Essie put it. As I experienced tests and trials as she had, an inner core of being would always remain with me. The recurrent help of inner figures was a theme I noted in her dreams as she recounted them to me, and in my own dreams, which I told to her. After our visit, I drove back to Berkeley, reassured and stronger.

I am now in my forties, a seasoned Jungian analyst and a psychological anthropologist. I think back to that time in my twenties and the meeting with Essie Parrish as the first outer manifestation of an inner experience of the Self in the form of the shaman, the ancient root archetype of healers. A shaman is, by Mircea Eliade's definition, a person who journeys in an altered state of consciousness for the purpose of helping others.[1]

I have sought contact with shamans and those who have learned from them because I feel there is much to discover and share. By studying with Michael Harner, I learned to enter the shamanic state of consciousness, traveling to the Upper World and the Lower World in response to the drum or rattle. Journeying is a powerful tool for connecting with shamanic wisdom which many people can learn to utilize under the direction of an experienced teacher. The skill of using monotonous percussion sounds to alter one's state of consciousness is a widespread shamanic technique that needs to be respected and approached with care.

On finding a teacher of shamanic techniques, it is well to post a note of caution: shamans vary in their authenticity just as psychologists, analysts, and medical doctors do, so it is important not to idealize practicing shamans. One needs to apply the same kinds of standards to the shaman's work as one would apply to the work of a physician or an analyst. In my experience, however, the real shaman is unmistakable: unpretentious, contained, playful, related, harmonious, and competent, emphasizing love, respect, and optimism. Above all, the true shaman is at peace.

Claude Lévi-Strauss compared the shamanistic cure to the psychoanalytic cure and concluded that "the shamanistic cure seems to be the exact counterpart of the psychoanalytic cure, but with an inversion of all the elements. Both cures aim at inducing an experience, and both succeed by creating a myth which the patient has to live or re-live."[2] A distinction is made by Lévi-Strauss between the "individual myth" of the patient in psychoanalysis and the "social myth" of the shaman's patient.

Today, contrary to Lévi-Strauss's point of view, modern shamans using shamanic techniques both inside and outside the tribal context seem to be increasingly creating individual myths for their patients much as the psychoanalyst does. The *prima materia* for the patient's myth in shamanism is the shaman's vision (or the patient's own vision in an altered state of consciousness supervised by the shaman), while the patient's myth in analysis comes from the patient's dreams as interpreted through dialogue with the analyst. Both ways, therefore, could possibly provide a doorway to individual myth. The shamanic tradition particularly emphasizes the connection of the individual to a social context that increasingly becomes the whole world or "all our relations" in its broadest possible sense.

In their work on shamanism, Lowell John Bean and Sylvia Brakke Vane emphasize the creative dimension of shamanism both historically and in today's world. They trace the beginnings of medicine, religion, art, music, dance, and literature to "revelations gained in states of trance." The social aspects of the shaman's role are well expressed by Bean and Vane:

> The full-fledged shaman is a person of power, controlling, directing, and persuading other members of a society, and usually stands at the apex of the power hierarchy. The power is derived not only from the knowledge and wisdom acquired during apprenticeship and initiation, but also from the confidence of the society, from the legitimacy of the role.[3]

In my own experience, I found that when I came close to the shaman archetype, synchronistic experiences began to multiply. I laughed more! I began to experience all things—nature and human beings, the inner world and the outer world—as more connected. I found an awareness that everything is alive. Order, pattern, and meaning became much more apparent. Each day brought new insight and surprise.

My meeting with another shaman in Soweto in South Africa illustrates newfound acceptance of synchronicity. Cecil Burney and I have traveled to Soweto to meet the Zulu sangoma (shaman) Credo Mutwa. When Cecil recounted his dreams, Credo Mutwa linked them to the lives of his own ancestors. When Cecil and Credo Mutwa exchanged gifts, Cecil received a sculpture of a lion—a central image from a dream he had not described but which had led him to visit Credo Mutwa. This story emphasizes that in approaching the shaman, one becomes aware of meaningful connections. The focus on ordinary, rational consciousness may be given up for the moment, and magic lives. There, all things are interconnected. With effort, I have learned to bring some of the magic back into my daily life.

In traditional non-Western cultures, the world of dream, myth, and ritual is considered to have its own reality. In some cultures, it is "normal" waking life that is distrusted and considered less fully real. The archetype of the shaman brings a sense of renewal through its ability to unite these worlds: to enter the supernatural world and bring back a vision that gives meaning to everyday life. Dreams, shamanic journeying, and visits with practicing shamans are three ways of approaching the archetype of the shaman. These three ways bring about a fourth: the experience of one's own inner shaman. This awareness gives us a connection to an ancient and democratic tradition in which each person finds a personal inner wisdom. We each can step through the shamanic door to discover our own inner truth. What we bring back heals and enlightens.

Christine Downing

The Healer

The idea that woundedness, illness, and suffering are a prerequisite for taking on the role of healer appears in the myths and rituals of traditional cultures throughout the world. Reflection on this theme conjures up for me remembrance of a particular dream, dreamed long ago and not by me but by a woman friend in Jungian training.

She dreamed that she and her training analyst were together undertaking the exploration of an undersea world, making their way through all of the fantastically beautifully colored coral and other plants that grow at the bottom of the sea. All around them were brilliantly tinted fish and other wondrously strange inhabitants of the sea. The passage was a difficult one. They knew it was important to make their way without brushing against the fatally poisonous coral and without disturbing the living creatures whose world they had entered. My friend's hands clasped her analyst's ankles as he led the way through the unfamiliar terrain. She found herself trusting his guidance, confidently following his lead, until suddenly he made a turn which seemed to push her directly against a sharp piece of coral. The wound was deep and began to bleed. Soon after, they emerged from the water. Feeling betrayed, she turned to him and asked, "How could you let that happen to me?"

"Only the wounded healer heals," he replied.

Those words reverberate because they are confirmed by my own experience. I know that it is my own fragility and vulnerability, my experiences of what I can only call "loss of soul" (one of its most painful dimensions was that the part of me that dreams seemed to have died) that underlie whatever power I have as a healer or teacher. I have also learned in a personal way that healing often involves wounding. To take apart carefully wrought defenses as part of his work, the teacher may often need to reveal ignorance and heighten confusion, and the therapist may often need to uncover hidden pain.

Freud and Jung, the two healers of the soul from whom I've learned the most, both clearly knew of this complex interrelationship between wounds and healing. Freud was initiated into his depth understanding of the psyche by the death of his father and the eventual discovery of the murderous resentment and unrelenting rivalry he had felt since childhood toward his father whom he knew he loved. Attending to the isolating depression and the disruptive dreams that preoccupied him during the next few years led him to acknowledge, "I am my most difficult patient." Through the exploration of his own patienthood Freud came to recognize the woundedness of all of us. It is not only neurotic or psychotic people who are ill, for to participate in civilization, as all humans must, is to be deeply discontent, dis-eased, inevitably restrained from true fulfillment of some of our most powerful longings. As a healer Freud could aid the transition from hysteric misery to common unhappiness; he could offer sympathy, understanding, and courage, but he could not cure; he could not eliminate our woundedness. In one of his last essays, "Analysis Terminable and Interminable," he acknowledges how, after a long, sustained analysis, one is changed and yet remains the same. He suggests that the most important task in analysis is the acceptance of our finitude and preparation for our death.

Jung's call came by way of the symbolic death of his symbolic father through his break with Freud. This led him into years of psychoticlike immersion in the unconscious which he reports so vividly in "The Confrontation with the Unconscious" chapter of *Memories, Dreams, Reflections*. Later, in *The Psychology of the Transference*, he reaffirms how important it is that therapists remember the experiences of woundedness that led them to become involved in therapy to begin with, and that they remain open to further wounding. Jung believes that in the therapeutic relationship therapists, too, get involved in a transformative process that, like their patients, they may often find difficult, confusing, and painful. Effective therapy depends on the therapists' readiness to risk being hurt in the process and changed by it, and their willingness to communicate that readiness. Jung also speaks of the importance of healers remembering that they, too, are wounded in order to protect themselves from the danger of inflation, the danger of being pulled into an identification with the healer archetype.

The wounded healer also plays an important role in Greek mythology. In the religious healing tradition of ancient Greece, it was assumed that the god who can heal is the one responsible for the wounding in the first place. Thus the sufferers must seek to discover which deity has been offended and which ritual acts must be undertaken to be purified of their pollution. Ritual healing was based on homeopathic assumptions: the agent of wounding and healing are one. The Greeks also believed that the deities had themselves suffered whatever they might impose on others.

The major Greek deity associated with healing is Apollo. To understand this connection is to let go of our superficial identification of this god with dispassionate abstraction, with formal perfection and invulnerable self-sufficiency. It means going behind Nietzsche's heuristic contrast between Apollo and Dionysus; it means going behind the Delphic vision of Apollo to older, more complex representations.

Though I know of no tale in which Apollo is literally wounded, there are many that portray his distress at the death of young beloveds, like Hyacinthus and Cyparissus. Apollo also received a serious wounding to his dignity as a god when he killed the Cyclops, who had made the thunderbolts with which Zeus slew Apollo's son, Asklepios. As punishment, Zeus sentenced Apollo to a year's stint as servant of a mortal king, Alkestis. The year with Alkestis represented a year of purification; the connection to our theme may be more evident if we remember that the Greeks saw pollution as homologous with a wound.

But the recognition of Apollo as a healer seems to proceed more from his being a wound*ing* rather than a wound*ed* god. His arrows brought disease and swift death to men, as the arrows of his sister Artemis were held responsible for women's deaths not caused by visible violence. The rarely visited mountaintop temple at Baasae was built by citizens of the faraway town of Phigaleia in gratitude for Apollo's finally bringing to an end the plague he had visited upon them. The sculpture known as the Apollo Belevedere is a Roman copy of a statue initially made in response to a community seeking to bring a similar devastation to an end.

As Apollo comes to be identified primarily with his temple at Delphi, his work as healer comes more and more to be accomplished through his oracular activity. Apollo had wrested control of the Delphic oracle from the primordial earth mother goddess, Gaia, by killing the Python she had established as its guardian. Originally the oracle had probably been incubational; petitioners received the directions they sought through dreams sent by Gaia. In Apollo's time, female seers, called Pythia, responded to the questions of those who sought to know how they might purify themselves or their city. Consultation of the oracle represented an attempt at a rational approach to the resolution of suffering; one came to learn the source of one's pollution and its remedy. Yet the answers were cryptic, and usually one's first or even second interpretation of what action they directed was wrong. Following the oracle often made things worse before it made them better.[1]

Remembrance that we are mortal and not divine is a prerequisite to receiving healing from Apollo. In his realm, healing depends on true knowledge of one's situation. Apollo's famous dictum, "Know Thyself," meant not as *we* might suppose: "Know the truth about your individual personal history," but "Remember that you are mortal." The god of healing remains the god associated with death.

Like all the major deities, Apollo is a god associated with many realms other than healing, although his particular way of being a healer is integrally related to his other functions and attributes. Often it is among members of the next generation, among the children of the Olympians, that we find more specialized divinities. Thus it is Apollo's son, Asklepios, who becomes preeminently *the* god of healing. His power derives from his father. Even at Epidauros, the site most identified with Asklepios, his temple is built above the ruins of an ancient Apollo temple. The Asklepian sanctuary in the gentle, peaceful valley was in classical times overlooked by an Apollo temple erected on the hilltop far above. Once long ago, as Apollo Maleatus, Apollo himself had healed the sick by visiting them in their dreams. But as Apollo becomes more and more the Apollo of Delphi, such visitations come to seem incongruous.[2] Now it is another god, his son, who makes nocturnal appearances.

The story of Asklepios's birth encapsulates much of who he is. He was the result of a love affair between Apollo and a beautiful mortal woman named (in the most widely accepted traditions) Koronis, a granddaughter of Ares, the god of war, and a sister of Ixion, the first human murderer. The genealogy thus again brings together the motifs of healing and death. According to the most often-cited version, when Koronis discovered she was pregnant, she decided to find a mortal man who might wed her and give her child legitimacy. Apollo, affronted that any woman might prefer a human husband to a divine lover, sent Artemis to kill Koronis and the bridesmaids; he himself kills the groom. Unwilling to have his unborn son die in this holocaust, Apollo, acting as surgeon and midwife, cuts open his dying mistress's womb to rescue the almost full-term child, and thus Asklepios is born (the first Caesarean, it is sometimes jokingly said), saved from death so that he might grow up to heal others.

Asklepios was placed in the care of Cheiron, the wise centaur who was teacher also to Jason, Achilles, and Actaeon. The centaurs, a race of creatures with the bodies of horses and shoulders and heads of men, who descended from Apollo or perhaps from Ixion, were wild and fearful. But Cheiron, whose genealogy was distinctive for he, like Zeus and many of the Olympians, was a child of Kronos, was wise and gentle. In his case his animal nature seemed to signify an attunement to instinctual wisdom and a deep understanding of embodiment, which informed his gifts as hunter, sculptor, and healer. Unlike the other centaurs, Cheiron was an immortal. But during the course of Herakles's battle against the centaurs, Cheiron had been wounded by an arrow dipped in the poisonous gall of the Hydra, whom Herakles had killed long before. This wound was deep and painful, and it would not heal. Indeed, so unremitting was his distress that Cheiron came to regret an immortality from which he could not escape. One senses that the incurably wounded centaur's gifts as healer were shaped by his own ineluctable fate.

For a long while, when I thought of the wounded healer, I had really had in mind the *healed* healer, the once-wounded healer whose wounds were now healed. Cheiron represents something different: the still-wounded healer. This suggests a perspective from which our wounds are not something to get over, to put behind us, to hide, but an integral part of our being. This does not mean that being wounded is true health, but that acceptance of our wounds is part of true health, as is acceptance that some wounds heal and some do not.

None of Cheiron's other famous pupils were as profoundly influenced by him as was Asklepios. The others gave or received healing in the course of their exploits as warriors or hunters; he dedicated his life to healing. In recognition of his gifts as a physician, Athene shared with him the vials of blood collected from the wound made when Perseus severed the gorgon Medusa's head from her body. The blood that dripped from the left vein was a magically potent poison; the blood from the right was reputed to have the power to restore the dead to life. On several occasions, perhaps in sympathetic remembrance of his mother's unjust death, Asklepios used the magic potion to bring back to life heroes unjustly punished by the gods, heroes prematurely sent to Hades.

Zeus, angry at Asklepios's presumption in transgressing *the* boundary between humanity and gods, struck Asklepios with his thunderbolts and sent him to Hades, so that he, though a god, might himself experience the fate of mortals. Thus Asklepios becomes the only god in Greek mythology to experience death.

For the Greeks, then, *the* god of healing is the one who knows what it is to die. Although his stay in Hades was only temporary, and although he can experience mortality without forfeiting his immortality, it is Asklepios's own experience of vulnerability to death that makes him seem to the Greeks a more kindly, benevolent god than any other.

As a god who had spent time in the underworld, it is not surprising that Asklepios was seen as a participant in Persephone's mysteries, an initiate of Eleusis. The god of healing has come to understand his work as subordinate to hers. Though not himself an underworld deity, he urges those who come to him to offer prayers to Demeter and Persephone. He can save one from death *now*, but not for good. The respite his healing provides gives those who are not yet ready for death an interval to prepare for the inevitable. The healing of the body gives us time to attend to the health of our souls. Those who sought Asklepios's aid believed that if the god refuses to heal, the time for one's death has come. Sometimes, of course, death is a *release* from illness.

Thus there is a shrine to Asklepios at Eleusis. But his own cult center was at Epidauros, and the rituals there were different from those at any other temple site. For this god was available to the individual whenever he was sought; his temple was open every day, not only on designated ritual occasions. Though not a chthonic hero associated with the underworld, Asklepios was also not an Olympian; he was a god who stayed on earth. Those who came to Epidauros were the hopeless cases, patients who had exhausted the medical resources of their own communities, who knew they were threatened with death and felt they were not yet ready. We should note, however, that the acutely moribund were not allowed within the god's precincts. Literal death was excluded from this realm of healing, as was literal birth, for pregnancy needs no cure. (Barren women, however, came to the shrine in the hopes of being impregnated by the god.) The ritually impure, the criminal, were also excluded.

One went through this ritual alone; it was not a communal event as the rites associated with other gods were. There were three days of ritual preparation—fasting, bathing, sacrificial offerings to Asklepios, Apollo, Mnemosyne (Memory, the mother of the muses; perhaps the prayers to her expressed one's hope of being re-membered), and Tyche (Success). Then, dressed in ordinary clothes, one was led by a *therapeute* to a small stone chamber, empty except for a simple stone sleeping platform, a *kline* (the origin of our word *clinic*), a space one might have visited in daylight during the period of preparation. The therapeute withdrew, leaving the patient alone with his or her dreams and with the god. After offering a prayer to Themis (right order), one settled down to sleep in hope that the god himself would come in one's dreams.

The Greeks believed that when we sleep, our *psyche*, that in us which is quiescent during waking life, becomes active. It is the psyche that dreams and that persists after the death of our bodies and lives on in Hades. "Psyche" represents the core of our individual being, our personal essence, the aspect of the patient that will encounter the god. The psyche *sees* dreams and receives them; dreams are god-sent and are theophanies. In the Asklepian ritual, the epiphany, the god's appearance in a dream, was understood as the healing event. His coming marked the hidden transition between illness and the return to health. Every cure was a divine act, a mystery, which could only happen in the dark. At Epidauros, unlike Delphi, it was the patient who had the healing vision rather than the priest or priestess. The vision itself accomplished the cure; there was no need for interpretation or for action based on the dream's prescription.

In the patient's dream, the god might appear in his humanlike form or in theriomorphic form as a snake or as a dog. Many of the recorded dreams describe a snake or a dog licking the afflicted part and thus healing it; barren women told of dreams in which a snake appeared and copulated with them. As in so many other religious traditions, the snake was seen as emblematic of the mysterious relation between death and rebirth. Dogs, too, were associated with underworld experience: three-headed Cerberus welcomes the dead to Hades but eats those who try to leave; night-roaming Hekate is accompanied by baying hounds, the restless spirits of those not given ritual burial.

When the god appeared in dreams as a humanlike physician, he acted on the pattern of rational medicine; his cures were medical cures. He applied salves, made use of drugs, and operated, though his procedures were often contrary to human theories of treatment, and his surgeries more radical than those any mortal healer would dare undertake.[3]

Dreaming, the patient was alone with the god. The therapeute returned in the morning to the sleeping chamber only to record the dream, though the patient's retelling may no doubt have had some salutary effect. In the retelling, the dream may have been subtly revised to accord with the culturally expected dream pattern.

Afterward the patient would offer a song of praise in gratitude for what he had been given and sacrifice a rooster to the god as a token that daylight had overcome the dark, and health has overcome disease. Despite his recognition of the ultimate power of the underworld deities, Asklepios remains a son of Apollo, dedicated to life on the sunlit earth and to the never ultimately victorious struggle against death.

Adolf Guggenbühl-Craig

The Invalid

Health and invalidism seem to be opposing ways of viewing life. One can either see oneself as healthy, strong, and "whole," or as deficient, lacking somehow in body and psyche. From the health perspective, deficiencies, disabilities, and *lacunae* are but temporary problems which must be overcome; from the invalid's perspective they are simply part of life.

If there is an Archetype of the Invalid, however, should there not be a mythological personification of it? Do not archetypes usually appear in mythology as gods or goddesses? Were not such collective representations the basis for Jung's theory of archetypes? Where then, in which mythologies, do we find the invalid as a collective image?

The Greek gods seem to be anything but invalids. In keeping with their exalted position they are portrayed as physically perfect beings. There are only two exceptions: Hephaistos, who limps, and Achilles with his vulnerable heel. Even the perfect, untouchable hero has a weakness.

Moving to Germanic mythology, we find a different state of affairs. Here there are numerous examples of invalids. In fact, the whole of Germanic mythology seems to be overshadowed by an atmosphere of foreboding—the Nidhoggr gnawing at the roots of Yggdrasil, the world tree, and the knowledge of the impending *Goetterdaemerung*. As an individual figure, we find Thor, the god of war, who has a mill stone embedded in his forehead—a painful memento of an early battle. Other Germanic gods suffer from severe wounds, are missing a hand, or something of the sort. Baldur, the shining one, is invincible against anything except the parasitic mistletoe. Invalidism seems to be of greater importance for Germanic mythology than it was for the Greeks.

Many non-European mythologies—the Mexican and the Indian, for example—often portray their gods as grotesque, distorted beings. Similarly, we find bizarre deity figures from prehistoric cultures which give a crippled impression.

Artists often create mythological images of this kind. I see the paintings of Velasquez, for instance, as an expression of the archetype of the invalid. His figures are frequently grotesque and distorted. The film-maker Fellini flavors his works heavily with invalids—the crippled, perverse, and abnormal aspects of the human race, the elephantine woman or skeletal man. The invalid as a mythical image and symbol appears also in classical adventure stores. One is reminded of the pirate stories, of Long John Silver with his peg leg in Stevenson's *Treasure Island* or Peter Pan's archrival, Captain Hook, with his metallic prosthesis. The figure of the pirate, in itself an image of the invalid, traditionally is missing an arm or leg or at least has a patch over one eye. Another familiar image of the invalid from literature is Hugo's Quasimodo, the Hunchback of Notre Dame. In general, the arts seem to point to the archetype of the invalid—what are the gargoyles on the Cathedral of Notre Dame if not invalids?

Given the archetype of the invalid, there must also be an invalid complex since archetypes draw parts of the psyche and psychic experience to themselves. This is what is meant by a complex. A man who has a father complex tends to experience life within the framework of the patriarchal, whether it has to do with "father" and "fathering" or not. A policeman, for example, makes him feel like a small boy being confronted by his paternal parent. There is, in point of fact, an invalid complex. In the course of my work as a psychotherapist, I have often encountered women—and men as well—who could only fall in love with invalids. They were sexually attracted only to those who were physical invalids.

Allow me to sketch out a brief "differential diagnosis" of the archetype of the invalid by way of definition and comparison. The invalid must not be confused with the archetype of the child. The child, like the invalid, is weak and inferior, lacking the qualities of the adult. The child, however, *grows*, changes, becomes adult, "kills the father." It has a future. The archetype of the invalid must also not be confused with that of illness. Illness, much like the child, has a future. It leads to death, to health or, even, to invalidism. It is temporal, a passing threat, a catastrophe. Illness may well impair psychic or physical functioning, but it is acute, dynamic, temporary. Invalidism leads nowhere, neither to death nor to health. It is chronic, a lasting deficiency. It is a chronic state of being "out of order."

Those who live out the archetype of the invalid can be very tiresome and annoying to those around them. I might note parenthetically that only one other archetype makes people so tiresome and annoying: the archetype or the fantasy of health. A person who goes on and on about his bad back is pretty boring, but is nothing compared to someone who never tires of telling about his physical prowess, how his heart still beats regularly and rhythmically after jogging six miles, how he gets up every morning at six o'clock to take an ice-cold shower.

Of course, an archetype in and of itself is neither good nor bad, neither interesting nor boring. Depending on the situation and our point of view, it can seem to be negative or positive. Our job as psychotherapists is to study and reflect on the archetypes and their characteristics, to allow ourselves to be amazed by them, to learn, in some small measure, to deal with them in actual experience. The archetype of the invalid can be very annoying; it can, on the other hand, be very pleasant as in the following example.

I knew a middle-aged man who suffered from chronic back pains, periodic depressions, and continual fatigue. At the same time, he was a nice person to have around—he made others feel helpful and useful. You could always do something for him, like finding him a comfortable arm chair. He seemed to appreciate gestures of this sort. He was in no way a threat to those around him; there was no sense of competitiveness for their time and attention. He made you feel kindly and generous, provoking a friendly, accepting attitude in others. It was most relaxing to be with him. If the archetype of the invalid is recognized and respected, it gives rise to reflection and discussion. In the case of this man, whenever someone would suggest going for a walk, he would reply, "No, thank you, my back hurts. Why don't we stay here and chat a little?"

The archetype of the invalid can be very fruitful for the person living it out. It counteracts inflation; it cultivates modesty. Because human weakness and failings are given their due, a kind of spiritualization is possible. Invalidism is a continual *memento mori*, an ongoing confrontation with physical and psychic limitations. It allows no escape into fantasies of health or away from an awareness of death. It promotes patience and curbs obsessional doing. In a way, it is a very *human* archetype. The fantasy of health and wholeness in body and soul may be suitable for the gods, but for mere mortals it is a tribulation. *Quod licet jovi non licet bovi.*

Because the archetype of the invalid emphasizes human dependence, because it forces acceptance of our mutual need of and for others, it is an important factor in relationships. We are haunted today by a psychological *fata morgana*—the illusion of the Independent Person. There are still those who believe it possible to be totally independent of others. *All* of us are dependent on someone—on husbands or wives, on fathers or mothers, on our children, friends, even our neighbors. Knowledge of our own deficiencies and weaknesses, of our own invalidism, helps us to realize our eternal dependence on someone or something. A person who is a "cripple" in regard to his feelings will always be dependent on those with a "healthy" feeling life. Mutual as well as one-sided dependency comes into its own with the archetype of the invalid. It serves as a counter-balance to the "rolling-stone-gathers-no-moss" image of the wandering hero, a popular figure among members of the younger generation. For them the ideal is to move like free spirits throughout the world with no attachments, no hindrances: today in India and tomorrow in Mexico. Freedom and independence are their alpha and omega, the be-and-end-all of their existence.

Another area in which the archetype of the invalid plays an important role is the phenomenon of transference in psychotherapy. Dependency in psychotherapy is generally understood as a father or mother transference and is viewed as a regression. Unfortunately, the child/parent regression fantasy in psychotherapy can be very damaging. More often than not a client's dependency reflects not the child, but the invalid. Sometimes clients remain dependent on their therapists for years—the child seems never to grow up. How can it? We are not dealing with a *child*, but with an invalid and his or her corresponding need to be dependent! In these situations the analyst often develops a guilty conscience. He asks himself if he is not, perhaps unconsciously, trying to maintain a full practice by constellating the analysand's dependency. The question is out of place. The analyst is not being unethical, but is serving in a legitimate fashion as the invalid's crutch. Although the analyst might attempt to shift the analysand's need for dependency to someone else, to a neighbor or a friend, one thing is certain: the crutch will always be necessary. The goal of total independence is simply unrealistic. If, on the other hand, the analyst identifies with the fantasy of health, of wholeness and growth, he simply will not see what is happening. He will believe himself to be dealing with the child archetype. He fails to realize that the absence of growth and healing points to the invalid, not to the child. The child, as we noted above, grows and requires help only for a time.

I must reiterate that the difficulties and attendant dangers in dealing with the invalid can never be overestimated. It is just these difficulties and dangers which frequently result in both a collective and individual repression, characterized by the slogan, "the invalid shall always be with us!" In our confrontation with invalidism, we all too readily succumb to a fatalistic attitude, to passivity that says, "Why bother? There is nothing we can do anyway!" Failing the proper understanding of the archetype of the invalid, we give up, we stop trying to heal that which can be healed. To some extent, the great strides made in both medicine and psychiatry are a result of the repression of the invalid. We have become so captivated by the fantasy of total health that we are indefatigable in our efforts toward its realization. Yet we analysts should not be the first to cast stones: the fantasy of health fills our practices just as surely as does that of invalidism.

If I appear *ipso facto* as a self-appointed attorney for the defense in the case "health vs. invalidism," it is because the archetype of the invalid has too long been ignored; it has not been granted the respect it deserves. My attacks on "health," the prosecution's position, are not intended to discredit, but rather to help achieve some semblance of balance between essential perspectives. In the sense of further developing my case, I should like to point out the pitfalls of the health/wholeness archetype, my worthy opponent.

According to the contemporary fantasy of health, we must become whole where wholeness is understood in the sense of perfection: "Be ye perfect . . ." The slightest defect, the least malfunction must be cured, removed or eradicated. Although there was a time when a melancholic temperament was accepted, even idealized, today melancholics are diagnosed as "depressive," are tranquilized and medicated to the point of being blissfully happy vegetables. Deep down inside we are all aware of our failings, our weakness, our invalidism. At the same time we repress this realization with whatever means possible. We struggle endlessly, senselessly, to maintain the illusion of wholeness through trying to achieve perfect health.

Our blindness to the place and importance of the invalid archetype becomes a moralistic attitude, holding health and wholeness as the ultimate good. It is not hard to imagine how devastating this attitude is in dealing with those suffering from neuroses and psychosomatic disorders. I am continually struck by the tone of moral superiority that creeps into psychotherapists' voices when discussing cases of this nature. Neurotics and psychosomatics are simply inferior; they cannot be healed because they do not want to be. They do not want to change; they do not want to grow. They refuse our attempts for their betterment. They will not even listen to their dreams! Like drowning men, they cling to their resistances, defending themselves, as we see it, tenaciously against the therapist who is only trying to help them. Such people, such poor, benighted souls are only worthy of our attention when they embrace our growth/health/ wholeness fantasy (is it a fantasy or is it a delusional fixation?). As therapists, we are only interested in them when they *want* to be healed.

I do not wish to leave the impression that all patients are chronic cases or cannot be healed. I merely wish to point out that, in instances where the archetype of the invalid is manifested, healing and wholeness are simply not possible. To accept this fact might seem immoral, both to patient and analyst. The positive effects will, however, soon offset any lingering doubts. Because healing and wholeness are so much in vogue these days, we desperately need reflection and acceptance of the invalid archetype.

To ignore or denigrate an archetype invites its wrath and vengeance, and the archetype of the invalid is no exception. It seems that the harder we try to heal chronic neurotic or psychosomatic patients, the more desperately they resist. They become more tyrannical, more demanding and claim more of our time and attention. Far from healing, our efforts seem but to exacerbate the condition. It would appear that many people are simply waiting for the moment when they can openly claim their invalidism. A minor accident, a slight decrease of some physical or mental capacity, and they give up their jobs, claim disability insurance, and expect that others will take care of them. In each of us they arouse guilt feelings. They seem to say, "Now I'm an invalid. Now it is up to you to take care of me." It is our failure to accept the invalid in each of us, our fantasy that human beings should be as healthy as those idealized Greek gods, that makes us unable to cope with the archetype of the invalid when we meet it. Our guilt forces us to pay homage to what we refuse to accept.

Human beings operate out of four basic modes or functions: thinking, feeling, sensation, and intuition. Theoretically we all have at least the potential of all four: one function is superior, another is inferior, and the remaining two are auxiliary. The High Priests of Health and Wholeness would have us help our patients to develop all four. However, many patients, for some reason or other, lack one or two of these functions. It is as if they were deformed or crippled. If, for example, they are missing the feeling function, it would be pointless to help them to develop what is not there. We would, rather, do better to help them explore the measure of their deficiency, show them how to live with it, and demonstrate how they might profit from someone who, for example, had a well-developed feeling function. Attempting to develop all four functions with such patients would only lead to disappointment and frustration for both patient and therapist. Instead of accepting and respecting the patient as he is, an invalid, there is the danger that therapist and patient will not only reject invalidism, but will also despise it. The result for the patient can understandably be disastrous. Are not we analysts really the advocates of the archetype of the invalid? Is not that what we should be about?

The psyche is viewed on one hand as being archetypal, functioning according to given, universal patterns of behavior and experience. On the other hand, it demonstrates completely individual, unique characteristics. The images of wholeness and invalidism are both universals—in other words, archetypal. Let us ask ourselves whether they are two, totally different archetypes or whether they belong together as aspects of the same archetype. The image of invalidism cannot exist without the image of wholeness; the figure of the Imperfect can only be seen upon the ground of the Perfect.

For purposes of discussion, it is easier to speak of two separate archetypes. In the final analysis, however, both Wholeness and Invalidism are aspects of the Self, representing basic polarities within our psyche. Unfortunately, when we talk about the Self, there is much too much said about qualities like roundness, completeness, and wholeness. It is high time that we spoke of the deficiency, the invalidism of the Self. I have always had difficulty with the fact that mandalas are regarded as symbols *par excellence* of the Self—they are much too whole for my taste. Man comes to the full realization of himself, of his Self, through his invalidism; completeness is fulfilled through incompleteness.

Mary E. Hunt

The Friend

Everyone wants to make friends, have friends, be friends. No one likes to lose friends, disappoint friends, or dishonor friends. The question is, how do we know any of this when so very little exists in the literature and lore of Western society to ground an understanding of friendship and to encourage its flowering? It is of the nature of archetypes to be so deeply woven into the fabric of individual and collective psyches as to be implicit, but such a loud silence on friendship seems to be going a step too far.

Contemporary psychology offers shelves of books on myths and stories, fairy tales and parables on every conceivable image, but few on the value of friendships. Amid the Great Mothers and the Cosmic Children, the Trickster and the Crone, it would seem that something as simple as Friends would emerge often as a common carrier of relationality. Strangely, friendships remain an afterthought, a catch-all category that takes a back seat to marriage and family-based archetypes, one that loses out to gender and activity-oriented models, one that is so common as to be passed over at peril to us all.

An Analysis of Friendships

I realized the insignificant place given to friendships in the relational panoply while reviewing theological literature. The few findings I encountered were interrelated: the usual model was based on Aristotle's pyramid, with men's experiences of friendship being normative; an inverse relationship applies between the number of friends and the degree of closeness (i.e., the closer the type of friendship, the fewer one is capable of, and only men are capable of achieving the pinnacle of friendship with other men); and marriage, rather than friendship, is seen as the ultimate relational achievement. In short, men have a monopoly on friendship. They freeze it in hierarchical form, and they contradict it publicly by getting married.

I found these shortcomings to be counterintuitive because friendship is central to my sense of self and my relationship to the world, and is deeply flawed from a feminist perspective because women seem to value friendship above almost everything else. My response was to use women's friendships as the starting point for a feminist theology of friendship.

I labeled my work *Fierce Tenderness* out of my experience, not all of it happy, with friends. The seeming emotional juxtaposition struck a deep chord in readers who, with little explanation necessary, found it consistent with their relationships of deepest meaning and value.[1] The powerful, sometimes brutal sense of honesty and passion is coupled with the gentle, always embodied sense of nurture and care that friends provide for one another. Far from being a romanticization of what are admittedly complex relationships, friendship is the relational context in which love and power find their expression, in which we dare to experiment, and in which we express the quality of life that we desire. Who but friends will tolerate our peculiarities? Who better than friends with whom we become ever more differentiated?

What became clear is that women's friendships with women are quite different from the male model, and that such differences can be helpful to women and men who are friends, as well as to men who seek to overcome their conditioning and be fierce and tender friends with men. Moreover, a feminist approach to friendship prioritizes quality and not quantity of friends. It encourages varieties of friendships rather than reserving for heterosexual marriage the mark of maturity. Above all, it begins with a friendly relationship with the self.

The best kept secret I found was that people like to talk about their friends. Everyone feels an expert on the topic. The very theme makes the consideration of it communal and participatory. In short, friendships function archetypally.

It remains a puzzle why Freud, Jung, and their followers did not immediately light on the notion of friendship as central to the psychological well-being of healthy humans. I do not bemoan this insofar as the shortchomings of their typologies are well articulated in the many critiques of the essentialism, cultural imperialism, sexism, and racism that underlie them.[2] Still, the fact that friendship is not often among the conspicuous categories is perplexing. I suspect it is something like what happens when I look into the cupboard for the pepper shaker. I can never find it amid the exotic herbs and spices that I use less frequently. The trusty pepper, used so often that the container is more smudged than the rest, is so ordinary it seems invisible.

Re-valuing Friendship

The reasons for friendship's obscurity seem to me to be precisely its strengths. I see four such reasons that encourage a re-valuing of friendship in a world that is unfriendly to most of us and those people and things we value:

First, *friendship is not a dualistic concept but a unitive one*. Most archetypes have their twin, their pair, their opposite. Gender balance (Mother, Father), age distribution (Puer, Senex), and other dualistic expressions are absent in friendships where two or more friends are virtually the same to one another. Of course, there are individual differences of race/ethnicity, class, age, sexual preference, gender, and so forth, but in relationship a friend is a friend is a friend.

To enter into friendship, to really experience its archetypal dimensions, one must love, respect, question, accept. Imagine friendship with a dear friend, a dead friend, a dubious friend. One finds many degrees of the same dynamics. Imagine it with an animal, with the earth, with the spirit realm wherein one feels the reciprocity of friendship, the being befriended. Note, too, how hard it is to say "friend" in the singular. It exists as a conceptual and grammatical place holder when in fact the reality is always plural. We are friends, we were friends, we would like to be become friends. Even as I befriend myself I am something more than singular, an insight into the unitive nature of the friendly beast.

Second, *friendship is a relationship that crosses ages, genders, sexual preferences, legal, social, and cultural barriers*. I do not mean to suggest that friendship is a relational cure-all, nor do I mean to freight it with expectations that would render most human efforts disappointing. Rather, I think friendship has been privatized and has become the subject of greeting cards instead of a serious tool for diplomacy, simply because it is so powerful. Few archetypes are so versatile: friendship is highlighted in children and elderly people alike, and can be seen in women and men in equal measure.

The most obvious ethical referent for friendship, passed over, I believe, to keep the status quo solid, is sex. How easy it would be if we formulated sexual norms on the basis of friendships and not gender, so that same-sex or mixed-gender relationships were equally subject to criteria of friendship, not sexual preference. Discrimination then would be against those who violate the demands of friendship, the expectation that we treat one another with reverence, that we have fun together, that we honor our unity and celebrate it with safe, sensual, and consensual delight. Sexual abuse and child abuse would be censured as unfriendly acts resulting in injury of those whose friendship we are taught to value. Far from leading to ethical chaos, a sexual norm based on friendship would level the moral playing field and sharpen the special obligations that come with such intimacy.

Friendship is not an elixir for erasing difference but a powerful motivation for bridging the enemy-producing social structure in which we live.[3] Racism is a paradigm in which obvious differences lead to discrimination and death. While it would be naive to say that friendships between people of different racial/ethnic groups are the solution to such deeply rooted social problems, it is equally unhelpful to label friendships a private solution to a public problem. Interracial friendships, as well as cross-class friendships, and friendships between people of widely varying ages are a promising part of a political solution to a world perched dangerously on the brink of the most unfriendly act of all, war.

Friends have an impact on one another. Friends make us do things we would otherwise never consider. We vote, protest, buy, bank, and worship in large measure because of the influence of friends. Friendships lead us to feel compromised when our political commitments and our personal choices do not jell. Friends force us to reconsider our politics, indeed to notice parts of the world that without them we would pass over. I am wary of placing too much weight on friendships for fear of collapsing complexities. Still, the transforming nature of friendship is so obvious—witness U.S. and Soviet children finding a way to be friends despite decades of propaganda, Friends of the Earth making the environment a political issue, friendly nations setting up trade agreements that shape global economics—that I cannot overstate its archetypal importance.

This leads me to the third reason, *that friendship is an inherently political relationship.* Some recoil at the notion that their sacred intimacies are not too private for politics. But insofar as friendship is a plural notion with the capacity not to transcend but to transfuse structures that keep us apart, it contains the seeds of social change. We are friends not only in the privacy of our living rooms, but in the glare of the *polis* where other people see and are affected by our bonds.

Some religions have seen this as the virtue of laying down one's life for one's friends. History is replete with examples of people who have turned friendships into social movements. Jane Addams and her Hull House companions were a group of friends; Dorothy Day formed the Catholic Worker Movement out of the religious commitment and political instincts of her friends. It is no coincidence that the "comrades" and "compañeros/compañeras" of political movements call one another by a word best approximated in English as "friends."

The danger, of course, is that friendship can be seen as instrumentalized love. Contacts and networking can replace altruism as a social virtue. I do not mean to confuse these quite different experiences. I mean instead to emphasize the fact that all friendships are predicated on a certain implicit sense of justice that goes by the code name "love," but which is obscured and hallowed into oblivion if it is not expressed concretely in the myriad struggles for social change that are today's definition of politics. This is why friendships need to be made explicit.

Happily, *friendships find expression in liturgy and lovemaking, in art and athletics, in food and fashion,* the fourth part of re-valuing them. The archetype takes over with friends turning up where we least expect them. Who are our co-religionists if not our friends? And with whom better to make love, make children, make a home, make a way, make a wave, make a move than our friends? In our time, especially for those who have access to resources, all of these things are possible and necessary for the quality of life we crave.

What is often missing is the symbolic expression of friendships, a situation being remedied by covenants and commitments, commissionings and celebrations that remind us of the richness that is friendship, the losses that we incur, and the possibilities that accrue when we simply pay attention to this powerful component of our lives.

Ecology is a cosmic expression of friendship with an earth that is neither Mother nor planet, finally, but Friend to us. The earth is not a static surface on which we rest, but the matrix of matter in which we find ourselves. Only friendship, admission of unity, awareness of plurality, political intent, and attention to the aesthetic beginning with our collective survival will usher us into a safe future.

Archetypes have their limits, as Christine Downing has observed in her introduction to this collection. But Friend as a category of personal experience, as a name for those voluntary relationships that we hold most dear, and as a transforming motivator for social change is, nevertheless, one of the most powerful archetypes available.

Epilogue

How Archetypal Images Reshape Our Lives

In examining these many archetypal images I hope to open us to their power to revitalize and reshape our lives. The hope is that we will discover images, perhaps in these pages, perhaps in myth, poetry, or fiction, perhaps in our dreams or in some eventful outward encounter, that will speak to our souls.

As Jung observed, it is never enough just to know about these concepts and reflect on them: "It is no use at all to learn a list of archetypes by heart. Archetypes are complexes of experience that come upon us like fate and their effects are felt in our most personal lives."[1] But once they have "come upon us," we must engage them, enter into dialogue with them, befriend them in order to tap into their creative, transformative power.

Nor should we expect that the images that directly appear to us will neatly fit into any of the forms we have explored in these pages, for living images will spill out of the categories. It is just that which makes them living and life-giving, their capacity to challenge any familiar understanding of the self. Nor will engagement with the imaginal and the archetypal resolve our problems or cure our ills. What it may do is draw us more deeply into the complexity of life, its richness, ambiguity, and challenge.

The point of attending to the archetypal is, after all, not simply to bring me to have a different relation to my psyche, to my self, but to help me toward a different relation to my surround, to teach me imaginal consciousness, to learn to attend to *die Dinge*, the things of the world. For self and world are transformed together. And it may be that this emphasis on archetypal images of the self is but a preliminary preparation for attending to the archetypal dimension of everything and of every thing. I remember Rilke's question:[2]

> *Are we* here *perhaps just to say:*
> *house, bridge, well, jug, fruit, tree, window—*
> *at most, column, tower. . . but to say, understand this, to say it*
> *as the Things themselves never fervently thought to be?*

Notes

Abbreviation

CW: C. G. Jung, *Collected Works* (Bollingen Series XX), translated by R.F. C. Hull and edited by H. Read, M. Fordham, G. Adler, and William McGuire (Princeton, N.J.: Princeton University Press; and London: Routledge and Kegan Paul). Cited by volume number and paragraph or page.

Prologue

1. C. G. Jung, *Memories, Dreams, Reflections* (New York: Random House, 1963), p. 392.
2. *CW* 8, p. 213.
3. Cf. Gaston Bachelard, *The Poetics of Reverie* (Boston: Beacon Press, 1971), pp. 97–142.
4. Jolande Jacobi, *Complex, Archetype, Symbol* (Princeton: Princeton University Press, 1971), p. 50.
5. James Hillman, "An Inquiry Into Image," (Spring 1977):70.
6. Jolande Jacobi, *The Psychology of C. G. Jung* (New Haven: Yale University Press, 1973), p. 45.
7. *CW* 9.1, p. 58.
8. Cf. Demaris S. Wehr, "Religious and Social Dimensions of Jung's Concept of the Anima," *Feminist Archetypal Theory*, eds. Estella Lauter and Carol Schreier Rupprecht (Knoxville: University of Tennessee Press, 1985), p. 27.
9. *CW* 8, p. 190.
10. *CW* 8, pp. 286–289.
11. Hillman, "Image," p. 65.
12. *CW* 9.1, p. 48.
13. Quoted in Jacobi, *Complex*, p. 65,6 from *Eranos Jahrbuch* 1934, p. 223; not included in *CW* 9.1 version of "Archetypes of the Collective Unconscious," though a similar passage occurs in *CW* 14, p. 463.

14. *CW* 9.1, p. 179.
15. James Hillman, *Puer Papers* (Irving, Tex.: Spring Publications, 1979), p. 13.
16. James Hillman, *ReVisioning Psychology* (New York: Harper & Row, 1975), p. 158.
17. *CW* 9.1, p. 31.

Part I Introduction

1. *CW* 9.2, p. 189.
2. *CW* 8, p. 195.
3. *CW* 7, p. 232.
4. *CW* 9.2, p. 21.
5. James Hillman, *Anima: An Anatomy of a Personified Notion* (Dallas: Spring Publications, 1985), p. 173.
6. Ibid., p. 179.
7. Cf., especially June Singer, *Androgyny: The Opposites Within*.

The Persona: The Mask We Wear for the Game of Living

1. E. A. Bennet, "The Double," *Studien zur Analytischen psychologie C. G. Jungs*, vol. 1 (Zurich: Rascher Verlag, 1955), p. 384–396.
2. Ibid., p. 393.
3. Ibid., p. 389.

Anima: The Inner Woman

1. M. Esther Harding, *The Way of All Women* (New York: C. G. Jung Foundation, 1970), p. 12.
2. *CW* 9.2, par. 34.
3. Ibid., par. 40.

Anima: Guide to the Soul

1. For a succinct study of kinds of oppositional pairs and some of the confusions arising when the kinds are not kept distinct, see C. K. Ogden, *Opposition* (Bloomington: Indiana University Press, 1967).
2. *CW* 9.2, section 422.
3. Cf. James Hillman, *The Myth of Analysis* (Evanston, Ill.: Northwestern University Press, 1972), pp. 183–190, and James Hillman, *The Dream and the Underworld* (New York: Harper & Row, 1979), pp. 55–59.

Animus: The Inner Man

1. Jung says in *Aion* (a late work): "Since the anima is an archetype that is found in men, it is reasonable to suppose that an equivalent archetype must be present in women: for just as the man is compensated by a feminine element, so woman is compensated by a masculine one." (*Collected Works*, Vol. 9, ii, p. 14).

2. In the chapter "Anima and Animus" Jung explains why men have animas, and, one would assume, contrariwise, why women have animuses as well. First, Jung asserts that the anima is the soul-image in men. Men's souls have a feminine quality. Personified, we call it the anima, and it is composed of: (1) the experiences of real women the man has known; (2) the man's own femininity; and (3) an *a priori* category. We have here, experience (social-cultural level), and innate biological tendency (biological level) and an *a priori* category (transcendent level). The woman's animus presumably is built on these same factors.

3. I do not quarrel with Polly Young-Eisendrath's reading of the animus and anima as complexes in her book, *Hags and Heroes*. Her reading is innovative and, most important, workable. I think, however, that Jung described both animus and anima more often as archetypal images than he described them as complexes. Many provocative and wonderful discussions with Polly have helped me clarify my own thinking on the matter.

4. Philip Rieff, in his book *The Triumph of the Therapeutic*, speaks of the difference between the sociological and the psychological perspectives regarding the individual and society. In a footnote on p. 3, he says: "From its beginnings, sociological theory has argued against dualist oppositions of human nature and social order, and against individualist conceptions of the self." My own view is an attempt to bring both perspectives—that of sociology and psychology—to bear on an understanding of the self.

5. This term, "abuse of Jung's psychology for women," was first used by Polly Young-Eisendrath. In a workshop we did together on "Animus" at the Pittsburgh, Pa. Jung Center, Polly and I agreed that the term "animus-possessed" is an abuse of language, and that it must be eliminated from the vocabulary of Jungians.

6. See "Sex-Role Stereotypes: A Current Appraisal," Inge K. Broverman, et al. (*Journal of Social Issues*, Vol. 28, No. 2, 1972), pp. 59–78.

7. "Religions centered on the worship of a male God create 'moods' and 'motivations' that keep women in a state of psychological dependence on men and male authority, while at the same time legitimating the *political* and *social* authority of fathers and sons in the institutions of society. Religious symbol systems focused around exclusively male images of divinity create the impression that female power can never be fully legitimate or wholly beneficient." *Womanspint Rising*, p. 275.

8. The anima for women may also be a symbol of our unlived life, if we women are identified primarily with a masculine mode of being. This is not unlikely in our society.

The Double: Same-Sex Inner Helper

1. Plato, "Symposium," *Plato with an English Translation*, vol. 5, trans. W. Lamb (Cambridge: Harvard University Press, 1913), p. 105.
2. 2 Sam. 1:26.
3. *CW* 17, par. 338.
4. J. Tolkien, *The Return of the King* (New York: Ballantine, 1965), p. 267.
5. Plato, "Symposium," pp. 76–77.
6. Thucydides, *The Peloponnesian War*, trans. R. Warner (Baltimore: Penguin, 1954), pp. 399–403.
7. Homer, *The Illiad*, trans. W. Rouse (New York: Mentor, 1950), p. 260.

The Self Is a Moving Target: The Archetype of Individuation

1. The difficulty of presenting all of Jung's conceptions and evidence for the Self archetype, and of presenting the many traditions and individual dream-sequences showing the existence and functioning of this transpersonal factor, may have led Jung's immediate followers to reduce everything to a few metaphors such as "the ego-Self axis." I chose to retain a greater quantity of metaphors for the Self. This approach risks confusion and the possibility that the essential simplicity of the Self will be obscured, but I chose it to be faithful to my experience and to the intimation I find in Jung's writings of many simultaneous and successive forms and forces from the Self.
2. *CW* 11, p. 259.
3. C. G. Jung, *The Visions Seminars*, vol. 2 (Zurich: Spring Publications, 1976), pp. 472–473.
4. C. G. Jung, "Answer to Job," *CW* 7, pp. 468–469.
5. Murray Stein, *Jung's Treatment of Christianity* (Wilmette, Ill.: Chiron Publications, 1986).
6. J. S. Mill, "On Liberty," *Great Books of the Western World*, vol. 43 (Chicago: Encyclopedia Britannica, Inc., 1986), p. 297.
7. *CW* 9i, p. 289.
8. C. G. Jung, *The Visions Seminars*, vol. 2, p. 341.

Part II Introduction

1. *CW* 9.1, p. 82.

Sons and Fathers: Or Why Son Is a Verb

1. Anonymous, "On Being a Father," *Parent's Magazine and Homemaking* 41 (1968): p. 49.

2. James Agee, *A Death in the Family* (New York: Bantam, 1981), p. 26.
3. Robert Penn Warren, *A Place To Come To* (New York: Random House, 1986), p. 9.
4. Stanley H. Cath, Alan R. Burwill, and John Ross, *Father and Child: Development and Clinical Perspectives* (Boston: Little, Brown, 1982), p. 62.
5. Warren, *A Place*, p. 335.

The Devouring Father

1. Aniela Jaffé, "The Creative Phases in Jung's Life," *Spring* (1972):164.
2. C. Kerényi, *The Gods of the Greeks* (London: 1961), p. 91.

Mothers and Daughters: A Mythological Perspective

1. The quotations in this chapter from C. G. Jung and C. Kerényi are taken from *Introduction to a Science of Mythology*, trans. R. F. C. Hull (London: Routledge & Kegan Paul, 1951).

Redeeming the Father

1. H. Kohut, *Analysis of the Self* (New York: Doubleday-Anchor Books, 1973), p. 66.

Great Mothers and Grand Mothers

1. For further application of the rhetoric of the fairy tale in relation to the motif of the grand mother and in relation to psychological perspectives, see David L. Miller, "Fairy Tale or Myth?" *Spring* (1976): 157–164; and David L. Miller, "Red Riding Hood and Grand Mother Rhea: Images in a Psychology of Inflation," in James Hillman, et al. *Facing the Gods* (Dallas: Spring Publications, 1980), pp. 87–100.
2. Robert Graves, *The Greek Myths*, vol. 1 (Baltimore: Penguin, 1955), pp. 118f, 104.
3. Cf. "To Demeter," *The Homeric Hymns*, trans. Charles Boer (Chicago: Swallow Press, 1970), pp. 91–135.
4. Catherine Avery, ed., *The New Century Classical Handbook* (New York: Appleton-Century-Crofts, 1962), p. 961.

Coming to Terms with Marriage: A Mythological Perspective

1. *CW* 17, pars., 331, 331b.
2. Murray Stein, "Hera Bound and Unbound," *Spring* (1977):107.
3. Ibid., p. 111.
4. Russell Jacoby, *Social Amnesia* (Boston: Beacon Press, 1975), p. 111.
5. C. Kerényi, *Zeus and Hera* (Princeton: Princeton University Press, 1975), p. 122.

The Twins: An Archetypal Perspective

1. Janet McCrickard's recently published *Eclipse of the Sun: An Investigation into Sun and Moon Myths* offers an extensive study of solar feminine psychology (Somerset, England: Gothic Images Publications, 1990).
2. J. Rendel Harris, *Boanerges* (Cambridge: Cambridge University Press, 1913). Provides much of the material summarized in the next several paragraphs.
3. Paul Radin, "The Basic Myth of North American Indians," *Eranos-Jahrbuch 1949*, Ogle Frobe-Kapteyn, ed. (Zurich: Rhein-Verlag, 1950), p. 359; Jaan Puhvel, *Comparative Mythology* (Baltimore: The Johns Hopkins University Press, 1987), p. 290.
4. Marie-Louise Von Franz, *Creation Myths* (New York: Spring Publications, 1972), pp. 70–75.
5. *CW* p. 106.
6. *CW* p. 226.
7. Joseph Campbell and Maud Oakes, *Where the Two Came to Their Father: A Navaho War Ceremonial,* 2d ed. Bollingen Series I (Princeton, N.J.: Princeton University Press, 1969), p. 36.
8. Edward F. Edinger, *The Bible and the Psyche: Individuation Symbolism in the Old Testament* (Toronto, Canada: Inter City Books, 1986), p. 36.
9. C.G. Jung, *Mysterium Coniunctionis,* 2d ed. Bollingen Series XX (Princeton, N.J.: Princeton University Press, 1970), p. 508.
10. Roger Woolger, "Death and the Hero," *Arche: Notes and Papers on Archaic Studies* 2 (1978):48.
11. Sylvia Brinton Perera devotes a chapter to "The Bipolar Goddess" in her *Descent to the Goddess: A way of Initiation for Women* (Toronto, Canada: Inter City Books, 1981), pp. 43–49.

Gay Relationship as a Vehicle for Individuation

1. See Robert H. Hopcke, *Jung, Jungians and Homosexuality* (Boston: Shambhala, 1989), p. 160, and "Eros in All His Masculinity: Men as Lovers, Men as Friends," *The San Francisco Jung Institute Library Journal* 7, no. 4 (1975):27–41.

Part III Introduction

1. *CW* 9.1, p. 154.

The Child Archetype

1. *CW* 6, p. 242.

The Puer

1. Ovid, *Metamorphoses* IV, 18–20.
2. *CW* 5, par. 527.
3. John Gillespie Magee, Jr., "High Flight," *The Family Album of Favorite Poems*, ed. P. Edward Ernest (New York: Grosset & Dunlap, 1959).
4. Gerhard Adler and Aniela Jaffé, eds., *C. G. Jung: Letters*, vol. 1 (Princeton: Princeton University Press, 1973), p. 82.

The Virgin

1. J. G. Frazer, *The Golden Bough*, Part 1, vol. 1 (New York: Macmillan, 1917), pp. 36, 37.
2. Robert Briffault, *The Mothers*, vol. 3 (London: George Allen & Unwin, 1927), pp. 169–170.

The Crone

1. Thomas M. Falkner, "Homeric Heroism, Old Age and the End of the *Odyssey*," *Old Age in Greek and Latin Literature*, ed., Falkner and Judith de Luce (Albany: State University of New York Press, 1989), p. 33.
2. Cf. Mary Daly, *Gyn/Ecology* (Boston: Beacon Press, 1979), pp. 16, 427; Barbara Walker, *The Crone: Woman of Age, Wisdom, and Power* (San Francisco: Harper & Row, 1985), passim.
3. Baba Copper, "Voices: On Becoming Old Women," *Women and Aging, Calyx*, 9.2 and 3 (Winter 1988):56.
4. Helen M. Luke, *Old Age* (New York: Parabola Books, 1987), pp. 92–94.
5. Barbara Macdonald, in Macdonald and Cynthia Rich, *Look Me in the Eye* (San Francisco: Spinsters, Ink, 1983), p. 19.
6. Carolyn G. Heilbrun, *Writing a Woman's Life* (New York: Norton, 1988), p. 130.

7. Luke, *Old Age*, pp. 44, 60, 63, 72, 73, 75.
8. Ibid., pp. 69, 95, 104, 106, 110.
9. Ibid., pp. 94–95.
10. Meridel LeSueur, *Ripening* (Old Westbury, N.Y.: The Feminist Press, 1982), p. 263.

Part IV Introduction

1. James Hillman, "An Inquiry into Image," *Spring* (1977):81.

The Hero

1. Joseph Campbell, *The Hero with a Thousand Faces* (Cleveland: Meridian Books, 1949/56), pp. 19–20.
2. Ibid., p. 4.
3. Ibid.
4. Erich Neumann, *The Origins and History of Consciousness*, trans. R. F. C. Hull, Bollingen Series XLII (Princeton: Princeton University Press, 1954), p. 127.
5. Campbell, *Hero*, p.16.
6. See Carol Gilligan, *In a Different Voice: Psychological Theory and Women's Development* (Cambridge, Mass.: Harvard University Press, 1982); and Mary Field Belenky, Blythe McVicker Clinchy, Nancy Rule Goldberger, and Jill Mattuck Tarule, *Women's Ways of Knowing* (New York: Basic Books, 1986).
7. See Naomi Goldenberg, *Changing of the Gods: Feminism and the End of Traditional Religions* (Boston: Beacon Press, 1979); and Demaris Wehr, *Jung and Feminism: Liberating Archetypes* (Boston: Beacon Press, 1987).
8. Michael E. Zimmerman, "Deep Ecology and Ecofeminism: The Emerging Dialogue," *Reweaving the World: The Emergency of Ecofeminism*, ed. I. Diamond and G. F. Orenstein (San Francisco: Sierra Club Books, 1990), pp. 145, 147. A version of my own conference paper had been published as "Getting Back to Gaia," *Anima* 13, 1 (Fall 1986):62–69.
9. James Hillman, *Re-Visioning Psychology* (New York: Harper & Row, 1975), p. 87.
10. Barbara Dunn, "James Hillman on Soul and Spirit," *Common Boundary* 6, 4 (July/August 1988):6.
11. Ibid., p. 8.
12. *CW* 13, p. 50.
13. *CW* 14, p. 358.
14. Michael Sexson, *The Quest of Self in the Collected Poems of Wallace Stevens*, Studies in Art and Religious Interpretation, vol. 1 (New York: Edwin Mellen Press, 1981), pp. 184–185.

The Female Hero

1. Carol P. Christ, "Margaret Atwood: The Surfacing of Women's Spiritual Quest and Vision," *Signs* 2, 2 (Winter 1976):317.
2. Penelope Washbourn, *Becoming Woman: The Quest for Wholeness in Female Experience* (New York: Harper & Row, 1977), p. 40.

The Monster

1. Erich Neumann, *The Origins and History of Consciousness* (Princeton: Princeton University Press, 1970), p. 276.
2. Mircea Eliade, *Myths, Dreams and Mysteries* (New York: Harper Brothers, 1960), pp. 219, 218ff; Joseph Campbell, *The Hero with a Thousand Faces* (New York: Pantheon Books, 1949), pp. 90ff.
3. Eliade, *Myths*, p. 223.
4. Frances G. Wickes, *The Inner World of Childhood* (Englewood Cliffs, N.J.: Prentice-Hall, 1978), p. 57.
5. *CW* 5, p. 419.
6. *CW* 5, p. 263.
7. Marie-Louise Von Franz, *Shadow and Evil in Fairytales* (Irving, Tex.: Spring Publications, 1974), p. 39.
8. Eliade, *Myths*, p. 184.
9. Joseph Campbell, *The Masks of God: Occidental Mythology* (New York: Viking Press, 1965), p. 334.
10. Mircea Eliade, *Patterns in Comparative Religion* (New York: World Publishing, 1963), p. 194.
11. Julie Stanton, *La nomade* (The Nomad) (Montreal: L'Hexagone, 1982), pp. 7, 42, 45, 50, 54. (Used by permission of the author; excerpt translated by Denyse Beaudet and David DeBus.)
12. Diane Kennedy Pike (aka Marianne Paulus), "Coming to Know Through Feeling, Through Direct Experience, Through Conscious Immersion in the World Mother, in Darkness," *Seeker Newsletter* 10, no. 1, p. 6.

The Victim

1. Russell Lockhart, "Cancer in Myth and Dream," *Words as Eggs: Psyche in Language and Clinic* (Dallas: Spring Publications, 1983), p. 56.
2. Simone Weil, *Notebooks* (New York: G. P. Putnam's Sons, 1956), p. 266.
3. Lockhart, "Cancer," pp. 57–58.

The Trickster

1. Susan Feldman, ed., *The Storytelling Stone: Myths and Tales of the American Indians* (New York: Dell, 1965), p. 126.

The Shaman

1. Mircea Eliade, *Shamanism: Archaic Techniques of Ecstasy* (Princeton: Princeton University Press, 1972), p. 5.
2. Claude Lévi-Strauss, *Magic and Religion* (New York: Harper & Row, 1963), p. 199.
3. Lowell John Bean and Sylvia Brakke Vane, "Shamanism: An Introduction," *Art of the Huichol Indians*, ed. Kathleen Berrin (San Francisco: Fine Arts Museum, 1978), p. 121.

The Healer

1. Joseph Fontenrose, *The Delphic Oracle* (Berkeley: University of California Press, 1981), ch. 7, asserts that this is true of the "legendary" responses but not of the "historical" ones.
2. Emma J. Edelstein and Ludwig Edelstein, *Asclepius*, vol. 1 (Baltimore: The Johns Hopkins University Press, 1945), p. 99.
3. Ibid., p. 154.

The Friend

1. Cf. Mary E. Hunt, *Fierce Tenderness: A Feminist Theology of Friendship* (New York: Crossroad, 1991).
2. The work of Naomi R. Goldenberg has enlightened feminist theologians in this regard. Cf. her *Changing of the Gods: Feminism and the End of Traditional Religions* (Boston: Beacon Press, 1979), and *Returning Words to Flesh: Feminism, Psychoanalysis, and the Resurrection of the Body* (Boston: Beacon Press, 1990).
3. The insight into "structural enemyhood" comes from Lois Kirkwood, who treats the question in her doctoral dissertation "Enemy Love in Racial Justice: A Christian Social Ethical Perspective," New York, Union Theological Seminary.

Epilogue

1. *CW* 9.1, p. 30.
2. Rainer Maria Rilke, *Duino Elegies*, trans. C. F. MacIntyre (Berkeley: University of California Press, 1961), p. 69.

About the Contributors

Denyse Beaudet is the author of *Encountering the Monster: Pathways in Children's Dreams*. She lives in San Diego, California, where in addition to raising a young daughter she lectures and conducts seminars on both children's dreams and adult development.

Jan Clanton Collins is a Jungian analyst practicing in Birmingham, Alabama, who received her training at the C. G. Jung Institutes of New York and Los Angeles. She is currently completing her doctoral studies in anthropology at Vanderbilt University.

Lyn Cowan is a Jungian analyst practicing in St. Paul, Minnesota. She is the author of *Masochism: A Jungian View* and has lectured widely in the United States. She is a former professor of psychopathology at St. Mary's College Graduate School and also teaches at the University of Minnesota.

David DeBus has degrees in literature, religion, and professional psychology. In addition to his private practice in La Jolla, California, he is Clinical Director at a therapeutic community for schizophrenia called Hanbleĉeya and teaches at the University of Humanistic Studies and California School of Professional Psychology.

William G. Doty is Professor of Religious Studies at the University of Alabama. He has published widely in professional journals in several fields, including psychology, classics, anthropology, literary studies, and religious studies. His most recent books include *Mythography: The Study of Myths and Rituals* and *The Daemonic Imagination:*

Biblical Text and Secular Story, coedited with Robert Detweiler. He is coeditor with William J. Hynes of a forthcoming volume of essays on trickster myths.

Robert H. Hopcke is a licensed Marriage, Family, and Child Counselor in Berkeley, California, and serves as Coordinator of the AIDS Prevention Program at Operation Concern, a gay and lesbian counseling agency in San Francisco. He is the author of *Jung, Jungians and Homosexuality, Men's Dreams, Men's Healing,* and *A Guided Tour of the Collected Works of C. G. Jung,* and has written numerous articles on homosexuality and men's issues.

Mary E. Hunt is a feminist theologian. She is the cofounder and codirector of the Women's Alliance for Theology, Ethics and Ritual (WATER) and the author of *Fierce Tenderness: A Feminist Theology of Friendship,* winner of the Crossroad Women's Studies Prize in 1991.

Mark Ledbetter lives in Macon, Georgia, with Margaret Cottle Ledbetter and their daughter, Ruth Weldon Ledbetter. He is Assistant Professor of Religion at Wesleyan College. His recent book is *Virtuous Intentions: The Religious Dimension of Narrative.*

River Malcolm is a Jungian-oriented therapist practicing in Del Mar, California. Before completing her degree in counseling, she sojourned through graduate programs in mathematics, molecular biology, electrical engineering, and creative writing.

David L. Miller, Watson-Ledden Professor of Religion at Syracuse University, has been a frequent lecturer to academic and psychological groups in the United States and Canada and has taught at Jung centers in Japan and Switzerland. Since 1975 he has been a member of the Eranos Circle. His books include *The New Polytheism: Rebirth of the Gods and Goddesses, Three Faces of God,* and *Hells and Holy Ghosts.*

Daniel C. Noel is Professor of Liberal Studies in Religion and Culture at Vermont College of Norwich University. He is the author of *Approaching Earth: A Search for the Mythic Significance of the Space Age* and the editor of *Seeing Castaneda* and, most recently, *Paths to the Power of Myth: Joseph Campbell and the Study of Religion.* His articles have appeared in *Spring, Anima, Quadrant,* and the *San Francisco Jung Institute Library Journal.* He lectures widely and leads summer seminars in the British Isles.

Annis Pratt taught English and Women's Studies at the University of Wisconsin for twenty years. She now lives in Michigan, where she continues to write about feminist archetypal criticism and transformational pedagogy. She published *Archetypal Patterns in Women's Fiction* in 1981 and is currently finishing a book on Medusa, Aphrodite, Artemis, and Bears in poetry by men and women entitled *Archetypal Empowerment in Poetry.*

Caroline T. Stevens is a Jungian analyst in private practice. She is active in the educational programs of the C. G. Jung Institute of Chicago and is the author of book reviews and articles on Jungian topics.

Howard Teich is a licensed psychologist in private practice in San Francisco and Sonoma, California. A pioneer in the field of masculine psychology, he lectures widely on the mythological theme of the twin heroes. Dr. Teich has also led classes and workshops on dream psychology. Currently, he is at work on a book entitled *Changing Man.*

Connie Zweig is a writer and editor living on a ridgetop in Topanga Canyon, California. A former columnist for *Esquire* and executive editor of *Brain/Mind Bulletin,* she is also editor of the collected volume *To Be a Woman: The Birth of the Conscious Feminine* and coeditor of *Meeting the Shadow: The Hidden Power of the Dark Side of Human Nature.*

Permissions and Copyrights

"The Ego: The Conscious Side of the Personality" is an excerpt from the essay "The Ego" by C. G. Jung from *The Collected Works of C. G. Jung, Vol. 9, Part II: Aion*. Bollingen Series 20, pp. 5–7. Copyright © 1959 Princeton University Press, reprinted with permission of Princeton University Press.

"The Persona: The Mask We Wear for the Game of Living" is taken from the essay "The Persona" by Edward C. Whitmont from Edward C. Whitmont, *Symbolic Quest: Basic Concepts of Analytical Psychology*, pp. 156–159. Copyright © 1969 C. G. Jung Foundation, courtesy of the C. G. Jung Foundation of New York.

"The Shadow: The Rejected Self" is an excerpt from Robert Bly, *A Little Book of the Human Shadow*, pp. 17–19. Copyright © 1988 by Robert Bly. Reprinted by permission of Harper & Row.

"The Shadow: Agent Provacateur" is comprised of excerpts from an essay "The Shadow of Training" by Patricia Berry from Patricia Berry, *Echo's Subtle Body*, Spring Publications, 1982, pp. 187–191. Reprinted with permission of the author.

"Anima: The Inner Woman" is comprised of excerpts from the essay "The Anima" by Edward C. Whitmont from Edward C. Whitmont, *Symbolic Quest: Basic Concepts of Analytical Psychology*, pp. 189–199. Copyright © 1969 C. G. Jung Foundation, courtesy of the C. G. Jung Foundation of New York.

"Anima: Guide to the Soul" is comprised of excerpts from James Hillman, *Anima: The Anatomy of a Personified Notion* (Dallas: Spring Publications, Inc., 1985), pp. 9–15, 23–25. Copyright © 1985 by James Hillman. All rights reserved.

"Animus: The Inner Man" is comprised of excerpts from the essay "Uses and Abuses of Jung's Psychology of Women: Animus" by Demaris Wehr from *Anima*, 12, 1 (Fall 1985), 13–23. Used with permission.

"The Double: Same-Sex Inner Helper" is comprised of excerpts from the essay "The Double" by Mitchell Walker from *Spring* (1976): 165–175. Copyright © 1976 by Spring Publications. All rights reserved.

"The Self Is a Moving Target: The Archetype of Individuation" is an original essay written especially for this collection by David De-Bus. Copyright © 1991 by David DeBus. Used by permission of the author.

"Sons and Fathers: Or Why Son Is a Verb" is an original essay by T. Mark Ledbetter. Copyright © 1991 by T. Mark Ledbetter. Used by permission of the author.

"The Devouring Father" is comprised of excerpts from the essay "Devouring the Father" by Murray Stein from Patricia Berry, ed., *Fathers and Mothers* (Dallas: Spring Publications, 1973), pp. 68–74. Used by permission of the author.

"Mothers and Daughters: A Mythological Perspective" is comprised of excerpts from *Woman, Earth, and Spirit: The Feminine in Symbol and Myth* by Helen M. Luke. Copyright © 1981 by Helen M. Luke. Reprinted by permission of the Crossroad Publishing Company.

"Redeeming the Father" is comprised of excerpts from Linda Schierse Leonard, *The Wounded Woman* (Athens, Ohio: Swallow Press, 1982), pp. 161–168. Reprinted with the permission of the Ohio University Press/Swallow Press, Athens.

"Fathers and Their Daughters: Walking Our Street" is a previously unpublished poem by David DeBus. Copyright © 1989 by David DeBus. Used by permission of the author.

"Great Mothers and Grand Mothers" is an original essay by David L. Miller. Copyright © 1991 by David L. Miller. Used by permission of the author.

"Loving Grandmothers" is an excerpt from the essay "Grandmothers" by Jane Rule from Jane Rule, *Outlander*, Naiad Press, 1981. Reprinted with the permission of the author and publisher.

"Song of the Self: The Grandmother" is from Alma Luz Villanueva, *LifeSpan*, Place of Herons Press, 1984. Used by permission of the author.

"The Grandfather Archetype: His Kingdom for a Hand" is an original essay by River Malcolm. Copyright © 1991 by River Malcolm. Used by permission of the author.

"Coming to Terms With Marriage: A Mythological Perspective" is comprised of excerpts from the essay "Coming to Terms with Hera" by Christine Downing from *The Goddess*, Crossroad Publishing Company, 1988. Copyright © 1981 by Christine Downing. With permission of the author.

"Sisters and Brothers" is comprised of excerpts from Christine Downing, *Psyche's Sisters*, Continuum Publishing Company, 1990. Copyright © 1988 by Christine Downing. Used by permission of the author.

"Sibling Mysteries" is from Adrienne Rich, *The Dream of a Common Language*, Poems 1974, by Adrienne Rich. Copyright © 1978 by W. W. Norton & Company, Inc. Reprinted with the permission of the publisher.

"The Sadness of Brothers" is an excerpt from the poem "The Sadness of Brothers" by Galway Kinnell, *Mortal Acts, Mortal Words*. Copyright © 1980 by Galway Kinnell. Reprinted by permission of Houghton Mifflin Co.

"The Twins: An Archetypal Perspective" is an original essay by Howard Teich. Copyright © 1991 by Howard Teich. Used by permission of the author.

"Orphans" is comprised of excerpts from Eileen Simpson, *Orphans*, Weidenfeld and Nicholson, 1987, pp. 240–243. With permission.

"Occupation: Spinster," is from *We Become New*, Lucille Iverson and Kathryn Ruby, eds., Bantam Books. Copyright © 1975 by the author.

"Gay Relationship As a Vehicle for Individuation" is an original essay by Robert H. Hopcke. Copyright © 1991 by Robert H. Hopcke. Used by permission of the author.

"Lesbian Family, Holy Family: Experience of an Archetype" is an original essay by Caroline T. Stevens. Copyright © 1991 by Caroline T. Stevens. Used by permission of the author.

"The Child Archetype" is comprised of excerpts from the essay "The Psychology of the Child Archetype" by C. G. Jung from *The Collected Works of C. G. Jung, Vol. 9, Part I: Archetypes and the Collective Unconscious*, Bollingen Series 20, pp. 167–179. Trans. R. F. C. Hull. Copyright © 1959, 1969 Princeton University Press. Copyright © 1987 renewed by Princeton University Press, reprinted with permission of Princeton University Press.

"The Puer" is an excerpt from an essay by Marie-Louise Von Franz. We gratefully acknowledge permission to reproduce pp. 1–6 from *Puer Aeternus* by Marie-Louise Von Franz. Published by Sigo Press, 1981.

"The Senex" is comprised of excerpts from the essay "Senex and Puer: An Aspect of the Historical and Psychological Present" by James Hillman from *Puer Papers*, ed. James Hillman (Dallas: Spring Publications, 1979), pp. 13–23. Copyright © 1979 by Spring Publications, Inc. All rights reserved.

"Phallos and Male Psychology" is comprised of excerpts from Robert M. Stein, *Incest and Human Love*, 2d ed. (Dallas: Spring Publications, 1984), pp. 81–90. Used by permission of Spring Publications. All rights reserved.

"The Virgin" is an excerpt from *Woman's Mysteries* by M. Esther Harding, pp. 101–105. Copyright © 1971 by the C. G. Jung Foundation for Analytical Psychology. Reprinted by arrangement with Shambhala Publications, Inc. 300 Massachusetts Ave., Boston, MA 02115, for publication in the USA and Canada and with Random Century Group in the British Commonwealth and Empire.

"The Conscious Feminine: Birth of a New Archetype" is an original essay by Connie Zweig. Copyright © 1991 by Connie Zweig. Used by permission of the author.

"The Crone" is an original essay by Christine Downing. Copyright © 1991 by Christine Downing. Used by permission of the author.

"Re-Visioning the Hero" is an original essay by Daniel C. Noel. Copyright © 1991 by Daniel C. Noel. Used by permission of the author.

"The Female Hero" is an original essay by Annis Pratt. Copyright © 1991 by Annis Pratt. Used by permission of the author.

"The Monster" is an original essay by Denyse Beaudet. Copyright © 1991 by Denyse Beaudet. Used by permission of the author.

"The Victim" is an original essay by Lyn Cowan. Copyright © 1991 by Lyn Cowan. Used by permission of the author.

"The Trickster" is an original essay by William G. Doty. Copyright © 1991 by William G. Doty. Used by permission of the author.

"The Shaman" is an original essay by Jan Clanton Collins. Copyright © 1991 by Jan Clanton Collins. Used by permission of the author.

"The Healer" is an original essay by Christine Downing. Copyright © 1991 by Christine Downing. Used by permission of the author.

"The Invalid" is comprised of excerpts from Adolf Guggenbühl-Craig, *Eros on Crutches: On the Nature of the Psychopath*, trans. Gary V. Hartman (Dallas: Spring Publications, 1980), pp. 12–25. Copyright © 1980 by Adolf Guggenbühl. All rights reserved.

"The Friend" is an original essay by Mary E. Hunt. Copyright © 1991 by Mary E. Hunt. Used by permission of the author.

About the Editor

Christine Downing is Chair of Religious Studies at San Diego State University and was for fifteen years a core faculty member at the California School of Professional Psychology. She has also taught at the C. G. Jung Institute in Zurich and at Pacifica Graduate School. Her books include *The Goddess: Mythological Images of the Feminine, Journey Through Menopause, Psyche's Sisters: ReImagining the Meaning of Sisterhood,* and *Myths and Mysteries of Same-Sex Love.* She is currently working on two books, *Orpheus and Eurydice: Male and Female Engagements with the Underworld* and *Women's Mysteries.*